Two Armies
and One Fatherland

TWO ARMIES
AND ONE FATHERLAND

The End of the Nationale Volksarmee

Jörg Schönbohm

Translated from the German by
Peter and Elfi Johnson

Berghahn Books
Providence • Oxford

First published in 1996 by
Berghahn Books
Editorial offices:
165, Taber Avenue, Providence, RI 02906, USA
Bush House, Merewood Avenue, Oxford, OX3 8EF, UK

© English-language edition Berghahn Books 1996
© German edition Wolf Jobst Siedler Verlag GmbH, Berlin 1992
Originally published as *Zwei Armeen und ein Vaterland.*

Library of Congress Cataloging-in-Publication Data
Schönbohm, Jörg, 1937-
[Zwei Armeen und ein Vaterland. German]
Two armies and one fatherland : the end of the Nationale Volksarmee /
Jörg Schönbohm ; translated from the German by Peter and Elfi
Johnson.
    p. cm.
ISBN 1-57181-069-2 (hardback : alk. paper)
1. Germany (East). Nationale Volksarmee--History. 2. Germany
(East)--Military policy.. 3. Germany--History--Unification, 1990.
I. Title.
UA719.3.S362 1995
355'.00943--dc20   95-38478
                                                              CIP

British Library Cataloguing in Publication Data
A catalogue record for this book is available from the British Library.

Printed in the USA on acid-free paper.

Contents

FOREWORD

From the days that Lieutenant-General Schönbohm and I were lieutenants, we trained to fight the Soviet military and its ally, the East German Nationale Volksarmee (NVA). We never viewed the East German forces lightly. The East Germans had somehow succeeded in making Communism work – even *more* productively than the Soviets who had forced them to adopt this system. This also led us to conclude that the East German military had probably improved on Soviet military doctrine and war-fighting capabilities. In short, in the event that the Soviets ever chose to attack, those of us in NATO felt that the East German forces would probably prove the toughest and most skilled of any forces we would meet in battle.

Then, in November 1989, the world witnessed a miracle. We all watched in awe as frosty-breathed West and East Germans tore down the Berlin Wall and rushed toward one another in open embrace. When the night fell, there were no East and West Germans – only Germans.

And so begins the story of *Two Armies and One Fatherland.* General Schönbohm was there from the beginning. He was the person to whom his nation turned to merge the two forces of East and West – to erase decades of attitudes, habits, and outlooks – to form a single military force. Although much has been written in Germany on this marriage, much of it has been contradictory, diffuse, and tentative. And very little has been translated for the outside world. General Schönbohm's account is the first definitive explanation of this enormous human endeavour.

This is a fascinating story, eloquently written, and told only as a participant and first-hand observer can. However, General Schönbohm was more than that. He was the architect; the blacksmith at the forge.

General Schönbohm had the daunting task of transforming a military force that was 103,000 members strong. His task was to integrate troops and units that had faithfully served the NVA, into a force that had stood firmly against every ideal and value the NVA had represented for almost fifty years. He had to close down a large number of redundant military installations, rehabilitate those that were to be kept, and exercise immediate and tight control over the weapons and munitions (over 300 metric tonnes of the latter) that had been the arsenal of the East German Army. To make matters more difficult, this effort had to be accomplished even as the Soviet forces were evacuating East Germany, leaving in their wake further problems and difficulties.

General Schönbohm writes frankly and clearly of the extraordinary problems he faced not only in disbanding the NVA, but also of the numerous challenges he faced back in Bonn. Let there be no mistake about it; integrating the NVA into the Bundeswehr was more a function of overcoming considerable institutional and personal prejudices on both sides and building mutual respect, than the mere transfer of people and equipment. That most Germans now consider the Bundeswehr's efforts at quickly ending the distinctions between East and West as a great success, is an irrefutable tribute to the superb leadership and the outstanding dedication of General Schönbohm.

Here in the United States, among the members of our military, the Bundeswehr has long been regarded as a military force of superb quality, expertly trained and prepared for battle; truly an ally whom we would be both proud and fortunate to have on our flank in battle. The same is true today. The Bundeswehr would be forgiven if it had relinquished some degree of its excellence as it strove to do its part in unifying its nation. But that is not what happened. Astonishingly, the Bundeswehr has maintained its excellence despite the considerable obstacles and challenges involved throughout reunification. And a great deal of the credit belongs alone to General Schönbohm.

Through this book General Schönbohm has done a historically vital service to his nation and to its allies. As we face the enormous challenges of the coming years – the Partnership for Peace and the expansion of NATO, for example – General Schönbohm has given us a better understanding of the concerns and difficulties involved in reforming military forces and integrating them into newly democratic societies.

Thus General Schönbohm's book is both a manual of proven techniques and a timely resource for the tasks before us. However, of even greater importance, this is a success story, and an eloquently written record of one of the most significant events in modern military history.

John M. Shalikashvili
General, United States Army
Chairman, Joint Chiefs of Staff
Washington, May 1995

PREFACE

The unification of Germany came quickly and surprisingly – hoped for and desired by many, opposed and obstructed by others. In that historic period, from 1988, under the Defence Ministers Rupert Scholz and Gerhard Stoltenberg, I was – as a Lieutenant-General – the head of the Planning Staff and a close adviser of the ministers.

German-Soviet relations started to improve in October 1988 with the visit of the Federal Chancellor, Dr Helmut Kohl, to President Gorbachov in Moscow. I was able to take part in this visit and gain initial experience of the Soviet negotiators. In this volume I will describe the developments which, two years later, led to the happy reunification of Germany, and also resulted in my appointment to my home area in Brandenburg near Berlin, as Commanding General of the former East German armed forces, the Nationale Volksarmee.

From spring 1990 it was clear to us that German unity was approaching, without knowing when it would happen or under what conditions. The conditions for the take-over of the NVA were not outlined until two-and-a-half months before unification: only after the conclusion of the Two-Plus-Four Treaty and Gorbachov's agreement that unified Germany could remain within NATO. We had to take over, at short notice, Communist-indoctrinated armed forces, formerly hostile to us and drilled to hate and be ready to attack and which up until now we had known only from situation reports or by observation through binoculars. These soldiers had to be persuaded to co-operate from the first day, so we could peacefully take over the heavily armed forces of the defunct German Democratic Republic (GDR) without violent reaction, desertions or 'losses' of arms and equipment. It had to be made clear to the NVA troops that all German soldiers must themselves take part in the task of uniting Germany, even though a very large number of the former NVA officers had no chance of remaining in the Bundeswehr (the Federal German Armed Forces) in the long term.

In my diary, from 2 October 1990 to 1 July 1991, I described the experiences and atmosphere, the challenges people faced and military decisions linked with the take-over and disbandment of the NVA and the formation of new Bundeswehr units. This record is taken from my personal diary, written under the impact of the varied experiences and necessary decisions. This book has been written not only for servicemen but also for readers concerning themselves with the human challenges arising from German unity and with overcoming the legacy of a totalitarian state.

In the GDR, Communist indoctrination in the state, the armed forces and society was more comprehensive than in all other states and armed forces of the now-defunct Communist Bloc. The GDR was able to explain its identity as a second state on German territory only through Communist or Socialist ideology – there could be no GDR without Communism and that is how it turned out. The other states of the former Eastern Bloc could exist with or without Communism; they were able to retain their national identity and to strengthen it after winning freedom. For their armed forces the changeover was not as radical as for the NVA, whose state had been swept away and its ideology shattered to pieces.

Against this background it is all the more remarkable that the troops and civilian staff of the NVA have taken part in this change and in the abandonment of their former attitudes which were linked to it. From the first the Bundeswehr approached this task as a joint challenge, and for the sake of our common future it relegated the memories and experiences of past confrontation and painful division. The achievements of the Bundeswehr in the process of unification have been fully recognised by our Federal President and Federal Chancellor. For instance, Chancellor Kohl, visiting troops in Potsdam in summer 1993, declared publicly: 'In such a way the Bundeswehr is rendering an important service towards the growing together of the two parts of our fatherland ... And I am sure that the achievement of the armed forces will later, in retrospect, stand as one of the most successful chapters, perhaps even the most successful chapter in the process of German unification.'

My comrades of all ranks regarded the take-over of the NVA as a personal challenge and as a happy occurrence in our history – Germany had been united with the approval of its neighbours and the Great Powers, the danger of a civil war had been banished and German soldiers were serving in the armed forces of our united fatherland.

Jörg Schönbohm
Bonn, June 1995

Chapter 1

FIRST EXPERIENCES
IN MOSCOW

On Monday 18 October 1988 the Federal Defence Minister, Professor Rupert Scholz, and a small delegation accompanied the Federal Chancellor, Dr Helmut Kohl, on a visit to Moscow. I took part as the Head of the Defence Minister's Planning Staff. This visit was intended to break the ice and place relations between the two countries on a broader basis. Accompanying the Federal Chancellor was a large delegation of business leaders – arranged to give economic relations, too, a new impulse.

We planned that the Defence Minister would also make his own contribution to the normalisation of relations with the Soviet Union, without annoying our allies. We knew that all of our steps were being watched carefully by the allies. It was important that we should be able to speak to the Soviet Union on a basis of complete equality, something the Federal Republic was more able to do because it was firmly embedded in NATO. It was intended that we would hold talks with the Soviet Defence Minister, Army General Dmitri Yazov, that a speech be made at the Malinovsky Academy and that we should visit troops in the Moscow region. After some to-ing and fro-ing our Foreign Minister had agreed that the Defence Minister could include in his delegation two senior aides, as well as his press spokesman and adjutant. This was really a minimal complement for the first talks since the Second World War between the Federal Defence Minister and the Soviet Defence Minister, together with his military chiefs. In Bonn there were some fears that this first meeting since the war could produce too much publicity. Our preparations were comprehensive and thorough; it was a new experience for us all.

By the Thursday before our departure the agenda for the visit had yet to be completed, in spite of repeated requests, so the Soviet Defence Attaché had to be called in. After this intervention the minister received – but not until Friday afternoon – the agenda for the visit that was due to begin on the Monday morning. The Soviets explained the delay in providing the detailed agenda by referring to Yazov's absence in Siberia, saying that he had reserved final approval for himself – as if there were no telecommunication links in the Soviet Union. To me this was an example of the way a Great Power treated a small but important medium-sized power. It was going to be an interesting journey.

We landed on Monday morning, on time and according to protocol, in two Luftwaffe B-707s. After the official welcome there was considerable confusion at the airport. The Defence Minister, the parliamentary leader of the Christian Democrats, Alfred Dregger, and the representatives of German industry had to wait for the cars which were to take us to Moscow. After some complications they finally arrived, and drove in a motorcade to the imposing Hotel Rossiya. Moscow made a grubby, grey impression. The hotel, on the whole, was decent, even though in most of the rooms the heating did not work and there were no plugs in the baths.

The first talks with Defence Minister Yazov took place in the building of the General Staff: a guard of honour of young soldiers, a burst of camera flashes; the tall, heavy-set Yazov looked as if he could crush the small, agile minister Scholz. However Scholz was relaxed and assured: an obvious contrast. Then we were introduced to the Soviet delegation. The Commanders-in-Chief of the army, air force, navy and missile forces, the deputies of the Chiefs of the General Staff, and various departmental heads in the Soviet ministry took part in these discussions. The balance of forces in the conference room mirrored that of the two countries' troops fairly accurately – and our Foreign Office had originally wanted to make our delegation even smaller!

We had expected Yazov to offer some words of welcome, but he opened the talks with the brief statement: 'Herr Minister Scholz, you have come here, what has brought you here and what interests you most?' Scholz spoke for a short time about the past, the Second World War, the division of Germany and further developments up to the present. He then spoke about the general situation in Europe, the state of arms control and about possible areas for developing future co-operation.

Yazov followed these remarks with lively interest, at times agreeing and at others making disapproving comments, while the other generals and admirals sat there stock still and silent. Only their rapidly changing expressions made it possible to gauge whether they agreed or not. During the subsequent discussion, which lasted for three hours, only Yazov spoke on behalf of the Soviets. The others simply sat and nodded in agreement. Finally Colonel-General Nikolai Chervov spoke, about the treaty on the limitation of intermediate-range nuclear forces (INF) and possibilities for circumventing it. Yazov showed, by the way that he led the discussion, that he was well prepared and in control. The atmosphere of the talks was business-like and frank. There was some tough talking and I gained the definite impression that, particularly due to his firmness, Scholz had impressed the Soviets.

On the question of overcoming the division of Germany, or even of a reduction in numbers of Soviet troops in connection with negotiations on conventional forces in Europe, no common ground could be found. The Soviets unswervingly held to the view that the division of Europe could only be overcome, in the long term, through the dissolution of the blocs. In addition there was no sign of movement regarding pragmatic proposals for co-operation. Yazov insisted on the necessity for Soviet superiority in order to guarantee peace in Europe. Just as tough and unproductive was the discussion on the theme of nuclear weapons. Yazov called for the de-nuclearisation of Europe and declared quite frankly that we Germans must consider ourselves hostages to nuclear strategy. He said that Soviet nuclear weapons were aimed, in the event of a counter-strike by the Soviets, at German industrial centres and at the general population. The threatening undertone, intended to blackmail or force good behaviour, was unmistakable to me; these were strange 'frank and neighbourly' discussions. He refused to accept our arguments for NATO's nuclear strategy. He did not recognise that, from our point of view, the nuclear weapons of the Western Alliance were deterring the Soviet Union from using its own armed forces.

We argued that only the United States, together with its allies, could guarantee our security against the massive military superiority of the Soviet Union; military stability was the precondition for détente. Yazov insisted that all nuclear weapons must be abolished – just as Gorbachev had proposed. He refused to understand that the Europeans would then be helpless in face of the overwhelming superiority of the Soviet conventional forces. The Soviet Union, he said, was a peaceful country. For our part, we tried to bring up the question of monitoring a ban on nuclear weapons but Yazov would not be drawn into such a discussion.

However, there were also moments of humour, as when Yazov, answering a question from Scholz about the cost of Soviet armaments, said he had no idea of what his weapons systems cost, he needed only to order them and he would receive them. He had no comprehension at all – and this was already autumn 1988 – of our system of cost accounting and budget estimates, which lead to budgetary negotiations with parliamentary committees.

At the end of the lively discussions a mutual interest in arms control negotiations was evident. There was no indication that the Soviets would ever give up their attitude calling for paritative – that is, numerically equal – reductions in the armed forces, which would have permanently assured them of a considerable superiority in Europe. They were neither ready to accept the simple principle 'whoever has more must disarm more' nor prepared to reduce the size of the armed forces on both sides to the same level.

In spite of the material disagreements, there was an atmosphere of frankness and better understanding – one could not expect more. At the close Scholz invited Yazov to Germany and it was agreed that, to start with, the Chief of Staff of the Bundeswehr and the Soviet Chief of the General Staff should meet to talk about improving relations in the sphere of military policy.

The next day we visited the Malinovsky Academy, where officers of the armoured formations were trained – including at that time personnel of the Nationale Volksarmee, the armed forces of the German Democratic Republic. Minister Scholz was given the opportunity to address those taking part in the training programme. Scholz's speech covered a broad range of topics, from the development of the overall situation, to questions of the strengths of both sides. We had translated the speech into Russian and brought three-hundred hard copies with us, for distribution to the servicemen. We wanted to introduce into the internal Soviet discussion German statistics about the balance of forces and our view of comparative strengths.

Before the speech the Commander of the Academy, a Colonel-General, had tea and biscuits served in his office. We discussed with him and some of his lecturers the tasks of the academy and the procedures for selection of course participants. The frank discussion showed that even here soldiers could talk in a business-like way about the nuts and bolts of their profession. However, as soon as political matters were touched upon, there was the usual discussion of basic principles and exchange of opposing arguments. Thus it was virtually impossible for us to explain to our host the concept of the integration of the armed forces into the state; he could not understand democratic control over the forces. The Soviet officers knew little about the democratic state based on the rule of law; they only knew of 'imperialism', whose tools we were supposed to be. They did not want to believe that the Bundeswehr was created purely for defence and that a war of aggression was expressly forbidden by the Basic

Law. In response, we quoted from Soviet sources which stated that the enemy was to be given an annihilating rebuff on their own territory – which quite clearly meant an attack.

As we toured the academy we saw signs of pride in the Soviet armoured units. Models of tanks and successful battles – particularly from the Second World War up until the victory in Berlin – could be seen all around. Everywhere victorious campaigns were displayed in glass cases; of their operations in Afghanistan there was not one mention.

Then came the speech. In the great colonnaded chamber several hundred staff officers were gathered. We were welcomed with dutiful applause. The flashing of press cameras, the television crews – this, too, was probably a new experience for the Soviet officers. Scholz's speech achieved its desired effect, particularly when he gave concrete figures about the strengths of both sides, and from these drew conclusions on disarmament. Subdued murmurs indicated what an impression this had made. After the speech an animated discussion developed. However, the Soviet questions had quite obviously been prepared in advance, as they only made indirect reference to the speech. Instead, they followed the themes provided by Soviet argumentation, from a nuclear first-strike to the 'aggressive manoeuvre concept' of NATO.

What effect was achieved by this speech and our behaviour I do not know. I had the impression that the business-like manner in which a civilian minister answered even military questions made an impact. Some prejudices against the 'aggressive West and the Federal Republic of Germany' might have started to crumble. I imagine that the Soviet officers went home with unanswered questions and perhaps with cause for thought. However, there was no narrowing of differences, and that probably could not have come about at the first meeting.

The next day we visited the Taman Division, famous in the Soviet Union, located about sixty kilometres from Moscow. We travelled along gravel roads, past small woods of birch and fir. The Taman division had distinguished itself during the Second World War, particularly in the defence of Moscow, and after the war had become the 'showpiece division' for visitors. It marched at the head of the military parades commemorating the October Revolution – accompanied by applause. We were shown a demonstration, with shots fired, of an engagement between tanks and infantry, the standard of which was lower than ours. The proportion of first hits was smaller, while conduct during the engagement, and firing while on the move were not as good as ours. There were different views among the journalists as to the Soviet intent.

I believe that the level really did correspond to the state of training of the troops: soldiers do not deliberately give a poor performance, particularly when distinguished visitors are present. Furthermore, the troops gave an impression of enthusiasm. But if this was in fact a showpiece unit of the glorious Soviet army, what was the state of the other units? Not until two years later was I to hear from former NVA officers, who had studied in the Soviet Union for several years, that this division had become purely a 'demonstration and showpiece division', which no longer had any regular training. Soviet units which had been stationed in the GDR had been of a better standard.

The barrack-rooms and living conditions of this elite unit were spartan. In each barrack-room there were from twelve to twenty-four men, with poor quality lockers and chairs. The conscripts had to stay mainly in the barracks, even at weekends; their families lived a thousand or more kilometres away. We were told that their military service was deliberately arranged far from their home areas; in this way the conscripts would contribute to the integration of the Soviet people. When we asked whether all the soldiers could communicate in Russian, even when they came from Kazakhstan, Kirghizia or the Tatar regions, the answer was evasive.

Our visit to the barrack-rooms showed that here, too, everything had been excellently prepared. The living quarters and the wash-rooms seemed to have been unused for days: greetings from Potemkin! Our visit to the training sections gave the impression of simple but effective training aids – particularly compared to our high-technology simulators. A captain in the tactical and operational training centre explained the tactical training and defensive dispositions – 'exclusively defensive dispositions, Gospodin General.' He was then unpleasantly surprised – and blushed – as I pointed through our interpreter to an enormous map which clearly showed an attacking operation. He excused himself by saying that the changeover to the new doctrine had not yet been completed. It would have been more honest if he had conceded to me, a soldier, that a tank division must of course be capable of a counter-attack and must therefore be trained accordingly. Were these the beginnings of a new feeling of insecurity?

In conversation with officers in their mess we got rather closer. Some officers talked about their time in the GDR; for most of them it had basically been a good experience. They had fond memories of their time in Germany, but admitted that they had little contact with the German population and had come together with Germans solely through the official Society for German-Soviet Friendship. They described relations with the NVA as normal – though I could not determine what they meant by normal. Only later did I learn that the Soviet forces in Germany had appointed liaison teams, which also had a monitoring function, at all levels from the GDR Ministry for National Defence down to the divisions. When the Soviets had concrete requests to make to the NVA they communicated them through the liaison organisation or had the local commanders come to them. Often, contacts were reduced to joint events on Days of German-Soviet Friendship. Then large quantities of vodka were consumed and there were mutual assurances of steadfast comradeship in arms. There were only a few joint military manoeuvres.

The officers of the NVA gained their experience of Soviet reality during training courses in Moscow or at other military academies. When they returned to the GDR after two or three years of training they were proud of the conditions in their own country where everything was so much better – a widely-held view until unification. Later, through discussion with former NVA officers, I learned that they were proud of the GDR, which had essentially been the showpiece of Socialism. In all of the other allied states of the Warsaw Pact, conditions for the general population were worse in every respect. How the GDR itself compared with the western world was only realised after the fall of the Berlin Wall.

At the close of our visit to the division each of us was given a loaf of bread and some salt as a sign of Soviet or Russian hospitality. Was this meant personally or was it merely a traditional, symbolic gesture? A few of the journalists accompanying us found that the bread was of poor quality and as they got onto the bus they simply dropped it on the grass. Fortunately a German press officer noticed this, picked up the bread and took it with him. Was this thoughtlessness also symbolic?

After the final delegation talks which were led by the Federal Chancellor and the Soviet President, Helmut Kohl stated at a press conference that the ice had been broken and that Gorbachev would visit Bonn in 1989, when the two sides would sign a treaty on mutual relations. He added that the two meetings, that in Moscow and that in Bonn, were closely connected and must be seen in that light.

So we flew home with the impression that we had taken part in an important meeting. Whether the breaking of the ice at the political level would be followed by a greater relaxation in the military sphere was not clear. The question remained as to whether Germany had any room for manoeuvre in the military sphere – as a divided country in the heart of Europe, with the greatest concentration of armed forces in the world.

Chapter 2

DEVELOPMENTS IN SECURITY POLICY AFTER 1988

The ice had been broken in Moscow but the military facts remained unchanged. More than 350,000 Soviet soldiers were still stationed in the GDR, with modern equipment and armaments, with nuclear and chemical weapons. The negotiations in Vienna on the control of conventional arms were stagnating, the talks on strategic arms reductions (START) were making no progress; only the agreements on mutual observation of manoeuvres within the framework of the Conference on Security and Co-operation in Europe (CSCE), as well as the related notification of manoeuvres, were still being complied with. Even here, there were already fierce discussions and disputes with the Soviet Union and some Eastern Bloc states about questions of pure 'protocol' such as, whether manoeuvre observers were allowed to use their own binoculars, a compass or even a dictaphone. These questions were dealt with by experts, far from high-level politics, but they influenced the climate and atmosphere of the negotiations which followed.

In spite of all the arguments the leadership of the Bundeswehr was prepared to reveal details of the potential and capabilities of our forces in order to win trust and reduce prejudices. On the other hand, we had to continue to maintain the credibility of our defence capability within the Alliance. At what cost could we make unilateral advance concessions, in view of the overwhelming superiority of the Soviet Union? The path between hope and risk was narrow.

Were the Soviet worries and caution about us based on the experiences and traumatic events of the Second World War, or was this experience merely being used to ensure their own superiority for the future? These questions were discussed in the Federal Defence Ministry in developing our approaches to arms control policy. The result was that we insisted, along with our allies, on equality in certain categories of conventional weapons systems throughout Europe, from the Atlantic to the Urals, between the members of NATO and of the Warsaw Pact Organisation (WPO). Out of this arose the demand: 'Whoever has more must disarm more.' This was logical, but the Soviets did not find it acceptable. They demanded instead, that naval forces, with their impressive capability to project power, should also be included in the negotiations. However, for the United States, as a large transatlantic and maritime power, this was, of course, unacceptable, as it could not carry out its protective function for Europe and maintain a world-wide balance of forces without a strong navy. So even after the Federal Chancellor's visit to Moscow, the lights were showing red on arms-control policy and in the military sphere.

In addition, the discussions on replacing the surface-to-surface Lance missile were straining our relations with the U.S. and the British. Further, in German public opinion they led to fierce, often emotional debates. The Alliance – especially the United States and Great Britain – wanted to decide in 1988 on the development and purchase of a replacement for the Lance. However, Bonn applied the brakes, and pointed out that for the time being no decision was necessary; they should wait for further developments within the Warsaw Pact.

At conferences of the defence ministers in the Nuclear Planning Group and the NATO Defence Planning Committee, these modernisation plans and the need for a change in NATO strategy were discussed. All participants agreed that joint defence efforts and nuclear armaments must take into account the effectiveness of the military capabilities of the Soviet Union and the Warsaw Pact, including the GDR. So, as before, heavily armed alliances continued to face each other. The Warsaw Pact was not prepared to reduce its superiority through arms control measures laid down in treaties, and subject to verification.

Not until Gorbachev's speech at the United Nations in December 1988, did the possibility emerge for a fundamental improvement of future relations between the blocs. Gorbachev rejected the use of arms to achieve Soviet aims, and committed himself to respect international law and to submit to verdicts of the International Court of Justice. He gave advance notice of unilateral withdrawals of Soviet troops and of reductions in Soviet forces. This was to take place without a treaty and could thus not be verified. However, Gorbachev had taken a first step to reduce Soviet superiority. His speech was sensational, even though its practical significance remained to be seen.

Up to the beginning of 1989 the Bundeswehr expected, on the basis of a Federal Government decision, that recruits called up on 1 June 1989 would serve for eighteen months instead of the previous period of fifteen months. The training programmes and the rhythm of the call-up had been changed and the conscripts starting service on 1 June 1989 had been promised better pay. However, in April 1989 the Federal Government decided to cancel this decision at short notice, and to keep to the fifteen months conscription. This required another change in planning by the forces; as a result massive cuts in training and in troop numbers were needed.

Against this military and political background, not all of us were fully aware of the extent and force of developments in the GDR. Above all, Bonn wanted to achieve improvements for the people and to reduce the GDR government's pressure on the population. A first sign of a change of climate in the East was seen in the expulsion of arrested dissidents in January 1988, and the advance announcement of a more generous application of the regulations on travel to the West, particularly for GDR citizens who had not reached pensionable age; pensioners were already allowed to visit the West. The East German leader, Erich Honecker, stated that the number of GDR citizens, apart from pensioners, allowed to visit the West would increase from 1.4 to 1.5 million annually.

On the other hand, journalists based in the GDR, from both the Eastern Bloc and the West, were subjected to restrictions on free reporting about developments in Moscow, and leading politicians and theoreticians of the GDR's ruling party, the Socialist Unity Party (SED), indicated that they had reservations in principle about Gorbachev's reforms. 'The GDR as a sovereign Socialist state does not need *glasnost* and *perestroika*, as it has no rigidities or shortcomings comparable to those in the Soviet Union – thanks to the policy of the SED.' The leading SED theoretician, Otto Reinhold, argued that a changeover to democracy in the GDR was impossible, on the grounds that the achievements of Socialism had created the fundamental distinction from capitalist West Germany; to give up those achievements would mean giving up the GDR's own identity. Did he really believe that the population would follow that ideologically based argumentation?

The GDR government did everything possible to underline its independence as a state. For instance, at the end of June 1988 at Honecker's invitation, a disarmament conference about nuclear-free zones was held in East Berlin, with participants from more than a hundred states. At this conference he proposed 'the creation of mechanisms for the peaceful settlement of crises and the prevention of military incidents in Central Europe.' The GDR was clearly trying, at all costs, to win more international stature but it permitted serious physical attacks to be made on West German television teams and journalists during the conference. True, this led to protests and angry reactions in the Federal Republic, but it did not stop the joint working-party on security policy of the West German Social Democratic Party (SPD) and the SED, from calling, a fortnight later, for the creation of a 'zone of trust and security in Central Europe'.

In September 1989, the federal government responded to Honecker's new travel regulations by agreeing to pay the GDR some ten billion Deutschmarks between 1990 and 1999, for surface transit traffic between West Germany and West Berlin. However, this did not influence the hard-line policies of the GDR government; evidently the leadership in East Berlin felt that any concessions made to other countries would lead to increased internal tension. In fact, despite the fact that the possibility of travel to the West had been put into law, there was increasing pressure on the GDR government for greater freedom of movement. People were no longer willing to be ordered around and they wanted immediate change. Gorbachev's adviser Datshishev, in a background briefing held in Bonn in summer 1989, stated that the Berlin Wall was a relic of the Cold War and was out-dated. Amazingly only one West German newspaper reported in detail on this revolutionary statement – and this report produced no echo.

Honecker was unmoved by this; he tried to underline the permanence of his frontier, and with that his state, by declaring that the Berlin Wall would remain standing for another fifty or a hundred years, as long as the reasons for its construction still existed. Apparently he saw no other chance of maintaining his party's rule than continuing to fence off the GDR. The old, obstinate man did not seem to see that such declarations deprived his citizens of any hope of early change and thus increased their readiness to flee.

In this state of change, where an upheaval had begun but had not yet been acknowledged officially, the NVA was firmly in the Socialist camp – as before it was standing on guard for socialism; inner tensions and disputes could not be seen from outside. It is true that we knew about the use of soldiers in the economy and as a result a possible reduction in the state of readiness, but the NVA remained a willing and powerful instrument in the hands of the political leadership. The soldiers remained alien to us, they were not neighbours we could trust. They stood for human-rights violations, repression by the SED party apparatus and the shootings on the Wall, and on the frontier between the two Germanies.

On 1 April 1989 the new travel regulations came into force. These regulations made the system already in force more precise and more extensive. On 7 May local elections were held in the GDR, with the usual high turnout of voters – over ninety per cent. But the elections also brought surprises for the regime. Of the roughly 12.5 million voters, almost 12.2 million voted for the listed candidates. This meant that there were more votes against the official list than at any time since the foundation of the GDR – and even so, some opposition groups cast doubt on the result. There was open talk of election fraud. Was this already the writing on the wall?

Meanwhile in the Federal Republic we were concerning ourselves with shop opening hours (including one evening with late opening), tax benefits for families, *(Familienlastenausgleich),* or taxation of unearned income at source. We, too, did not seem to realise that the GDR was being shaken right to its very foundations. At the end of May it became known from church sources in East Berlin, that at least twelve people had lodged charges with the Prosecutor-General of the GDR alleging election fraud. The objections made against the election result became more numerous and the spirit of resistance among the population grew. However, the SED leadership appeared unimpressed; Horst Sindermann, President of the Volkskammer, East Germany's rubber-stamp parliament, defended GDR Socialism and rejected reforms such as those in Poland and Hungary. The GDR system, he said, needed no reforms.

Further demonstrations against the local elections, planned by groups affiliated to the church, were prevented by strong units of the Stasi and the police. Even the state visit of Gorbachev to Bonn in mid-June, and the obvious improvement of relations between the two governments, did not bring the SED to relax its obstinate stance. The GDR became more and more isolated in the Eastern Bloc, but refused to acknowledge this fact. It seemed not to take notice of the joint declaration by Helmut Kohl and President Gorbachev on 13 June 1989, regarding human rights, the self-determination of nations, the free choice of political and social systems, overcoming the division of Europe, and about the Basic Treaty between the two German states. Honecker merely announced that the methods of guarding his frontier were to be made more humane; border guards were now allowed to shoot only in self defence or at deserters from the forces or other armed formations.

By the end of June it was clear that the numbers of East Germans moving West were increasing rapidly. In the first half of the year 30,000 Germans had already left the GDR legally and the federal government forecast that the figure would reach 80,000 by the year-end. This flood of emigrants was growing like that of the embassy refugees who, by fleeing into the Federal German embassies in Prague, Budapest and Warsaw, wanted to win freedom on their own initiative. The Hungarian government promised not to send back any Germans to the GDR against their will – whereupon a third reception camp for Germans had to be established in Budapest. The numbers of refugees increased, as did the numbers of demonstrators in Leipzig. On 10 September the Hungarian government allowed six thousand Germans to leave for the Federal Republic. The perfect, almost impenetrable system for preventing escapes to the West, had been opened for our fellow countrymen by a country in the East and thus could never again be closed or repaired. Hungary became, for many, the land of hope. This turned out to be the breaching of the dam. Was it to be the beginning of the end of the GDR?

All over the GDR, citizens' movements were formed virtually overnight, hoping to force a democratic renewal. However, the GDR Ministry of the Interior continued to deny recognition to the 'New Forum' movement, which had applied for registration in eleven of the fifteen regional capitals. On 25 September in Leipzig eight thousand people took part in the largest demonstration so far, which demanded, above all, the legalisation of the 'New Forum' but also, in general terms, human rights, freedom of opinion and association and the release of people who had been arrested during the earlier 'peace prayers' organised at one of the city's churches. Fifty people were arrested but it soon became evident that this could not halt developments. On 2 October, eight to ten thousand people marched through Leipzig and demanded the legalisation of the New Forum.

Meanwhile, on 7 and 8 October the GDR leaders marked the fortieth anniversary of their state, together with delegations from all the Eastern Bloc countries. However, they were forced to protect themselves with strong security forces who acted brutally against demonstrating citizens: this was a 'state festival' protected by police and soldiers. Gorbachev came to Berlin for the anniversary, and in his speech he encouraged the GDR leaders to make changes and reforms, and to co-operate with all the democratic groups.

After this, events moved quickly. Ten days later, on 18 October, Erich Honecker resigned and Egon Krenz, who had long been seen as his 'crown prince', took over Honecker's party and state offices. Many old functionaries were dismissed or resigned voluntarily, and every citizen was given permission to visit the West for up to thirty days each year. The system was crumbling everywhere. Even the prospect of free elections was proposed. Even so, this was all happening too late, the avalanche could not be stopped. On 9 November the regime had to open the border with the West and the Wall; the population could travel 'abroad' (to West Germany, as well as other Western countries) for the first time since the building of the Wall nearly three decades earlier.

The SED still went on trying to save whatever could be saved in the GDR. Reforms were to start very quickly and Krenz declared that the SED intended to give up its power monopoly – 'such a position cannot be fixed, but must be earned.' But events accelerated further. On 18 March 1990 the first free elections to be held in the GDR took place. Against all expectations the Christian Democratic Union (CDU) emerged as the strongest party and Lothar de Maizière formed a government. The civil-rights activist and Protestant pastor, Rainer Eppelmann, became Minister for Disarmament and Defence (MAV). He was soon to become one of our most important partners in talks. However, the Soviet troops continued to be stationed in the GDR on the basis of the victors' old rights.

When the Wall came down, our NATO partners turned their gaze towards Germany and we were faced with questions which indicated the extent of their worries. It was now important not to let the slightest doubt arise in the West about our reliability and loyalty to the Alliance, but at the same time energetically to develop the opening to the East.

In order to achieve a joint stance, I flew to Washington shortly before Christmas with the relevant permanent secretary and the head of the staff department for military policy. In talks with Pentagon politicians concerned with security issues we saw the developments in the East as positive, regarded a relapse into confrontation as very unlikely, and tried to assess the possible military risks of the economic developments and ethnic tensions in eastern Europe. However, at that time none of us felt able to propose a radical change in our strategy and a regrouping of the forces. The development of the successor to the short-range Lance nuclear missile was adhered to, as was the doctrine of forward defence. In addition, low-level flights were to continue, even though it could be foreseen that it would be increasingly difficult to explain their military necessity to the public, in view of the crumbling Warsaw Pact.

However, in time the changing world situation was bound to influence NATO strategy, and the future tasks of the Alliance. This raised a whole series of problems. Above all we were concerned with the question of the military challenges which we would face if German unity came sooner than expected. What would happen to the NVA then? How many U.S. soldiers could remain stationed in Germany if Soviet troops withdrew some day? And could the integrated forward defence close to our eastern frontier be retained if the eastern European states became free democracies? Finally, would not the Bundeswehr have to be reduced by far more than the 75,000 to 95,000 soldiers already planned?

These questions, with all their national and international consequences, were to occupy us a great deal in the months ahead, and they decisively influenced our planning. In the Foreign Ministry they were seen as 'subsidiary technical questions' which had to be subordinated to the prime interest – the hopes for the early unification of Germany. That attitude threatened to worsen the naturally tense relationship between the foreign and defence ministers which was already latent because of their different tasks.

These differing views were to become clear at the start of the new year. It was evident from interviews and speeches by the Foreign Minister, Hans-Dietrich Genscher, that he opposed both the stationing of the Bundeswehr on the territory of the GDR, and an extension of NATO's jurisdiction beyond its present limits. 'Anyone who wants to extend the frontier of NATO to the Oder and Neisse,' said Genscher in an interview with the newspaper, *Bild am Sonntag,* on 28 January 1990, 'slams the door on a united Germany. On the other hand it is undisputed that we shall remain in NATO.' This statement had not been agreed upon within the federal government, and it left the future security status of the unified Germany completely unclear. Would West Germany be under NATO protection in the future, while the East would not be? Did this not amount to the danger of a new division? In addition, there were the justified questions from our allies to the defence minister, as to how this idea could be put into practice.

Even during the security policy *(Wehrkunde)* conference held in Munich in early February 1990, none of the participating Germans, except for the new defence minister, Gerhard Stoltenberg, gave clear support to Germany's membership of NATO. Egon Bahr, a leading security expert from the Social Democratic opposition party, caused particular disquiet with his statement: 'A unified Germany and membership of NATO are mutually exclusive.' U.S. senators present put their position very clearly: without Germany there would be no NATO and without NATO there would be no U.S. troops in Europe and there would no longer be a nuclear guarantee for Germany. Questions posed by our allies were very serious; they were worried that a unified Germany could split NATO and as a result strengthen tendencies in the United States towards isolationism and quitting the alliance. That is why they wanted us to give a clear and unambiguous declaration of loyalty to NATO as the basis for European and German security. Was it possible that German unity would become dynamite for NATO?

In view of this uncertainty, Gerhard Stoltenberg decided in mid-February to make the position of the Defence Ministry absolutely clear at a press conference.

The federal government, he said, had to fulfil a commitment to protect all Germans, a commitment that was indivisible and after unification would apply to the whole of Germany. It was in the interest of the Federal Republic that Articles Five and Six of the NATO treaty (which include the commitment to defend member states'territory in the case of attack) should be confirmed and should in future be made valid for the whole territory of Germany. Germany would remain in the military integration of the alliance and had committed itself not to station any integrated command bodies or units assigned to NATO on the territory of the former GDR, although the former GDR territory would not be demilitarised. He added that NATO protection would apply to the whole of unified Germany. These remarks by Gerhard Stoltenberg led to heated disputes with sections of the liberal Free Democratic Party (FDP), of which Genscher was the outstanding figure, and to the accusation that Stoltenberg was recklessly endangering German unity.

The public discussion ultimately ended with a joint declaration of the two ministers concerning their previously differing viewpoints. It was stated that none of the 'NATO-assigned or non-assigned Bundeswehr forces' were to be stationed on the territory of the GDR. The ministers' declaration, brought about thanks to the intervention of the Federal Chancellor, also stated that the GDR would not be demilitarised, but it nevertheless ruled out the transfer of whole Bundeswehr units to the GDR for the time being. However, a future all-German government was not denied the possibility of independently selecting personnel for the forces of unified Germany. That made it possible for us to decide, following unification, how many servicemen were to be taken on from the former NVA.

Chapter 3

First Talks with the GDR Leadership

After the democratic elections in the GDR and the formation of a government by Lothar de Maizière, Pastor Eppelmann became Minister for Disarmament and Defence. He was willing to have talks with his West German colleagues as soon as possible. However, he did not want them to take place at the Hardthöhe, the Federal Defence Ministry in Bonn, but on neutral ground. So the meeting of the two ministers on 27 April 1990 took place in the Holiday Inn Hotel at Cologne-Bonn airport – the first meeting of two German defence ministers since the foundation of the two states. By then there had also been an end to the shoot-to-kill policy at the Berlin Wall and the GDR frontier.

While Stoltenberg and Eppelmann conducted long and detailed talks alone, the two delegations met to discuss general issues. To our surprise, at the start of the talks Minister Eppelmann's parliamentary secretary, Dr Wiczorek, thanked the Chief of Staff of the NVA, Lieutenant-General Manfred Grätz, and the other NVA officers for preventing army intervention during the dangerous period of upheaval in the GDR. He said that this had earned them the trust of the new government, and that we could speak frankly with each other. However, for those of us from the West, this was not at all obvious. Up until that time there had been no sign of a changeover to democracy in the NVA, or that there had been the necessary self-criticism had taken place, or that there was a readiness for self-cleansing. The chief of the NVA was now the former defence minister of the GDR, Admiral Theodor Hoffmann, and there had been no visible change in the personnel of the military leadership. During the discussion between the delegations this subject was avoided. The changeover process from a party army to the forces of a democratic state, had evidently not yet been seriously tackled. The peaceful revolution was behaving peacefully towards the armed forces of the collapsed SED state and was not affecting them at the core. But, could a genuine new beginning be achieved with the old 'professional cadres'? It seemed doubtful to me.

There were also very different views about what constituted joint German interests. Eppelmann and his delegation saw no important differences between NATO and the Warsaw Pact. They hoped that both alliances would become part of the CSCE process or some as yet undefined European security system, and that the GDR would thereby be able to assume a bridging function between East and West. Our view, that Germany must remain in NATO and that not NATO, but rather the Warsaw Pact, had lost its reason for existence, was met with incomprehension. There was equally little support for the idea that U.S. troops should remain in our country while Soviet forces should withdraw. The other side could not yet be convinced of the importance of the United States and the presence of its troops for European and German security.

For this reason, I awaited with some apprehension the speech that Eppelmann was to make on 2 May to the first conference of NVA commanding officers to be held under his leadership. He declared that the aim of De Maizière's government was German unity, but that after unification there would still be a second German army on the territory of the former GDR; an army that would not be part of any alliance, but would have its own function in ensuring territorial security and would have to be structured, equipped and trained accordingly. 'As regards the NVA,' Eppelmann said, 'I am convinced that it will continue to exist as long as two military alliances, NATO and the Warsaw Pact, exist in Europe.' On this occasion too, Eppelmann failed to mention the role of the armed forces in the old regime, their SED past and the consequences for their personnel. There was only mention of a military reform – that the internal structure was to be changed and democratic principles based on the rule of law were to be introduced – but with unchanged personnel.

At the next conference of senior officers, on 23 May 1990, Admiral Hoffmann was able to explain his view of the Warsaw Pact and the NVA:

> I am convinced that the other countries of the Warsaw Pact will also do all they can to strengthen the Warsaw Pact in order to transform it into a political and military alliance. It is my personal opinion that as long as we remain a member of the Warsaw Pact, our republic, and we the military, should do all we can to strengthen the Warsaw Pact. The Warsaw

Pact is one of the security structures which have evolved in Europe. It stands for security and peace in Europe. That means the NVA has a secure place in these structures and can be proud that we have made a great contribution to the maintenance of peace. None of us wants to do without this membership. We have many friends there as well as our political and military home. Therefore, we want to do all within our power to fulfil the set tasks reliably.

On 28 May the next talks with Minister Eppelmann took place in his ministry in Strausberg, east of Berlin. We were picked up from our hotel in West Berlin. Owing to Berlin's Four-Power status I was not allowed to wear uniform there, so I wore civilian clothes at the initial discussions in the East, which caused some irritated questions. The meeting took place in the conference room of the ministry; present were the permanent secretaries, the chiefs of the NVA and their staff. On our tables were leather-bound writing-cases decorated with the coat of arms of the GDR and the words: 'For the Defence of the Workers' and Farmers' Power'. Three days later the old coat of arms was removed from public buildings.

It once again became clear that Admiral Hoffmann, as the head of the NVA, was hoping to maintain the Warsaw Pact as a 'stabilising element' for as long as possible, and to establish for the NVA a bridging function between East and West. He argued that the NVA could contribute its experience of co-operation with the Soviets and its East European neighbours for the benefit of Germany. Minister Eppelmann also approved of this idea. The political and military leadership of the NVA seemed to have a mutual interest aimed at, initially, retaining the NVA and in the long term, dissolving the two blocs – NATO and the Warsaw Pact – in favour of an undefined European security system. The officer corps of the NVA believed that it had a secure future. There had been no apparent self-cleansing of the NVA; the old leadership cadres were confirmed in office by a government which had emerged from a peaceful revolution, and thus avoided self-critical discussion about the state, the party and the system they had served. Experience of earlier self-cleansing processes in the ruling party were of little help now.

The meeting ended with the signing of framework regulations for official and unofficial contacts between the Bundeswehr and the NVA, as well as an agreement to continue the talks in September, utilising the experience gained in the meantime. From now on there would be reciprocal visits between personnel of the two armies and, as a result, closer contacts between them – but this was to be done cautiously in order not to concern either the allies or the Soviets unduly.

At the Bundeswehr senior officers' conference on 13 June 1990, Minister Stoltenberg took the opportunity to state clearly some basic principles on the issue of the future German forces. After reviewing the current situation in the alliance and the development of the CSCE, he declared that the reliable Western security and economic system based on NATO and the European Community (EC) must be complemented by co-operative, comprehensive security structures for the whole of Europe. Germany would continue to rely on the integration of German forces in the NATO structure on the territory of the present Federal Republic, but the Alliance's security guarantee must now apply to the whole of Germany. The units on the territory of the GDR must therefore be restructured as part of a comprehensive territorial organisation. The aim would be, after a short transitional phase, to create one German army in the united Germany. Until then, Stoltenberg proposed, the initial political and professional contacts should be continued – in addition to meetings between military personnel and civilian staff. This would help to convey the Bundeswehr's self-image as an armed force in a parliamentary democracy, as well as its experience in organisation, in *Innere Führung* (troop education intended to increase the serviceman's readiness to defend freedom and the rule of law), and training.

The minister strongly emphasised that this German army must also continue to abide by the principles of our constitution. 'The conception of *Innere Führung* sets out the principles which must guide the formation of the future German forces.' This made it clear that all members of the NVA would have to break with their SED past and identify themselves with our Basic Law if they wished to remain in the Bundeswehr.

Stoltenberg's guidelines had left no doubt that the NVA could not continue to exist in the unified Germany. Details of the transition and of the size of future German forces had still to be worked out. For the time being we had to decide upon the structure and size of the units to be stationed on the territory of the GDR.

Meanwhile, it had become clear that after the dramatic changes in the states of the Warsaw Pact, the arms-control agreements, and the reduction of Soviet forces in Europe, there was no compelling operational need for the present size of the Bundeswehr. As a result, in early July an understanding was reached within the federal government about the future size of the forces, and at the Federal Chancellor's meeting with Gorbachev in the Caucasus in mid-July, it was decided that unified Germany would, from 1995, have 370,000 service personnel instead of the existing 495,000 in the Bundeswehr and 175,000 in the NVA.

Even before the meeting in the Caucasus, a working-party of the Bundeswehr planning staff had already examined these questions in detail, and in early July had proposed that the units and installations of the NVA should be taken over as Bundeswehr units, then disbanded step-by-step in order to set up new, mixed units according to Bundeswehr criteria. However, until the end of 1994, the final withdrawal date of the Soviet forces, these units would be subject only to German command; there could be no link with NATO structures.

To ensure that from the start there was unified command of all the forces by the person placed in charge, the GDR Ministry for Disarmament and Defence (MAV) had to be closed down. For a transitional period a joint Bundeswehr headquarters would be set up in eastern Germany to take over part of the military duties of the MAV, to ensure there was a unified command, to disband the land, air and naval forces on the basis of the same criteria, and begin the formation of new units of the three services. The Bundeswehr headquarters would then be closed down and responsibility transferred to the commanding officers of the three services. Duties of the MAV in the civilian sphere were – if necessary – to be carried out by the Federal Defence Ministry's office in eastern Germany, or by a new regional office responsible for military administration.

In the GDR, apparently, little was known about these plans – or they were not believed. In mid-July Minister Eppelmann once again took a stance, and repeated that even after the unification of Germany there would be an independent army on the territory of the GDR – the NVA, though reduced in size. He said that it could be under the command of an 'organ' subject to the MAV or linked to the new Länder. New uniforms had even been designed for it already.

The career and short-service personnel of the NVA took new oaths of loyalty on 20 July, the anniversary of the 1944 officers' plot against Hitler, and five days after the historic Kohl-Gorbachev agreement which set the size of future German forces at 370,000 service personnel, provided for the withdrawal of Soviet troops from Germany by 1994, and for the NATO membership and unity of Germany. At the oath-taking, members of the anti-Nazi resistance in the Second World War were commemorated in a military ceremony. Minister Eppelmann thanked the officers of the NVA for preventing 'a Chinese situation' in 1989 – a reference to the Peking massacre of dissidents in 1986. He pointed to parallels between the events of 20 July 1944 and those of November 1989. The choice of the 20th of July, he said, was a plea to the NVA soldiers 'to declare their support for the new, constitutional system and for the democratic and humane political and social order.'

The new oath of allegiance, to the now democratic GDR, had been approved by the Volkskammer some time previously, on 26 April 1990, to supersede the Socialist oath. But, however understandable this was, the new oath-taking was controversial both in the NVA and in the Bundeswehr. Did it not appear that an army which had not yet accounted for its own history was being styled as an army of resistance through this linking to the events of the 20th of July? In addition, it could be foreseen – although evidently not everyone had realised this – that this army would not exist for much longer.

However, while the NVA commanders continued to believe in the theory of two armies in one state, and also to communicate this to their soldiers, the troops themselves were made to feel insecure due to reports in West German newspapers about the imminent disbandment of the NVA. During an internal official meeting in the MAV early in July 1990 the NVA Chief of Staff denied these reports and continued to back the concept of two armies in one country, although he did point out the problems of such a solution. However, the demands of a well-known journalist that the past history of NVA career soldiers should be investigated was met with an angry refusal: this commentator, it was claimed, was proving that he did not understand democracy.

All the same, taken as a whole, the responsible GDR military leaders were determined, in spite of the many difficulties, the tense psychological situation and the lack of concrete orders, to do everything possible to ensure calm and good sense in the NVA and to prevent rash, incalculable reactions. According to the minutes of an official meeting in July, the NVA Chief of Staff stated that:

> We survived the autumn of 1989 without the use of force. We also survived the critical days in the first half of January 1990 without the use of force, and we should also see it as our obligation to survive critical phase which is now approaching without the use of force. Nothing would be more tragic than if, as a result of thoughtless, ill-considered acts by this or that group of servicemen, in this or that base, situations arose which got out of control. The NVA cannot be compared with other professions which can demonstrate by using equipment associated with their work. What the refuse collectors in Berlin can do with their lorries we cannot have the NVA doing with their tanks. The results would be terrible, this must be stated quite clearly.

The NVA held to this position right up until its disbandment – an achievement that must be given great credit. Whether this resulted from the realisation that there had to be a fundamental change from the Socialist system to a democratic state based on the rule of law, or whether it was based on the pragmatic assessment that the NVA could no longer use its methods to influence the revolution and the peaceful changeover, must remain in question. There were certainly differing motives, but in the end the result was the same: the NVA remained until the end a controlled and calculable force. It may have been difficult for some senior officers to take part in the disbandment of their own army, but perhaps some saw an opportunity to prove themselves and thus qualify for service in the Bundeswehr.

On 10 August the two ministers met again and Eppelmann agreed to Stoltenberg's proposal to send a civilian and military liaison group from Bonn to Strausberg in order to improve the preconditions and information for the planning of all-German forces. Only a few days later this liaison group began work. Time was pressing, only two months remained before the unification of Germany. People were working under pressure in all departments of the Defence Ministry in Bonn to put the minister's instructions into practice.

Meanwhile the crisis in the Gulf had reached a new pitch and a German minesweeping unit had been sent to the eastern Mediterranean to free U.S. ships for operations in the Gulf. In parliament and among the political parties demands were being made that the Bundeswehr participate in international operations outside the NATO area; other voices called for the creation of a European peace-keeping force to include the Bundeswehr. Discussions were concluded only at the end of August, after a series of talks at government and parliamentary level. Government and opposition were in agreement that Bundeswehr operations outside the NATO area would only be possible after the clarification of matters through an amendment to the constitution.

During this turbulent political phase I was preparing myself for leaving my post as head of the minister's planning staff on 1 October 1990, and taking over duty as the Commanding General of 3rd Army Corps in Koblenz. However, things did not go as planned. On 14 August Gerhard Stoltenberg informed me in a very private conversation that he intended to make me commander of the Bundeswehr-Kommando Ost (BKO) – the Bundeswehr headquarters in eastern Germany. He said he considered this task as particularly difficult and politically explosive, and wanted to give it to me as I had the necessary experience in the ministry and in the political sphere, and as the head of his planning staff I was most familiar with the background. He felt that I was the best man for the job. Although I had some idea of the kind of problems I was going to encounter, I accepted: 'Minister, I shall take on this task with a warm heart and a cool head. I'll be happy to return to my homeland in the East, near to my birthplace.'

I was aware of what an important and challenging, but also very risky task I had taken on. I had now become responsible for ensuring that the strategies we had developed for disbanding the NVA were carried out, and could thus make a decisive contribution to the creation of joint German forces. If I, as the senior officer, were to fail, there could be serious consequences – extending to possible mutinies which had been acted out in various scenarios. One could not even exclude the possibility of efforts by the terrorist Red Army Faction or isolated members of the Stasi to use the opportunity to worsen the dangerous situation through attacks on property or assassinations.

After intensive discussions among the top military personnel, and in a committee including the defence minister, his permanent secretaries and the Bundeswehr Chief of Staff, the minister made the basic decisions on which we urgently needed clarity:

1. The NVA will cease to exist, and from 15 October, the (originally) planned Day of German Unity, the personnel of the former NVA will temporarily become members of the Bundeswehr, with duties according to the *Soldatengesetz* (the federal law governing the Bundeswehr).

2. The units of the NVA will be gradually disbanded. The new units of the Bundeswehr will be formed from members of the Bundeswehr and of the former NVA.

3. Up to about 20,000 career and short-service personnel of the former NVA can, after proving themselves, be taken on as short-service personnel for two years, or as career soldiers. The total strength in eastern Germany, 50,000, will comprise up to 20,000 former members of the NVA, as career or short-service personnel, up to 5,000 Bundeswehr career or short-service personnel and 25,000 conscripts and volunteers.

4. The training of the GDR conscripts who are called up on 1 September will be changed to accord with our training methods and legal system.

5. The armed forces in eastern Germany will be under the central command of the BKO, a body directly subordinate to the Federal Defence Ministry.

In a subsequent ministerial order the function of the BKO, under my command, was described as follows:

The Bundeswehr-Kommando Ost is a central superior headquarters of the armed forces, set up for a limited period, responsible for all three services and manned by mixed (Western and Eastern) personnel. It is directly subordinate to the Federal Ministry of Defence. The military superior of the commanding officer is the deputy of the Inspector-General. From the time that the Federal Defence Minister takes over command, all units, offices and institutions of the former forces of the part of Germany which has acceded shall be subordinate to the Bundeswehr-Kommando Ost. Main points: The military command over all sections of the land, air and naval forces, which continue to exist in the acceded part of Germany from the time of the take-over of command until the introduction of the Bundeswehr structure, will be concentrated in the Bundeswehr-Kommando Ost. In the main the Bundeswehr-Kommando Ost will be responsible centrally for military command and for transitional and winding-up matters. Initially the Bundeswehr-Kommando Ost will be in charge of all matters necessary for the introduction of the

Bundeswehr structure. After the Bundeswehr regional administration for the East has assumed responsibility for military administration, according to Article 87b of the Basic Law, and has taken over the sections which have previously done this work, the Bundeswehr-Kommando Ost will be exclusively responsible for commanding the armed forces in the acceded part of Germany, as well as for their disbandment or transfer to the decentralised command organisation.

Five main tasks were emphasised: the direction of the subordinate sphere; that is, all military offices, training colleges and units of the entire NVA; the supervision of the introduction of the decentralised command organisation in the following departments: army, air force, navy, Bundeswehr central military service, Bundeswehr central medical service; the disbandment of units and institutions which did not accord with the Bundeswehr structure; the taking over and storing of equipment of the former forces for possible further use or hand-over to allies; assistance in the withdrawal of Soviet troops.

In short, we had to take over the NVA, to maintain security and control, to disband the units step-by-step, to dismiss the overwhelming majority of the personnel, to collect the enormous quantities of equipment, arms and ammunition, to establish new units of the Bundeswehr and to co-operate with the Soviet troops and help in their withdrawal. For the internal structure of the BKO we planned: the commanding officer, a lieutenant-general; the commanding officer's deputy, a major-general; and a chief of staff, a brigadier; with the usual personnel in support; directly subordinated to the commanding officer were the liaison staff to the Western Group of the Soviet forces, the department of legal advisers and the subordinate commanders. The Staff itself had eight sections with a planned strength of 240 officers and non-commissioned officers from Western Germany and 360 from the East, plus about two hundred civilian staff.

After we had made the basic decisions, we had to put them into effect. Above all, we had to avoid the danger of chaos during the transfer of the NVA into the Bundeswehr. I feared that indiscipline could break out, that whole units might split off and that we might no longer be able to adequately protect arms and ammunition. For this reason, I argued that we must try to convince sufficient members of the NVA to co-operate in the orderly disbandment of the NVA and the establishment of the new units. The capability to exercise command, the guarding of equipment, the re-organisation of logistics, as well as medical provision – all this could be guaranteed only if we had sufficient personnel. We needed the help of officers and NCOs of the NVA, but were unable to conceal the fact that in the long term we could incorporate only a small number of personnel. Instead, we had to convince them that there was a common task to carry out in the Germany that now belonged to all of us. Through the orderly disbandment of the NVA and the establishment of the new forces, we said, they would be able to show that they were masters of their military craft and were doing their duty even under such unusual conditions; the goal, we pointed out, was an all-German Bundeswehr with service personnel from all parts of the country.

It was also of decisive psychological importance that in the united Germany the soldiers of the *one* army should wear the same uniform. We had realised by the middle of August that this could only be the so-called field uniform, of NATO olive, as it was impossible to supply all the soldiers of the NVA with the walking-out uniform. As for the NATO-olive uniform – actually a kind of working uniform – it was available in sufficient numbers and in all sizes, with the necessary badges of rank. To avoid the impression that the NVA personnel were second-class troops, I proposed to the minister that we should issue the field uniform exclusively – that is, for the officers from the West too. If even the commanding officer of the BKO and his officers were wearing the uniform of NATO olive, there would be no longer be any external distinction.

During all of these preparations a stormy debate was continuing about the dismissal of NVA generals and admirals. Eppelmann wanted some of them to be incorporated into the Bundeswehr. Among the senior officers of the Bundeswehr, too, it was suggested that some NVA generals should be taken on for specialised professional tasks. Even one or two parliamentarians felt that we should not dismiss all of the top-ranking officers. It was argued that they should not be made into martyrs. In view of the political good sense which had, until then, been expected from Bundeswehr generals, I was surprised by such statements.

The decision was delayed for a long period of time, which was particularly harmful to the officers concerned, whose future remained completely uncertain. In mid-September Stoltenberg informed Eppelmann of his intention not to incorporate any of these officers into the Bundeswehr. It was our view that the imminent new beginning must be stressed in particular at the highest level; a general of the NVA, who had achieved high rank through fighting for Socialism and the class struggle, could not convincingly stand up in the Bundeswehr for our Basic Law, our concept of humankind and our legal system. We also felt that neither the young conscripts nor the population in the former GDR would support the incorporation of such NVA figures. Only after some hesitation did Minister Eppelmann agree; a few days before 3 October (the day of German unification) he instructed his Permanent Secretary Werner Ablass, to dismiss the generals. Thus the dismissals were carried out at very short notice, which caused bitterness among many people.

The senior Bundeswehr officers who were to work alongside me were selected during this period. In view of the challenge facing us, I insisted on taking to the East only highly motivated officers. The numbers who volunteered were far greater than those needed – and this occurred at a time when the conditions and remuneration were still absolutely unclear.

The imminent disbandment of the NVA and the incorporation of some of its officers into the Bundeswehr had sparked off lively discussion in both parts of Germany, particularly in the media. Reactions differed, ranging from approval to strong opposition. These sometimes very emotional and heated debates can be understood only if one appreciates the manner in which the NVA depicted the enemy, and that until the end of 1989 'hate education' was part of the basic training of every member of the NVA. Even in the summer of 1988, the *Armeerundschau*, the official organ of the NVA, stated:

> Our hate is not blind and does not express itself violently. It does not stem from inhumanity, is not motivated by personal antipathy and is not rooted in discontent about the state of the world. On the contrary: just because we love life and want to preserve it, because we want everyone in the world to have a life worth living and are therefore fulfilling our soldierly duties – just for that reason we can hate from the bottom of our hearts all that and all those who stand in the way of realising those longings ... Our hate is inflamed by the crimes of imperialism ... by attitudes such as those of the Defence Minister of the FRG, Wörner ...

In addition, a book entitled *What it Means to Be a Soldier*, which was given to the service personnel when they took their oaths, included detailed passages about the class enemy and about imperialism and its soldiers:

> Your enemies are the mercenaries of imperialism, who have been whipped up into anti-Communism and drilled for aggressive war, and who would not hesitate for a moment to shoot at you when ordered. Whatever language they speak, whether German or English, whatever uniform they wear, that of the Bundeswehr or another imperialist army ... whoever bears arms for imperialism and acts on its behalf is our enemy.

In view of this attitude of mind and these statements about the Bundeswehr and its soldiers, the public disputes in Western Germany were understandable. And, of course, the career and short-service personnel of the NVA discussed whether they were willing to serve in the Bundeswehr, the army of the former class enemy. They had no idea of what they could expect, how they would be treated and how they would cope with the quick changeover. They were all extremely unsure of themselves.

To give an impression of the differing attitudes which prevailed, following are two contributions to the discussion, one made by an officer from the West and another from an officer from the East:

The NVA: Not Our Comrades

At last the time has come: now that, thanks to the agreement of President Gorbachev, the last bastions preventing the integration of united Germany into NATO have fallen, there are also no more obstacles to military reunification. The call is: soldiers of both German states – stand to attention for unification! Over here and over there the representatives of both ministries are zealously operating as match-makers of the forced marriage; they are only haggling about the amount of each side's military 'household goods' which can be brought into the new life partnership – 50,000 NVA men are, according to the Unification Treaty, to be taken over by the Bundeswehr.

But in their costing acrobatics the planners seem deliberately to be ignoring one thing: that in civilised society a marriage needs the agreement of both parties. In the case of the Bundeswehr this seems very doubtful. Its readiness for a rendezvous to enable the two to get to know each other, to talk, to give assistance, does not yet mean at all agreement on living together permanently.

The Bundeswehr can now look back on nearly 35 years of democracy in the Federal Republic, whose freedom and peace it helped to ensure. Its structure is imbued with the ideas of *Innere Führung* which, by the way, was largely developed and put into force by an officer of the former Wehrmacht – but one who sympathised with the resistance against the National Socialist dictatorship.

This concept and this tradition of *Innere Führung*, which has grown up over nearly 35 years, distinguishes this Bundeswehr from all other forces of the past and present. The Bundeswehr serviceman knows very well: a soldier can do wrong, and he knows which system he can serve, which strategy he can follow and which order he may carry out – and when he must refuse.

On the other hand, the NVA: not only did it outwardly resemble the old German Wehrmacht but its internal structures were analogous. Outwardly it appeared as a compliant instrument in the hands of the Soviet General Staff, greatly praised and respected for its efficiency.

Internally this army, and particularly its hated leaders, were a criminal dictatorship's instrument of repression. Its officers were rewarded with a privileged standard of living for the tough job of oppressing their own people, according to the motto: whoever bumps off enemies of the people on the anti-fascist protective wall can help himself in the Intershop.

No one was forced against their will to become an officer or non-commissioned officer in the NVA. On the contrary, the precondition for service as a volunteer in the NVA was a high degree of identification with the regime; almost all officers and most of the non-commissioned officers were members of the SED. Someone who has achieved a high degree of identification for many years does not change overnight into a convinced democrat.

Scientific research has shown that by about the age of thirty the development of the ability to make moral judgments has come to an end. It follows that by that time at the latest a serviceman can realise and judge the cause he is working for and for which he is ready, if necessary, to sacrifice his life. This also applies to an officer or non-commissioned officer of the NVA: either he has realised the type of system he is serving, in which case he is unscrupulous, or he was actually not able to make judgments, then he was just stupid. The Bundeswehr is, however, no refuge for stupid or unscrupulous military leaders.

A forced unification of the two German armed forces is unacceptable for the Bundeswehr; and for the members of the NVA, who would be seen for a long time as second-class servicemen, it would be an injustice. There remains only the quickest possible disbandment of the NVA. All former members of the NVA, not only those who are not needed in the Bonn plans, should be retired with appropriate remuneration. The costs would scarcely matter compared to the total costs of unification.

Written by a Bundeswehr captain, a lecturer at the Bundeswehr Academy for Information and Communication in Waldbröl, near Bonn. Source: *Die Zeit,* 14 September 1990.

We have only served loyally

What are the private and social attitudes of German servicemen in a united Germany? The spectrum of opinions is very wide among us as well, and our dilemma is certainly greater than that in the Bundeswehr.

Who were we and whom did we serve? The easy way would be to put the past behind us and instead to plan future possibilities.

But the fact remains that for decades we trod different paths. Well, one could say we were sent down different paths – it was not Germany's wish, the Cold War was not a German invention. But even from this point of view the decisive question is: did I serve loyally and could I also reconcile my service with my conscience? When I answer: yes, I could, and so could many comrades I know, some readers will certainly express doubts.

I don't know the thinking of officers on the frontier, who were confronted daily with shootings on the Wall, lethal shootings, but I imagine they were constantly having pangs of conscience. Anyone who has done military service will remember his 'first shot' because there are many questions linked with this 'first shot' which each of us can answer only for himself. Everyone who was no 'killer', or did not only see the 'job', put these questions to himself. Of course, there was the question of obeying orders, there were military and legal regulations, and the conviction that we were protecting the state frontier of a sovereign state. But the individual situation was decisive because only here can there be guilt in the legal sense. If this can be proved, there must be prosecution – even bearing in mind differentiated grades of guilt, as formulated in 1946 by Karl Jaspers.

The reader could also ask: 'You protected that criminal state with your bayonets. Were there never any doubts as to whether you were doing right?' I was born in 1948 and am in my twenty-third year of service. What motives caused me, in 1967, to put on the NVA uniform? There were subjective reasons – such as technical interest and also lust for adventure – but also objective motives. What my father had told me about his experiences in the war strengthened my feeling: that must not happen again. And as a citizen I felt the duty to do something to maintain peace. Of course I, too, believed in an ideology which, like all other ideologies, sought to get individuals to identify with it. I identified myself with it because I, too, was convinced that the GDR should be developed as an alternative to the FRG. And the chance of that, at the start of the 1970s, was by no means a small one.

Thus we had a firm structure of standards, ideals and thought processes. Nearly everything was subordinated to our army duties – even family life. A platoon leader who was on duty for sixty hours or more did not watch the clock; what was decisive was that an order was carried out and the squad was still fit for action. As there was no payment by the hour this must have been our 'Modus des Seins' [Way of Living] as described by Erich Fromm in his book *Haben und Sein* [To Have or to Be]. Collective work and achievements, and collective success, were the basic principle which one accepted voluntarily.

Naturally there was information about some shortcomings of the system, which soldiers brought from 'outside' or which one learned about oneself. But this was often suppressed, we saw only what we wanted to see, also because we assumed that those 'outside', the leaders of the party and state, would succeed in the end. This attitude naturally did not encourage critical thought. I had my first doubts in 1987, asking myself: 'Why aren't we using the "Gorby effect"?' Today this is clear to me. but then I could not see the links between party, state and ideology.

These thoughts are not intended to absolve guilt. When, at the end of 1989, people went on to the streets shouting 'We are the people', we at first saw that as 'counter-revolution'. But then we began to have doubts: the demonstrators were peaceful and they were united. They were not radical. They had many questions and they were always given the same answers. With the demonstrations of 4th of November 1989 the wheel had turned full circle. Anyone who was honest cut out 'counter' – the revolution remained. Although I am not a Christian, at that time I wanted to thank God and all the others who prevented a civil war.

That does not, of course, amount to legitimation for a democratic army. But we had first of all to realise that we were not a democratic army. After the removal of the political leadership the introduction of democratic institutions began. Naturally, the democratisation of an army does not come about just by pressing a button. But the possibility of changing from a 'party army' to an army of the people does exist; coupling acceptance of the facts with commonsense remains the greatest virtue. By that I mean that the NVA can contribute something to all-German armed forces but it does not have to do so if the political leadership decides otherwise.

The author of this piece was a lieutenant-colonel of the NVA in Neubrandenburg. Source: *Die Zeit,* 14 September 1990.

The above discussion shows that clarity had to be achieved as quickly as possible, in order to achieve unity among the service chiefs and reach a consensus about the way in which to create common German forces. The armed forces of the NVA and the Bundeswehr were faced with a unique challenge; they would either master the problem together or fail. So the Chief of Defence Staff, in a letter to Bundeswehr personnel, explained the position of the military leadership:

From the day of unification, in accordance with the guidelines of the Unification Treaty, we shall all be members of the Bundeswehr. I expect that the duty of comradeship will be taken seriously. Our varied backgrounds and differences of opinion must not endanger the process of growing together. There must be no sweeping judgments or condemnations. Extreme statements and behaviour are not fair to individuals. They call in question the credibility of our values and our view of humanity and do not help us in our work. Only together can we achieve the reorganisation and changeover.

This clarification came rather late but it did have a calming effect. In addition, some officers and NCOs had meanwhile had an opportunity to gain experience in units in the East. They had by then obtained a differentiated picture, were being careful in making judgments and were convinced that many members of the NVA, too, would be ready to revise their old concept of the enemy.

Chapter 4

THE NVA PRIOR TO
3 OCTOBER 1990

On 18 January 1956 the Volkskammer approved the law which established the NVA and the Ministry for National Defence. The NVA evolved from the barracked units of the Volkspolizei and already comprised 120,000 soldiers in the year it was founded; it was a volunteer army. In order to underline the claim, both internally and externally, that the GDR was a sovereign, national state, the uniform of the former Wehrmacht was introduced.

When the NVA was founded, the ruling party, the SED, had claimed – and obtained – the right to run it. The 1963 party programme states: 'The most important source of the strength of our armed forces is their leadership by the party of the working class. The party seeks to ensure that all members of the armed forces become class-conscious fighters for socialism ...'

In order to instil Communist ideas, Socialist military education was practised; it was found throughout the whole sphere of education, from kindergarten to training at work. Socialist military training, 'like every educational process, speaks both to the mind and the feelings. It is systematically differentiated according to political and military needs, to age and occupation ...' (NVA *Military Encyclopaedia*). This form of education served the overall development of the Socialist personality and reached its climax during training in the NVA.

Thus, it was thus only consistent that, in January 1962, conscription was decided upon and its length fixed at 18 months. The young citizen of the GDR swore the following oath to his fatherland:

I swear to serve the German Democratic Republic, my fatherland, loyally in all respects and, on the order of the Workers' and Farmers' Government, to defend it against the enemy. I swear to be always ready, along-side the Soviet armed forces and the armed forces of the Socialist countries allied with us, to defend Socialism against all enemies and to risk my life to achieve victory ...

Before joining the NVA the young conscripts usually went through military training at several levels. After the kindergarten came the *Ernst Thälmann* young pioneers' organisation, which included about eighty-five per cent of six to fourteen-year-old children, who could already prove their military skills in 'children's manoeuvres'. In the Society for Sport and Technology young people aged between sixteen and eighteen were prepared physically, and in various subjects, for basic military service and military careers, while the official youth organisation, *Freie Deutsche Jugend* (FDJ), the Free German Youth, was supposed to awaken the young people's defence readiness and their willingness to serve in the forces. The GDR Youth Law of 1974 states: 'It is the duty of young people to obtain education on military policy, initial military knowledge and skills as well as to serve in the National People's Army and the other organisations of national defence.' With this, pre-military training practically entered the schools, and it was only consistent that in 1978 military education was made a compulsory subject in the higher classes of secondary schools. An important part of this military training was teaching the children to hate as a necessary addition to the 'respect and love for the working class and its party, to the well-being of the GDR and particularly to the peoples of the Soviet Union ... Because we deeply love everything progressive, everything that is noble and serves the dignity of human beings, we deeply hate those forces which hinder or threaten such things. Our hate has therefore a different ethical and moral basis than that of the imperialists and their henchmen.' (From recommendations on Socialist military training). These obscure conceptions were trickled into the souls of the children and hammered into the brains of the youth.

By means of a comprehensive organisation the party was able to watch over every soldier in the NVA. To do this it had four different organisational paths, which were linked to each other. They were the political organs, the party organisations, the FDJ organisations and the SED functionaries in officers' uniforms. A large number of paid chief instructors, chairmen and aides were employed for all sections of party work. More than ninety-five per cent of the officers and more than fifty per cent of the NCOs were members of the SED; promotion was to be obtained only with the support of the SED and not in opposition to it. The party had the whole NVA firmly in its grip – 'political and ideological education is the centrepiece of Socialist military leadership.' The training of officers and NCOs served to shape the Socialist 'soldier personality', as described in the following extracts from the *Military Encyclopaedia*:

The Socialist soldier personality
• is fully loyal to the working class and its Marxist-Leninist party ...
• is imbued with deep hate against imperialism and its mercenaries ...
• is one of the most important factors in the superiority of a Socialist army over any imperialist aggressor.

The NVA was on the side of the party – it belonged to the party – and was firmly in the Socialist camp. On 20 November 1965 the party newspaper *Neues Deutschland* stated that the NVA belonged 'to the first strategic formation of the Socialist military coalition.' This classification meant that the military build-up had been concluded and the quality mark of Socialist reliability and combat readiness had been awarded. The NVA was thus among those formations which, in case of military conflict, would together with the Soviets, have been the first which could attack central Europe – that is, the FRG. In 1968 the NVA demonstratively proved its Socialist reliability during the invasion of Czechoslovakia.

Service personnel of the NVA were part of a readiness and mobilisation system which was able to react quickly and which could be activated directly from Moscow. One third of the air-defence forces were in constant readiness. The land forces could leave barracks within two hours, their weapons systems fully supplied with ammunition and assured of further supplies. In addition to six active army divisions the NVA had five motorised infantry divisions available for mobilisation in training centres and camps – everything was excellently organised.

The personal demands on officers and men were extremely high and they meant that the career soldiers led a life apart from the civilian world, in their own housing estates. The level of eighty-five per cent readiness meant they had only one free day and evening each week. Both the career and short-service personnel had to accept this situation. A double discipline was applied: that of the party and that of the military. Careful selection of personnel, political indoctrination, a one-sided information policy and a ban on contacts with the West made the career personnel of the NVA into reliable, elite functionaries. They were rewarded with social privileges which were met by disapproval and opposition from the rest of the population.

The career cadres of the NVA, as the career soldiers were called, were largely officers. The proportion of officers was at least three times as high as in the Bundeswehr. Professional training was intensive and led to many academic qualifications; specialisations which had been obtained were further developed in the management of personnel. In this lay a certain strength for the leadership apparatus; the price, however, was that officers were narrowly restricted to their own sphere of work and knew little of other areas. The Bundeswehr practice of ordering a soldier to carry out a mission but letting the individual decide on the method – *Führung durch Auftrag* – did not exist in the NVA, and the almost complete separation of fields prevented any exchanges of professional and personal information. Training in the Bundeswehr is in complete contrast. We train the career and short-service soldiers to be able to carry out orders in an independent manner. This means that when an order is given only the goal, but not the method of achieving it, is specified, and this gives the responsible person on the spot greater freedom of manoeuvre. This procedure requires appropriate training and the ability to take one's own decisions. Because of this, considerable demands are made of the individual, in order to achieve suitable training and education of junior officers and NCOs.

As for NVA officers, they were intentionally prevented from making independent decisions. Only at the highest level were the many threads of specialised knowledge brought together and assessed. The NVA required highly specialised experts who had no overview of the whole system. Room for manoeuvre was restricted by numerous regulations and all details were laid down beforehand.

A further particular aspect was that in the GDR military administration – which according to the Basic Law is, in the Federal Republic, carried out by civilian officials – was executed exclusively by servicemen. In addition, the NVA undertook many duties which in the Federal Republic are the responsibility of civilian officials or private bodies: ranging from telecommunications installations and the subsidising of sport in armed forces' sports clubs, to running school and kindergarten canteens. Furthermore, in small garrison towns in particular, the NVA carried out many public functions and consequently had a dominant role.

From 1985 the economic situation of the GDR grew dramatically worse. From this time onwards up to 55,000 NVA personnel had to work in the general economy, while the armed forces continued to be kept at an eighty-five per cent state of readiness. It became obvious to the servicemen that the order to maintain a high state of readiness, while having large numbers of absent personnel, made little sense militarily. In this period the internal decay of the NVA began – a process which was to speed up after the *Wende,* the changeover from Communist rule to democracy. On 3 October 1990, the day on which the NVA was taken over, it was no longer the highly trained, militarily and ideologically reliable army of previous years. Political developments in recent years had left deep scars which finally led to considerable insecurity among officers and men, as well as to acts of indiscipline. The extreme example of this was a mutiny of conscripts in January 1990 at the Beelitz base, south-west of Berlin.

Owing to this insecurity, after the events of November 1989 efforts began to be made to alter the internal situation in the NVA by means of military reform and also, through ideas borrowed from the Federal Republic, to begin changing attitudes. The aim was to change the NVA from a party army, to an army with democratic legitimacy. The armed forces of the GDR were subordinated to the Volkskammer, while the democratic parties, organisations and movements were given equal rights to carry out political activity among the soldiers and civilian employees of the NVA. Moreover, a number of instructions were issued regarding conditions in the barracks. A forty-five hour week was established, with duties to be performed only from Mondays to Fridays. The servicemen were addressed as 'Herr' instead of 'Genosse' (comrade) and were allowed to keep their passports and identity cards. When they had local leave, the soldiers were permitted to go beyond the garrison limits, something which previously even the officers had not been permitted to do, owing to the high state of readiness. In off-duty hours they were allowed to wear civilian clothes. The requirement to obtain permission for possessing a tape recorder or a car was rescinded, as well as all previous restrictions on receiving western radio and television broadcasts. And, of course, in off-duty hours, they were now permitted to take newspapers and periodicals from 'non-Socialist foreign countries' into barracks.

However, while officially the 'old thinking' was dropped and changes in the command and the training of the forces were promised, there was a failure to inform the servicemen about the principles and spirit of the armed forces of a democratic state. For this reason, but also because of the rush of events, the military reforms progressed no further than their initial stages, while the signs of disintegration increased. Internal discipline was relaxed, often by publishing ministerial orders in the media before informing superior officers, so that officers learned from their subordinates of the new situation before they themselves had been officially informed. Here the press was quicker than official channels – a new experience in the GDR. Loss of authority was the result.

On 3 October 1990, the day of German unification, all generals and admirals, as well as officers aged over fifty-five, were dismissed, along with officers of the so-called Political Main Administration, the Politoffiziere. The size of the NVA – while it was still under the GDR government – had been reduced by mid-September from 175,000 to about 103,000; the military intelligence service, the military prosecutors and the propaganda units had been disbanded. Thus on 2 October we had new information about the number of personnel and the amount of equipment available. According to that information we estimated the personnel strength at about 103,000, including 32,000 officers and 20,000 NCOs. We assessed the equipment strength as consisting of 2,300 battle tanks, 7,800 armoured fighting vehicles, 2,500 artillery pieces, 400 fighter aircraft, 71 warships, 50 attack helicopters, 1.2 million small arms and 300,000 tons of ammunition. As no one knew how many career and short-service men would really still be in the NVA after 3 October, the decisive question for us was: how could we take control of these enormous quantities of equipment and guarantee that it was securely guarded. What is more, it was not clear how far the officers, who had been indoctrinated by the Communists and trained to hate us, were really ready to serve, at least for a transitional period. Would a sense of responsibility be stronger than the Socialist military training? I was optimistic.

Chapter 5

LAST DAYS
BEFORE UNIFICATION

September-October 1990

Discussions are still continuing in the Hardthöhe and in parliament about how many soldiers should be dismissed on 3 October. In view of budgetary cuts the Bundeswehr Chief of Staff and the state secretary in charge of the budget and finances want, immediately on takeover, to drastically reduce the size of the NVA in order to reduce running costs. However, in the NVA there is already much commotion and insecurity; mass dismissals could cause the situation to get out of control. On top of this, we do not know where to put the arms, the ammunition and the rest of the equipment. Supported by the minister, I successfully oppose unduly hasty dismissals, but in the discussions I am accused of being too timid.

Gerhard Stoltenberg, too, has been told that there are fears the NVA could break up if the future is not soon made clear. Stoltenberg shows concern. Danger is threatening sooner than we had all imagined. The Chief of Naval Staff tells me the naval chief of the NVA fears that most of his officers could leave the service on 2 October as their future prospects are slim, while conditions offered for leaving on 2 October are relatively favourable. In this situation, he states, security can no longer be guaranteed in his service. Moreover, rumours are circulating that there are plans to scuttle a few ships out of desperation – ships that the Federal Navy will not take over anyway.

In this tense situation the two ministers and their delegations hold talks on 11 September in East Berlin, in order to make concrete and detailed agreements for the transition after 3 October. The Federal Minister explains that after 3 October most units will continue to exist for a period and disbandment will take place step-by-step according to a schedule yet to be worked out. By 1994 at the latest, the target of 50,000 men must be reached. In addition, the head-quarters would be partly taken over by generals and admirals of the Bundeswehr, and the subordinate units partly taken over by Bundes-wehr officers. Those NVA commanding officers who remained would be assisted by Bundeswehr training teams.

Over a snack I talk with some generals of the NVA who remain in responsible positions. They have few illusions about their future. We have an intensive discussion about military questions, and what is going to happen after 3 October. They have a high opinion of their personal contribution to the peaceful changeover, and upon this they base their claim for fair treatment; the Communist past does not appear in their argumentation – I have to remind them of it. They assume that they will be dismissed but want to be clear now about their personal situation, and demand that they are told the truth. They accuse the existing leadership of wavering and of having provided too little information, but they are ready to ensure the changeover to the Bundeswehr. I think back to the speech by Min-ister Eppelmann on 2 May, when he spoke about the tasks of the NVA in a united Germany. He has been unable to keep any of his promises; political developments have not only been much more rapid, but also more radical than any of us had expected.

The talks between the two ministers bring greater clarity – for the NVA too, at last. On 12 September Minister Eppelmann holds his last meeting of senior officers and asks me to participate. However, I decline because I do not wish to say anything until I have taken charge. I want to hold my first meeting of senior officers on 10 October.

We now have a mountain of problems before us. The question of the future prospects for members of the NVA, of training for civilian jobs, pensions and transitional payments, the remuneration of those 'still in use' (servicemen who, for a time, are staying on with a special status without becoming short-service members of the Bundeswehr) – all of this remains unclear even though it is of decisive importance for those concerned. We are going to be on a tightrope and it will be difficult to remain credible. I am determined to make things clear after 3 October 1990, even if that won't always be easy.

I use a weekend in September to make a visit, with my wife, to our old and new home area, in Brandenburg. We also want to have a look at Strausberg, my future base.

As we leave Berlin on the autobahn towards Potsdam, the sight of the frontier control installations creates an oppressive atmosphere. Involuntarily we think of our passports but there is no one who wants to see them, they have become unnecessary – at last! The autobahn towards Frankfurt/Oder and Poland is in bad condition but heavily used. We leave it near Fürstenwalde on the River Spree; from here the road leads to our hometown, Bad Saarow.

The former Chaussestraße, today the August-Bebel-Straße, is unchanged, still with the old cobblestones. Everything has a sad, grim look – no bright colours, no new buildings. My parents-in-law's house is as it was in 1953 when the family fled to the West; although paint and plaster are flaking off, the flats are evidently occupied. In the downstairs corridor are the old electricity meter and wiring dating from the 1930s. Nothing has been changed, it has just been worn out. In the small shop on the ground floor are two women who greet us in a friendly way and can remember my wife's maiden name. At the bakery next door – it is shortly before six in the evening – they are cleaning up. We get ourselves some pancakes – they taste of *Heimat*. When we say we'll come again in the morning, the woman shop assistant reacts with surprise: 'Tomorrow? Tomorrow is Saturday; in the GDR bakers are closed!'

Then a visit to the one-time car business of my father-in-law, which since he fled has been a state-owned firm with seventy-five employees, now owned by the *Treuhand*. At our request a friendly doorman showed us around. Although the firm has been enlarged with a boiler house, whose three great boilers are heated by peat when coal is scarce, a paint shop and a one-storey office building, everything looks temporary. The courtyard which used to be so well cared for and tidy looks like a scrap-yard, with pools of oil on the ground. Later we are told that they had to make many spare parts themselves – axles, engines, screws. A real work creation programme! 'But that was the only way we could survive under socialism,' the doorman tells us.

Later, we drive on minor roads through the Brandenburg countryside with its pines and lakes, near to the town of Buckow, where we have arranged to stay the night with relatives of West German friends. Our hosts, roughly the same age as ourselves, have grown up in the GDR. The husband is a self-employed craftsman, and his wife used to be a teacher, but was sacked because she went to church more often than to party meetings. They do not yet know of the job I shall soon be taking on in Strausberg. They live in a small house which they bought from the local authority in the 1950s. Now they fear a possible claim from former owners in the West.

Their son-in-law tells us about his experiences in the NVA where he is doing his conscript service. 'Everyone feels insecure. Our immediate superior says he's staying in the Bundeswehr because he's needed. They say that our commanding officer is selling lots of equipment and will then leave the service on 2 October. We're not having any more training, we just do guard duty but no one takes that seriously any more. Our superiors don't know how to maintain discipline any longer and no one knows what's going to happen after 3 October. It's not an army any more!' The evening is long and I begin to grasp something of the reality and the depressing experiences of our fellow countrymen.

Next day a drive to Strausberg, and a visit to the conference centre where I shall take up my quarters from 2 October. It had been proposed that I should live in Wilkendorf House, the guesthouse of the GDR Defence Ministry, but I turned that down, as I could already see the headline: 'German general lives it up in the East.' Any good reason for taking those quarters would not have helped then.

The conference centre is a kind of hotel and conference complex belonging to the ministry. As we enter the large hall, we are surprisingly welcomed from the wall opposite by the heads of Marx, Engels and Lenin, made from Meissen tiles – they are still gazing masterfully into the future. Evidently up until now no one has had the courage to get rid of the three 'plaster saints' of the GDR. Only shortly before the hand-over of command on 3 October are the three heads – at our request – at least covered up.

At the reception I give my surname and ask to see a room. The hall porter – a civilian employee – stands to attention and reports that the installation is operating normally and that at present a meeting of the association of Bundeswehr personnel is taking place.

My apartment is luxurious, even though it is decorated according to socialist taste and has dark wooden panelling. In the bathroom hangs a plush bath robe, by the bath is a pair of plastic flip-flops. The plastic information folder contains instructions in German and Russian. During Warsaw Pact meetings in the GDR this room was used by the Commander-in-Chief.

Afterwards we visit the spa town, Bad Saarow, my birthplace. Even though it was 1945 when my parents fled with us, I find our house straight away – it just seems smaller and greyer than it used to be. Here, too, in this pretty little place hardly anything has changed, nothing new has been built, no streets have been widened or narrowed, no by-pass, no new spa centre, no department store – unimaginable for us West Germans.

Some of the villas on the nearby Lake Scharmützel had been commandeered by the Soviets in 1945, changed into a type of sanatorium and closed off with fences and gates. After the *Wende* this hitherto hermetically sealed area was opened to pedestrians during the day thanks to a citizens' campaign. As we walk there, memories return of the last winter of the war. We celebrated Christmas of 1944 in one of the villas belonging to friends of my parents. Now the houses look dead – no one is to be seen anywhere.

However, the promenades by the lake on the other hand, are already filled with Berliners, and in the newly opened Cafe Dorsch they have western coffee and cakes, still at low eastern prices. The landing-stages are all clearly named; they belong to 'firms owned by the people' or 'agricultural production co-operatives'. On one sign I read 'association for recreation' and wonder what it might mean. Later on our drive we discover a 'laying-hens production co-operative' – do the famous GDR *Goldbroiler* [roast chickens] come from here?

This first visit to my new sphere of work makes me realise that I have still a lot to learn in order to find my bearings and to understand our fellow countrymen. The signs of Communism run deep – much is inconceivable for us. We will need to talk to each other in order to understand each other again. Both sides will have to make an effort. I am reading *Schwierigkeiten mit der Wahrheit* (Difficulties with Truth), the depressing essay of the idealistic Communist Walter Janka, and am re-reading *Verführtes Denken* (The Captive Mind), a book by Czeslaw Milosz, to learn about the thinking and experiences of my countrymen.

A few days later I call a meeting at the Hardthöhe of all the commanding officers and general-staff officers who are going to Eastern Germany, in order to familiarise them with their new duties. I say that our mission is to take over formerly hostile armed forces, to disband them in a controlled manner and to build up new units of the Bundeswehr which will include former members of the NVA. I add that this will require patience and, above all, understanding for the former servicemen of the NVA who are under great psychological pressure. So we must approach our countrymen in an open-hearted way and make it clear that we are coming to them not as victors but as Germans to Germans, and that we are ready to listen to all of their worries and concerns. From the first, I tell them, we have to prove our credibility and thus create trust. The population of the five new Länder must be shown that the Bundeswehr is a quite different armed force from the NVA. It is therefore important to make contacts as soon as possible, particularly with mayors, ministers of religion and local representatives, to give them an initial impression of the Bundeswehr.

The contributions and comments of the officers present show confidence, even though we are all facing a special challenge which can still only be seen in outline. However, the officers have grasped that they must show a pioneering spirit, a readiness to make decisions and the ability to deal with people whose self-confidence has been badly shaken. They all want to play a part in this historic task. We end the meeting with the firm conviction that we shall be able to meet the challenges facing us, with the support of those Bundeswehr units which have been chosen to act as sponsors for the new units, and also the support of the Federal Defence Ministry.

However, commanding officers throughout the NVA still do not know whether they will be replaced by Bundeswehr officers and, if that is the case, who will replace them or what will happen to them after that. One reason for the uncertainty is that details of the structure of the forces and their bases were only received very late from the GDR ministry. In addition, it is only a short time since we concluded our discussions on whether or not all battalions would be commanded by Bundeswehr commanding officers. It was decided that, under divisional level, about half the commanding officers would be provided by the Bundeswehr. This was intended to act as a transitional period in order to use the experience and knowledge of the NVA commanding officers and to achieve a smooth changeover. In addition, it has still not been decided finally and in detail which units will be disbanded on 3 October and which will be kept in service for longer.

On top of all that *Neues Deutschland* has published an alleged interview with me which I never gave. During a background discussion, a *Neues Deutschland* journalist had a tape recorder running, and from the various questions dealt with, had put together an interview which was falsified even further by leaving out two important sentences in one section. The statement which *Neues Deutschland* produced by this method says in short: 'Lieutenant-General Schönbohm: "We shall keep the NVA officers in the service for a time and then dismiss them; we need them only for the transition but not for the future."' This shortened version has naturally led to much annoyance in the NVA, as this newspaper is still read a great deal in the barracks. I thereupon print out the complete statement from a tape recording and send it to the liaison group by teleprinter. In this way the forces are informed about the whole text.

To prepare for the duties of the BKO, I sent an advance party led by the Chief of Staff Brigadier Jacobs, to Strausberg in mid-September in order that he could prepare for the hand-over there, together with the NVA generals who were still on duty. We must keep the military leadership operating after midnight on 2 October, primarily to guarantee that there will be no interruption to air safety which, as a sovereign country, we shall be taking over.

In countless individual discussions and group work the necessary preparations are made; finally, in Bonn, I sign the order which is to bring about the smooth hand-over of command from the NVA to the Bundeswehr, which is to take effect at midnight on 2 October. To prevent the forces from being leaderless, even for a moment, the whole command network of the former NVA will be kept in operation for the time being.

On the afternoon of 1 October I fly by helicopter to Hanover in order to take part, at the army officers' training college, in the instruction of 850 army officers and sergeants on their future duties. The soldiers are in an enthusiastic mood. I once again go over the work that awaits us, and add: 'Before you and your families lies a tough and demanding time. But we are taking part in an historic process which will be envied by our successors. We are laying the foundation stone for joint German armed forces – the goal is clear, the way is long, everyone's effort is worthwhile.'

Chapter 6

IN THE BUNDESWEHR-
KOMMANDO OST

Tuesday, 2 October 1990

I leave from Cologne-Bonn airport at midday, with my wife, in a transport aircraft to fly to Marxwalde, now called Neuhardenberg , with a stopover in Dresden. The pilots show us our flight path on the map. We have to get used to the old place-names again. In Marxwalde an NVA officer welcomes us and we fly in a Soviet MI-8 helicopter, 'saloon version', to Strausberg. The crew are still wearing NVA uniforms, the helicopter is from Honecker's former flight – dark-red upholstery with plastic edging, grey, tufted carpeting.

In Strausberg as the day's duty ends, the servicemen and civilian staff stream from the ministry – wearing, for the final time, the uniform of the 'Workers' and Farmers' State.' Some of them will return tomorrow – in the NATO-olive uniform of the former class enemy. Pieces of the old uniforms are already lying on the rubbish heaps.

On my arrival the first letters are waiting for me: suggestions regarding my duties, complaints about dismissals and unfair treatment, but also good wishes. Even before I take over my duties I am asked for help. General Richter, the head of our liaison headquarters and an old school-friend of mine, tells me about the situation on the eve of the unification of Germany. He reports that the situation as a whole is tense, but he considers that overnight, from 2 to 3 October, no unusual occurrences are to be expected, though one cannot be certain. He recalls the atmosphere at Eppelmann's last meeting of the commanding officers on 12 September, and also the threats of some of the regimental commanders, who stated that they had still enough arms and ammunition in their units to be able to defend themselves. His report indicates that high hopes are being placed in the Federal Defence Minister and the Commanding Officer of the BKO, and that it is expected the future will at last be made clear. Then he says to me very forcefully: 'Jörg, everything now depends on whether you manage to show who is in charge. The officers want to be led and to have the feeling that someone is on their side and will back them if needed. Your first decisions are therefore of the greatest importance. You can lose much trust if you make the slightest mistake. You are on a tightrope and I wish you all the best for the way ahead.' I am conscious of the special nature of my situation and that of my comrades; the responsibility is great but not oppressive.

In the evening my wife and I want to drive to Berlin to take part in the celebrations of German unity. However, Herr Ablass, who is still in office as Permanent Secretary in the GDR Ministry for Disarmament and Defence, has invited us to a small reception; we accept the invitation.

As we enter the ministry through the guardroom at around nine, soldiers on guard duty, wearing NVA uniform, check our identity cards. The reception takes place in an office. About twenty people are present, including three generals of the NVA who at midnight tonight will leave the service. Their co-operation up to the take-over of command tonight by Federal Minister Stoltenberg – and, with that, by us – has been good and also personally pleasing. But is this smooth co-operation at the beginning a blank cheque for the future, and does it mean that the past can be forgotten?

We are all wearing civilian clothes, the atmosphere is subdued and strained. Some of the men present appear to be uncomfortable in their badly fitting suits. As my wife and I enter the room we have the impression that the conversation stops. We do not know most of the people present. We feel a tense, almost oppressive atmosphere. It is difficult for us all to start talking naturally, everyone has their own thoughts and worries. We introduce ourselves and hear names which mean nothing to us newcomers. Only after a while do we start talking about the time that lies before us – a theme that concerns us all. I get the impression that most of the NVA officers, the civilian staff and their families are primarily interested in clarifying details of their own personal futures, even when those futures do not look too rosy.

At midnight we drink a toast together to the unity of Germany and the future of all Germans. From this moment on I am directly responsible for most of these people. So I fell that the time is right to say a few words:

> Germany has once again been unified. We all wish that the hopes of so
> many people are fulfilled. Difficult tasks lie before us, and great chal-
> lenges – many are facing an uncertain future. As members of one nation

we can again meet together freely, as servicemen and civilian staff we are serving the same state which commits us to its support for human rights, justice for all and social responsibility. In this state we have the greatest chance for a common, peaceful future.

But we all need time, basing ourselves on our different backgrounds, to find the courage and strength to gain experience together, and to achieve mutual understanding and trust in our common future.

The population of the defunct GDR has freed itself from a criminal regime without the use of force. We are thankful for that and we feel that we have a commitment to help you, which we must fulfil. We from the West have merely looked on for long enough. Now we can join together in doing something. Let us then, with confidence and perseverance, get down to the shaping of our common future in our united fatherland.

As we go past the guardroom at midnight the soldiers on guard are in Bundeswehr battledress, the NATO olive we know, with new berets. Germany is united, the soldiers have donned the uniform of the former class enemy and one of them reports in a correct military manner: 'Herr General, nothing to report!' The change of uniform has gone as planned. However, what is to follow is still shrouded in mist.

Wednesday, 3 October 1990

A bright sunny day. In the morning I fly to Berlin in a Soviet-made MI-8 helicopter marked with the Iron Cross national emblem. It feels strange to fly over the Brandenburg region, to cross over Berlin, passing the Alexanderplatz. The Brandenburg Gate lies under us, as do the Tiergarten and the Siegessäule. In a wide arc we fly to Tempelhof airport.

This is the first time I have visited Berlin as a soldier in uniform. I look at the beautiful but ravaged city from the air. Parts of the Wall can still be seen, only around the Brandenburg Gate has it been largely removed. I have also been given responsibility for the removal of the Wall and frontier defences, the mine-clearing and the disbandment of the former frontier troops. Now that the divided city lies beneath me I realise that the removal of the Wall must be given priority above many other things, even though it is not really the job of the Bundeswehr. But, with the units of the former frontier troops and the support of pioneer units of the former NVA we shall, I hope, soon be rid of this hated structure.

When we land at Tempelhof the U.S. base commander, an air force colonel, welcomes us as 'representatives of the free, sovereign and united Germany in the capital, Berlin.' I reply only: 'I thank you sincerely for this friendly welcome. I know that, as the German Commanding Officer of the Bundeswehr-Kommando Ost, I am only able to land here today because you and our other allies have remained in Berlin during the past forty-five years. For this persistence and for your commitment I thank you and your comrades. We shall never forget it.'

We attend the state ceremony celebrating German unification, held in the West Berlin Philharmonie concert hall. During the reception that follows I receive good wishes from many sides for the task that is ahead of me; then I fly back to Strausberg to take over command. The hand-over of the BKO, of the branch office of the Federal Defence Ministry and the armed forces administration of Military Region VII take place at half-past four in the afternoon. Many guests attend. The Bundestag commissioner for the armed forces and the members of the Bundestag defence committee are present – this, too, is a sign of public interest and the support of all political parties.

The speeches at this ceremony are interspersed with music from a symphony orchestra which has symbolic significance. The musicians come from East and West, they wear the same uniform and together they play the works of old German masters. At the request of the Bundeswehr Chief of Staff, I do not make a speech about my intentions – I would have been the only serviceman to have spoken.

Federal Minister Dr Stoltenberg states the direction of our future work in an Order of the Day:

> On 3 October 1990 the German people have again come together in one state. Walls and frontiers have fallen. More than four decades of forced division have not been able to break the feeling of the German people that they belong together.
>
> The population of the former GDR has approved by a large majority accession to the Federal Republic of Germany and has actively supported the process. With this, it has opted for the political system of the Basic Law. We are all committed to our country with its freedom-loving, democratic constitution based on the rule of law.
>
> Our united Germany is firmly integrated in the western community of values. We are a member of the European Community, as well as the Atlantic Alliance and the Western European Union. From this stem the orientation and commitments of our forces. These commitments have not been forced upon us; rather we have accepted them freely and consciously. They are an important part of our self-image.
>
> To stand up for Germany today means to stand up, at the same time, for freedom, for democracy, for the rule of law and for cooperation with our allies in Europe and North America. It means, too, on the basis of the treaties which have now been concluded, to strengthen cooperation with the Soviet Union and the young democracies of central and eastern Europe.
>
> The division of our country has been overcome. Now it is up to us to also to remove that which divides us in thought and feeling. The members of the armed forces are in this respect faced by a particular challenge, they must find their way from opposing each other to working with each other.
>
> The reduction of tension makes it possible to conclude disarmament agreements and to cut the size of our Bundeswehr. In a few years we shall have 370,000 servicemen. That will lead to a reduction in numbers in both the West and the East of Germany.

Important pre-conditions and framework regulations for the incorporation of servicemen and civilian staff of the former NVA into the Bundeswehr, have been laid down in the Unification Treaty. Many will have this chance and will use it. Others must be dismissed in the coming months according to the arrangements set out in the Treaty. I hope that they will not be despondent, but that they will make a new start in order to take part in the reconstruction of the economy in the new Länder. As far as possible we want to assist this far-reaching change through qualification schemes. From those who apply for service in the Bundeswehr I expect a readiness to learn, the willing acceptance of responsibility and an open-minded approach to new duties. I call on the servicemen of the Bundeswehr to accept the new servicemen without prejudice, to give them comradely help and further their speedy integration.

As of 3 October I have taken over command of the armed forces of united Germany as Federal Minister of Defence. At the same time the military constitution laid down in the Basic Law becomes valid for the whole of Germany.

We must now carry out the process of integration and troop reductions in such a way that after German unification we can achieve a united Bundeswehr which can fulfil its constitutional duty in the whole territory of the state.

For this we need the co-operation of the servicemen and civilian staff, not only to bring about an orderly hand-over and integration but above all to actively shape our future Bundeswehr.

In the evening I have dinner with all the heads of departments, who will be my closest colleagues, in order to discuss our common tasks. We all know what a mountain of work awaits us, but it becomes evident during our talk that we are a good team, that we have the same ideas about the future and will tackle the tasks facing us with drive and optimism.

Thursday, 4 October 1990

At 8 am Major-General von Scheven, my deputy, reports that the personnel of the BKO are drawn up on an inaugural parade in front of the main building of the former ministry in Strausberg. We did not know beforehand exactly how many servicemen would be present at this parade and how many of the civilian staff would attend. There are many more than the six-hundred servicemen we had reckoned with. They come from the East and the West. Although it is a mixed group the former members of the NVA can be identified by their stiff berets, which they are not used to, and their new battledress. It is not yet the usual military scene, but after all we are in a completely unusual situation. A clear sign of this is the federal service flag, which is fluttering over the parade-ground for the first time.

I have intensively prepared myself for what I am going to say and am as tense as the soldiers in front of me. I know that with this speech – one of the most important in my life – I am laying the foundations for all of our work. In the speech I must consider the reaction in the West and the East and cannot wriggle out of certain questions. Moreover the speech must not last longer than the ten minutes which are usual at a parade.

So it was that on 4 October I made the following speech on the activation of the Bundeswehr-Kommando Ost, on the hand-over of the NVA air force, of the Regional Command VII in Leipzig and of the army headquarters for Eastern Germany:

> Servicemen of the Bundeswehr-Kommando Ost, civilian staff, as of yesterday Germany is once again united. The Federal Minister of Defence has put me in command of German forces in the five new Länder and Berlin. With this parade I officially commission the Bundeswehr-Kommando Ost. I thank all of those who have carried out the preparatory work – above all the former members of the NVA – which has enabled us to function since yesterday.
>
> For us servicemen this is a special hour, an hour of hope for the future of our people. But it is also an hour in which many of us are worried about our own future.
>
> Our people now live united in a free, democratic social state based on the rule of law. We all bear the responsibility for ensuring that, in this part of Germany too, democracy is filled with life. The Bundeswehr-Kommando Ost has the task of transferring the units of the former NVA into the forces of democratic Germany – this can succeed only if we work together, and not against each other.
>
> It is our goal to shape the forces, in this part of Germany too, according to the concept of the free, responsible citizen. We can succeed only if we bear in mind and use the experiences which we have undergone, or been forced to undergo, in our past – our common past, and our separate past in the last four decades.
>
> I expect that the former members of the NVA, who from today will carry out the same duties as I, as servicemen of the Bundeswehr and therefore wear the same uniform, will fulfil their duties conscientiously. I expect them to be ready to make the Basic Law and the military law of our Federal Republic of Germany the basis of their actions. To this also belongs our self-image as citizens in uniform.
>
> From the servicemen of the previous Bundeswehr I expect open-mindedness, readiness to help and patience towards their new comrades. There is no reason for self-righteousness – try to get to know each other. We are serving a common cause – the future of Germany.
>
> There are difficult tasks ahead – tasks which, in this form, servicemen have never been faced with; this applies to all of us. Parts of the armed forces built up by the SED and trained in the spirit of the class war are to become units of the Bundeswehr: that is, the armed forces which used to be seen as the adversary and the class enemy.
>
> In spite of all previous differences and conflicting attitudes, in the future we must bring about the unity of the all-German armed forces in order to fulfil our joint mission of defending and maintaining the peace and freedom of our democratic state. This unity and togetherness can be attained only on the basis of a clear rejection of the basic principles of the GDR and its former armed forces.

The class war, the class mission, class hate and the conception of the enemy – all that kind of thing – have no place in the Bundeswehr. Respect for the human rights of each individual and compliance with international law are just as much a state goal of united Germany as they have been in the Federal Republic of Germany up to now.

It is up to you alone to break with the past, when you were serving a state which infringed these principles. Your entry into the democratic armed forces will only be successful if, beforehand, you have broken with the ideology of the GDR out of good sense and conviction. In that we want to help you – as comrades.

Your personal future is uncertain. I promise you today that I shall approach you frankly and with understanding – and that I will clarify your future prospects at the earliest possible moment. From you I would like frankness and honesty. This is the basis for the growth of cohesion and comradeship which the Bundeswehr needs and which we all wish for.

Our work will be attentively watched by our parliament, the public, by everyone in our country, but also by our neighbours in the East and West. We must show that we are succeeding in this difficult task of amalgamation, reform and reduction. We must visibly complete what was started on 9 November 1989. All of you, but above all our young conscripts, must quickly realise that from now they are serving in armed forces that are different; armed forces which demand only responsible rather than absolute obedience; armed forces for which the statement in the Basic Law 'the dignity of man is inviolable' is more important than any service regulation. From that stems the spirit of the army. That is a great challenge to us all. Let us master it together.

We who have now come to you, partly as your superiors but also partly as your subordinates, have not come as victors or conquerors. We come as Germans to Germans. We are German soldiers who have grown up in freedom, have been brought up under the protection of, and subject to the demands of, democracy and have been trained according to the principles of *Innere Führung*. Basing ourselves on these values and experiences we want to help to attain the unity of the nation within a free state based on the rule of law. We also want to achieve unity in our armed forces too: one people, one democratic state and united armed forces. Our reward is the unity of the nation in the democratic state based on the rule of law. To be allowed to take part in this task is a privilege. Now we must show that we are able to shape a common future, to overcome challenges and to create an all-German Bundeswehr for our fatherland.

As, from now on, all young Germans are to serve in the united Bundeswehr, instead of facing each other in two opposing armed forces, conscription takes on additional importance. It becomes the visible expression of the will to maintain unity and one's own personal freedom. Just as our federal flag and our national anthem are symbols of German unity, the armed forces must become likewise – offering experience of togetherness in the armed forces of united Germany. Each one of us here and in the units has to make his contribution to that. We are ready to do so.

After the parade I install, in Strausberg, the new Air Force Commander for eastern Germany and in Potsdam, the new Army Commander, while Major-General von Scheven installs the army Regional Command VIII in Neubrandenburg and the Naval Com-

mand in Rostock. The modest parades are intended to make it clear
that today is a new start. At the close the national anthem is played.
In this way we aim to show that servicemen in the same uniforms are
committed in the same manner to work together for united Germany. The content of our national anthem has come true, so we can
now sing from the bottom of our hearts: 'Let us strive fraternally,
with our hearts and hands, for unity, law and freedom.' A civil war
is no longer imaginable.

In Leipzig, after installing the Army Regional Command VII, I
take the opportunity at the following lunch to talk to servicemen of
various ranks. The young conscripts appear insecure and are not
forthcoming. This does not strike the officers as being unusual. 'They
do as we say. No problem.' Only obedience is important. I try to find
out whether they can picture future conscripts being more question-
ing, and perhaps more ready to disagree. They tell me: 'Herr General, until now we haven't had that here and I don't think we shall
have it in the future.' When I make it very clear to them that in this
respect some things will have to change, their faces betray their surprise at their top military commander expressing such unusual views.

The younger officers and NCOs hope to be able to remain in the
Bundeswehr because they know that conscription is to continue and
new units are to be established. On the other hand the older officers
are full of uncertainty. It is clear to them that in the long term they
have very little future in the Bundeswehr. Those who are under fifty
know that if they are dismissed they will have no further income
apart from unemployment benefits. For instance, a colonel tells me
he has served for more than thirty years, is not quite fifty and will get
a pension of only twenty-three per cent of his previous salary – very
much less than unemployment benefit. When I point out that there
were too many staff officers in the NVA and therefore reducing their
numbers is unavoidable, he expresses understanding, but complains
about the lack of prospects for finding other work. 'Who will give me
a job at forty-nine, Herr General? After all I've learnt nothing except
how to be a soldier.'

It becomes clear to me during these first discussions that our
problems lie primarily in the sphere of social security, and here in
particular we must prove our credibility. Meeting individual soldiers
reveals that the questions to be dealt with cannot be solved by
bureaucracy alone, but primarily through discussions with the men.

Back to Strausberg, where we have invited all of the members of
the BKO – most of them are former NVA servicemen – for a drink,
as well as the mayor and the chief administrative officer of Strausberg and the superintendent of the protestant church. They accept
our invitation with surprise and interest. For all three it is a com-

pletely new experience to be invited to such a function in the ministry. As we know that there was no social life in the NVA in our sense of the term, we are particularly keen to introduce a new style in this sphere.

Out of the roughly one thousand civilian and military members of the staff of the BKO six to seven hundred attend. The first discussions begin – about routine matters but also about the past and the uncertain personal futures facing many. We get to know each other. However, we still seem to be putting off the former NVA men with our frankness and matter-of-fact approach.

Among the guests there are three former generals, who are now working with us as advisers. In a short speech I again emphasise the credit gained by the NVA at the time of the changeover from Communism and praise the work of the three generals who had worked very closely with our advance party until 2 October. The recognition of this contribution to the united German forces visibly pleases the former members of the NVA. To make my short speech I climb on to a chair and whistle loudly through my fingers in order to gain people's attention. Later, I learn that by doing so I have, for many of the former NVA members, shaken the image they had of a Bundeswehr general.

After the reception I call the departmental heads to the first staff meeting in the so-called operational command centre, which was used by the Defence Minister of the GDR to command the armed forces during manoeuvres and crises. The senior officers sit on a raised platform in front of a series of computer monitors, which are not switched on, while the departmental heads are seated facing the other way. Only the person who is speaking has any eye contact – therefore a discussion with several people is not possible. We know that everything we discuss in this bunker installation with the departmental heads – all of them officers from the West – is being listened to by former members of the NVA still working here. In addition, we must assume that all of our telephones are being monitored and that bugs are installed in all of the rooms. Thus I can only discuss particularly sensitive questions with my staff by taking 'protective measures'. This, too, is a part of the new togetherness!

First of all we need to clarify what, in fact, we have taken over as far as personnel, equipment and property are concerned. As regards our headquarters staff we must discover why, instead of the planned 350 servicemen we have seven hundred; as our first task, we shall have to dismiss many men in order to make it possible to oversee and lead the personnel. To do this we have to find out which of the former members of the NVA are really willing, together with Bundeswehr officers, to take part in the disbandment of the NVA and the reconstruction of Bundeswehr units. Moreover we must distinguish between the military and civilian responsibilities and transfer these, where appropriate, to the military administration which, however, is still being established.

As far as the servicemen are concerned, we can only hope that the take-over of the formations by officers from the West functions smoothly, and that the servicemen of the NVA will accept that a few Bundeswehr officers are now their superiors who will set goals, issue orders and also check that they are carried out. Will the officers succeed in doing this with sensitivity, but also with the necessary decisiveness? In the press and also among some members of the Bundestag there has already been speculation that some officers might behave too high-handedly. However, I do not believe it.

In carrying out our future tasks it is important that the different services select Western 'sponsor units' which are to give prompt and unbureaucratic help when needed. (As became clear later, this decision was of extraordinary importance because it was only thanks to the active help of the sponsor units, through unbureaucratic, direct help, that we were able to solve many difficulties – from obtaining photocopiers, military regulations and office material to the short-term transfer of specialists in all kinds of spheres.)

Sadly, it turns out that there have been some initial quarrels between the military administration and the actual military staff, as they have been unable to agree about the allocation of rooms. On top of this, there have been disputes about certain orders. I am disappointed that, on only the first day of duty, the common vision of the unity of Germany and the joint task is receding into the background and withers amid bureaucratic in-fighting. We shall have to learn to talk as much about our common goal as about current problems.

Friday, 5 October 1990

In the morning I have detailed talks with the few NVA generals selected to work for us in the future as advisers, in a civilian role. Owing to the command structure of the NVA, organisational matters and knowledge only came together at the highest level in the ministry, which resulted in only a few generals having an overview of the whole military system. We are now in urgent need of their help. This is why we are now discussing together the contribution they can make to disbanding the armed forces which they themselves have built up, which they have served for several decades, and which is now threatening to disintegrate.

Each of us is under a certain amount of pressure and it is still uncertain how we shall get along with each other. I start by going through the duties of each one individually. Retired Major-General Berger will work closely with Major-General Mende, who has taken over the air force. Retired Major-General Engelhardt, who for a short time was the Army Commander, will advise our liaison group to the Soviets and will assist me regarding all general questions relating to the army. Retired Major-General Schlothauer, who was briefly Chief of Staff of the NVA, will work with my Chief of Staff, Brigadier Jacobs, and retired General Baarß will advise my deputy on all questions regarding general military duties and training. The former chief of the naval forces, Admiral Born, whom I did not request to make the journey specially from Rostock, will assist our Naval Commanding Officer.

After these instructions and detailed talks I have the impression that we have obtained knowledgable and willing colleagues. They see themselves as experts but they overlook all that must be changed – above all their own attitudes and ideology; we shall have to discuss and learn a great deal. Can we really work trustfully and openly together for the good of the common cause? Have we come to terms with the past?

Afterwards, the first weekly situation report at which it emerges that the beginning of the changeover from the NVA to the Bundeswehr has evidently succeeded without incidents or resistance. Kitting-out with the NATO battledress has been completed and all servicemen have come on duty. Even where commanding officers and their deputies resigned voluntarily shortly before 3 October, other officers of the NVA have carried out their duties until relieved by Bundeswehr officers, or higher-ranking officers of the NVA. The take-over of air sovereignty has also functioned smoothly, the link to the states of the Warsaw Pact has been disconnected. The number of men on guard duties has been increased by 5,500 other ranks, because extra sentries have had to replace the high-voltage security installations at ammunition depots. The NVA used this kind of installation to secure all big camps and depots; it comprised several barbed-wire fences and an arrangement of electric wires with lethal voltage. As this kind of security does not accord with our view of a state based on the rule of law, these installations were switched off during the night of 2/3 October. However, this has greatly increased the burden of guard duties, which allows less time for basic training and leads to considerable problems, as many ammunition depots are far from the garrisons and have no quarters for the guards.

However, what is decisive for me at the moment is that the security situation as a whole is stable, and that our orders and telexes can be received throughout the whole region, although during the discussion of the situation report it is revealed that there are also some problems in that respect. True, we have taken over an intact telecommunications system, through which we can reach all units of the former NVA by telephone and teleprinter, but these networks are hopelessly out of date and require too many staff. What is more, there are 'branch lines' everywhere leading to the former telecommunications monitoring system of the Stasi. Although we believe that we have cut off all these connections, we hear they still exist here and there – no-one knows where they lead. In some telephone exchanges former Stasi staff have gone 'underground', and are continuing to work as 'ordinary personnel' in this sphere, which is sensitive from a security point of view. (It takes us a long time to weed them all out.)

Previously, the telephone network of the NVA was linked to the fifteen regional capitals of the GDR with their SED party leaderships. Now we are also linked to civilian bodies such as the police, the ministries of the Länder or the *Treuhand*. However, there are scarcely any lines to western Germany. At first there are only a few links to the Federal Defence Ministry which, in addition, are almost always engaged. Calls made over post office lines to western Germany, as well as return calls to the East, are difficult or at times even impossible, and during the day not even car telephones are usable, as the network in the Berlin region is constantly overburdened. The fast exchange of information between East and West is of course very important and work is continuing at high pressure to improve matters.

At 6 pm I hold talks with four colonels of the former NVA. In a telex to me on 2 October, they had complained that the commanding officer of their division, a major-general, had been dismissed from all his functions and retired. They wrote in part:

> Herr Kohl has spoken frankly of the fact that the changes in this country took place without the use of force. We say that this would not have been possible without the loyalty, good sense and the political attitude of those who had weapons in their hands. We are shattered that our commanding officer, Major-General N.N., with effect from 2 October 1990, has been dismissed from his post and retired. Dr N.N. is one of the most loyal and professionally competent military men in the air force and air defence, who, through his personal actions, has ensured that the division has fulfilled all of its duties in all matters related to the changes in society, and has maintained the security of weapons and ammunition right up to the present. We see, from what has occurred that not fairness, partnership, loyalty and professional competence but political calculations are the basis of personnel decisions. This serves to instigate still more the insecurity and demotivation among the career servicemen.
>
> We know that personal, personnel and structural decisions are imminent. What is questionable is how such necessary decisions are made. After careful checks on the person concerned or with the political lawnmower? From our point of view it would have been a matter of course that our commanding officer, advised by representatives of the Bundeswehr, should himself lead the division during the restructuring and should finally disband his headquarters. If this style of personnel decision is continued after 3 October, then human walls will be erected instead of the Wall made of concrete.

I conduct the discussion in the presence of Major-General Mende, Commanding Officer of the 5th Air Force Division, who has taken over responsibility for the whole air force of the former NVA. The officers make their points calmly and in a business-like way and point out that their commander – generally liked and respected by the men – has been retired at only three days' notice. As he is under fifty, they say, he receives no pension but only unemployment benefit and is now among the mass of unemployed which, in their opinion, he does not deserve. Above all, they add, the manner of his dismissal has disturbed the servicemen. In the NVA, generals were normally appointed by the Chairman of the State Council, whereas their commander had not even been dismissed by the minister, but only by his permanent secretary in a short, uneasy retirement ceremony. Was this the style, they asked, which was to be expected in the Bundeswehr?

I try to explain my point of view to the officers. The Bundeswehr, I say, is in every respect different from the NVA, and this must also be shown by the fact that the old generals of the NVA, trained under the Socialist system and given all kinds of privileges in the former regime, can have no place in the Bundeswehr. The new beginning of the Bundeswehr in Eastern Germany must be made apparent, particularly through personnel changes at the top – the population could surely not understand any other decision. In the future many more officers would have to be dismissed, and for those of us who were bearing the direct responsibility it was clear that as citizens of the Federal Republic of Germany they had a right to fair treatment and support, according to the rule of law.

I promise, too, that in spite of the large number of impending dismissals we shall try to consider each individual's situation as far as possible and, together with the regional military administration and the unemployment exchanges, to organise professional training for the servicemen. I say we shall also try to retain officers and NCOs in the Bundeswehr for as long as this is justified by the needs of duty.

After initial tension the talks continue in a relatively open and business-like way, and after an hour and a half the officers express thanks for my statements. They say that they were surprised that I received them at all – and, in addition, so soon. This was a previously unheard-of style, which would quickly become known. It should be made known throughout the air force that it had commanders who would not evade problems, who had an understanding for the servicemen, were making efforts on behalf of the personnel and were trying to come to acceptable solutions.

This evening in the 'Report from Bonn' on television – as well as in the main daily newspapers – there are very positive reports on the hand-over of command. This pleasing echo must not deflect us from the challenges which lie ahead. We must now put our ideas and intentions into action through painstaking, detailed work.

Saturday, 6 October 1990

We travel by helicopter to Bad Salzungen in Thuringia. We want to propose to the minister that we hold the first public oath-taking ceremony for conscripts there. One of the former NVA generals who is advising us proposed the town after I had explained to him the aim of a public oath-taking ceremony. We want citizens, as soldiers, to publicly make a commitment in support of the state – in the market-place of a small town and with the participation of the inhabitants. As none of us knows the situation or the atmosphere in this place, but trusting that the recommendation is a correct one, I fly, for two-and-a-half hours on Saturday morning, in a helicopter to Bad Salzungen.

The flight over the countryside is impressive. After the lakes of Brandenburg and the autumn-tinted forests come the treeless plains and then the depressing sight of the opencast brown-coal mines and the chemical industry. Lunar landscapes: not a bush to be seen, far and wide the earth split open, dug over, exploited. Close to the great chemical works an industrial landscape is visible, recalling the era of industrialisation in the nineteenth century. Smoking chimneys, rusting industrial plants and pools of effluent in different colours near the few, dead conifers. It is a miserable sight. I must involuntarily think of the words of a West German acquaintance: 'The country is smashed up. And just as it appears in the environment, so it is in the minds of our countrymen. It's not their fault, but the fault of the terrible system! Believe me!' Will he be proved right? I disagreed with him at the time and would do so again. For on many chimneys and high-voltage pylons the German flag is flying as the symbol of unity, expressing hope, and faith in the future. Let us hope that we can fulfil their expectations.

A little later – green Thuringia, then the Wartburg, full of tourists. We land at the barracks in Bad Salzungen. Welcome from the commanding officer of the regiment, a Western officer of the Bundeswehr, and his present deputy, a major, previously a lieutenant-colonel and commander of the regiment. In the officers' mess are the civilian administrative head of the area and the mayoress of the town. Open sandwiches with marinated pork and thick slices of ham are served. The tablecloths are of plastic and there is a smell of disinfectant. I thank the two local representatives – of the town and the surrounding area – for coming, and explain what we want to achieve with the oath-taking ceremony. I tell those present that we do not want to hold the ceremony on the edge of the town, as the NVA did twice a year, but in the marketplace, among the population. In this way we want to show that the Bundeswehr is not hiding away in the barracks but coming out into the community. The people need to realise that soldiers and citizens belong together and that the serviceman of the Bundeswehr is really a citizen in uniform.

The mayoress and the administrative chief understand my explanation but nevertheless they have certain reservations. When the regiment was moved to Bad Salzungen in 1978, about 3,400 hectares of land were simply commandeered, a barracks was built and a live-ammunition firing range constructed. The population has not yet forgiven this method of taking over land, and the barracks is still seen as something alien. Did my advisers not know that, had they forgotten or do they regard it as unimportant?

During our discussion I point out that on 19 October the minister will take the opportunity to discuss all important questions with the mayoress and representatives of the town and the surrounding area. From that point of view the public oath-taking would be advantageous for both the administrative area and the town. In addition, the Bad Salzungen area would become known through the television reports. After a long discussion the mayoress and the administrative chief agree to the holding of the ceremony, but make it clear that by doing so, they are in no way approving retrospectively the take-over of the land. In any case, the detailed planning required by the garrison and the town authorities can now take place.

A subsequent visit to the barracks reveals a sight that will later be repeated again and again: although the building is not old, the barrack-rooms are in a miserable condition, revealing the great drawbacks of the prefabricated building methods. The furniture in the other-ranks' rooms – occupied by eight to ten men – consists, for each man, of a bed, a narrow locker and a stool. There is only one table for all the occupants of the room. The walls are bare – there are no personal effects. In an other-ranks' common room chairs are grouped around a television – dark distemper is flaking off the walls. Depressing grey everywhere. There is no room where one could feel comfortable and enjoy oneself. The kitchen and shower equipment, too, in no way accord with our regulations.

On the other hand, the technical equipment, that is, everything to do with the armoured vehicles of a motorised infantry regiment, is excellently housed, and the training installations are good. Although ammunition has by now been removed from the combat vehicles, some of it is still stored in the technical areas, a situation which is acceptable only for a short time. The whole regiment, with fifty per cent of its personnel strength and more than a hundred per cent of its normal equipment, is exclusively employed on guard duties.

Will this remain in the memories of the conscripts as the result of German unity?

The catastrophic state of the barracks, which I find again and again on my later visits to other units, had many causes. When it was founded, the NVA could only make use of existing barracks in exceptional circumstances, as the barracks, as well as most of the training areas, were being used by the Soviet troops. So the party and state leadership were forced to have the mass of the NVA barracks built in the 1950s and 1960s under the prevailing tight economic conditions. The necessary land for barracks and training areas was expropriated and the owners were only partially compensated, if at all, and then with tiny amounts, which usually resulted in the continuation of tension between the population and the NVA.

Some of the barracks were built from scratch on completely new sites; the best-known example is the major garrison at Eggesin, where an armoured division was stationed in an area with poor infrastructure. The newly built barracks accorded with the living conditions of the time and the concept of military service. They were built in part with the simple equipment of the forces. As there was no efficient building industry the NVA formed several pioneer construction regiments, exclusively for building barracks.

The old barracks were heated by coal stoves in the barrack-rooms, the somewhat newer ones by central heating of varied quality. Most of the central-heating boilers were fired with brown coal. The degree of pollution they caused was much higher than our standards would allow, while the heat that was produced was much less. In the washrooms there was, as a rule, only cold water and there were either no showers or they did not work. In the 'more modern' barracks shower blocks were built in the 1970s – for 2,500 servicemen one 'shower-room' with fifty to seventy showers. If showers were to be taken, each unit had to report beforehand, so there was enough warm water. If it was a cold winter and the boilers were over-burdened, there was often no warm water for the mass showers.

In the units there were shabby mess-halls for the other ranks and NCOs. On the other hand, the commanding officer and a few other officers ate in the commander's dining-room at tables covered with oilcloth, and received special food. In Strausberg too, until September, there was a dining-room which could be used only by generals – and that in the armed forces of the 'Workers' and Farmers' State'.

Once the barracks had been built, for decades nothing was invested in kitchen equipment or in the whole catering department. Later, 141 kitchens were inspected and it was found that all of them would have been closed due to unsatisfactory hygiene, if our standards had been applied. As a rule there were no extractor fans, so that floors and walls were smeared with fat – the feeling for cleanliness and hygiene had evidently been lost. There were also no automatic dishwashers, the servicemen had to take turns at washing up, and often there was not even any washing-up liquid.

Living quarters, kitchens and medical sections in the barracks were, as a rule, run-down, although to differing extents. However, the 'combat parks', where the weapons systems were kept in readiness, were generally in good condition. As the responsible commanding officers had little money in their budgets for maintenance, they concentrated on 'infrastructure of importance for action' in the combat parks. Furthermore, there were no building materials to be found anywhere, so it was hardly possible to improve the living quarters on one's own initiative. In any case, the superior officers were not interested in that. Superiors and subordinates had got used to these miserable conditions, and even now there was evidently little desire for change.

Postscript, Autumn 1991

In a barracks area an armoured personnel carrier accidentally drove against a pillar of an open storehouse which thereupon collapsed. Fortunately no one was hurt. An immediate check of the structural calculations and the materials used led to the discovery that a large number of the storehouses breached our safety regulations and could no longer be used. Even in this sphere external appearances had misled us.

Sunday, 7 October 1990

Preparations for the commanding officers' conference, in which 420 officers will take part, half of them former members of the NVA. During some discussions with the latter I have got a rather better feeling for their situation. I intend to first give them a survey of the security policy situation, in order to make it clear that the reduction in size of the former NVA is bedded in an overall security-policy concept, which in no small measure has led to the unity of Germany. Moreover, I want to underline that in a democracy the prime role of politics is expressed in a different manner than in totalitarian systems. The officers must realise that in a democratic state the results of an opinion-forming process do not always agree with what an individual or a professional group might wish.

But for me the central question in my preparation is: how honest am I, what can I say, what is binding? I shall have to make it clear that the majority of the staff officers have no chance of being retained in the long term, even though a small proportion of them are being employed on a temporary basis for two years. For that reason it is necessary to explain that the NVA had far too many staff officers.

Out of the total of 175,000 servicemen there were 2,110 colonels and naval captains, compared with 1,800 officers of the same ranks in the Bundeswehr, which had 495,000 men. This numerical comparison alone shows how necessary a structural reduction is.

On Sunday evening I agree with the head of the branch office of the Federal Defence Ministry, Herr Ablass, that we shall work together very closely. The branch office of the ministry and the BKO must not allow themselves to be divided. We must make a point of speaking to the 'Bonn people' in one voice. We must make joint use of our room for manoeuvre – keeping together is the motto.

Chapter 7

DAILY ROUTINE

Monday, 8 October 1990

I attend a discussion in Berlin with the Federal President, Dr Richard von Weizsäcker, who encourages us and increases our confidence ... A visit to the operational centre of the air force for eastern Germany in Fürstenwalde. This is in a bunker, the so-called 'fox's earth' which had been classified as 'secret'. It was here that the airspace situation reports of the former NVA were produced and – when necessary – transmitted to the neighbouring eastern states. Now not only is the airspace monitored from here, but also the air-rescue service organised; it is available both to the civilian and the military sectors. Former NVA officers, whom one can recognise only by the white seams of their new boots and the absence of name-tags on their uniforms, are working side by side with their comrades from the Bundeswehr – experts together. Here, in a short time, the kind of co-operation has grown up that we would wish for in all spheres.

Afterwards, a visit to a large ammunition depot which is hidden in a forest and in which about 45,000 tons of ammunition are stored. The fence, twelve kilometres long, was until recently secured by a high-voltage security system and guarded by only a few soldiers. The switching off of the system means that ninety servicemen must be transported from a garrison 250 kilometres away and are quartered in temporary, scarcely acceptable sanitary conditions in order to do guard duty in shifts for a week. At least arrangements are later made, with some effort, to accommodate the conscripts in a Bundeswehr building fifty kilometres away, where they can be regularly supplied with warm meals. However, this means they have to be driven daily fifty kilometres to and fro. The conscripts do not see why they have to do so much guard duty after the political changeover merely because the high-voltage system has been switched off. 'After all I will still have to shoot, Herr General, if someone comes,' said one.

The commanding officer of this depot – formerly an NVA officer – is already complaining about a shortage of personnel, because some of the qualified armourer NCOs have left the service and gone into civilian industry. He has insufficient officers and NCOs, but at least an adequate number of civilian staff. It becomes evident that part of the ammunition, which is in danger of being stolen, must be better protected. I give the necessary orders and can only hope that there will be no nasty surprises. Here, too, it becomes obvious that visits to the units are a must. Written reports often do not show the specific problems clearly enough – paper is patient.

In the evening I move from my temporary office into my permanent one, which first had to have the electronic bugs removed. I have not taken over the imposing room of the Commander-in-Chief of the NVA, so as to avoid people making comparisons with him, if only in their minds. So I am now sitting in a room partly panelled with light-coloured wood, with a yellow-brown tufted carpet, green curtains and four uncomfortable, bright yellow armchairs. In front of my desk four chairs stand by a work table against the underside of which one bangs one's knees when sitting down. I tolerate the grotesque furnishings and leave everything as it is, so as not to forget where I am. The bulky telephone equipment, the folding bed on the wall, as well as the collection of crockery in the built-in cupboard indicate that this room, too, had an important previous occupier.

Tuesday, 9 October 1990

A flight to Leipzig, to visit the artillery regiment, and a discussion with recruits who are very reticent. In a large group they scarcely answer my questions, only when there are just a few of them are they responsive. Only then do I learn who is unemployed, who receives no money under the law providing for the payment of allowances to families and children, and who wants to volunteer for a longer period. On 1 September the soldiers were called up into the NVA, and did four weeks of basic training, which they are now having to go through again – according to the principles of the Bundeswehr but led by a former NVA officer. Officers and NCOs from the West have been brought in to help. They are doing their duties well, are motivated and treat their new comrades in a frank and friendly way, without being condescending.

The commanding officer of the artillery regiment tells me of his worries, which in the main are the uncertain future of his officers and NCOs, the lack of training facilities, the shortage of personnel and, above all, the great burden of guard duties.

Afterwards a visit to the 4th Motorised Infantry Division in Erfurt. I learn that only half of the personnel and only one-third of the drivers remain, but that the materiel is still complete, including all of the weapons and equipment which had to be taken over from the Stasi and the frontier troops. The full extent of the problems is made evident. The pay rates of the soldiers has not been fixed, there are difficulties concerning medical care, there is a shortage of personnel, the storage of ammunition does not accord with our regulations, and petrol and oil are dripping from tanker-trains which have become leaky, but cannot be emptied because there is a shortage of suitable storage capacity. Everything – absolutely everything – is run down, insofar as it was not important for the weapons systems. Even the asbestos-covered roofs of the barracks are causing us concern, as it is unclear how they must be dealt with.

Talks with the mayor of Erfurt and a representative of the state government of Thuringia. They would like us to put a building at their disposal, so that the new state parliament which is shortly to be elected can hold a meeting. We are able to help quickly and unbureaucratically – this indication that we are making a new start together is understood.

Flight back to Strausberg. In the evening talks are held with the directly subordinated commanding officers of the army, air force and navy, during which we make final arrangements for the conference of commanding officers taking place tomorrow, and we exchange our initial experiences. The question of the training for civilian jobs, of servicemen who are to be dismissed confronts us like a wall. We know that we must act but we do not yet have a plan. All that is clear is that the Federal Defence Ministry has agreed to send officials of the vocational support service to the five new Länder as quickly as possible in order, within the framework of assistance between official bodies, to act for the Federal Minister for Labour and Social Affairs. It is most important that advice is given to the servicemen who are leaving, as they are finding themselves helpless in a completely different world thanks to bureaucracy and legal regulations.

Late in the evening I learn that a department of the BKO, with the best of intentions and in order to give advance information, has sent out a teleprinter message detailing those units which are to be disbanded as a first step. The basis of the message is a plan which has not been agreed as a whole and which has not been approved by me. To send that message direct to the units, to a very large number of recipients, and without any explanation, must cause confusion and perplexity. So I cancel it on the same evening because I want to personally explain to the commanding officers how things will proceed, and only then shall I make individual decisions. It is clear to both my chief of staff and me how important it is to have firm leadership if the basic line which has been laid down is really to be carried through.

Wednesday, 10 October 1990

In Strausberg the first commanding officers' conference of the BKO takes place with more than four-hundred participants – about half each from the old Bundeswehr and the former NVA – down to the level of regimental commanders and commanders of independent units. I had arranged this conference so soon in order to explain to the officers, as soon as possible, the basic ideas behind the measures which will follow, to get to know the officers and to underline to them in discussion that we, as German officers, have a common task to fulfil and will be judged later on whether and how we have mastered it together. As there is no living accommodation available in Strausberg the conference cannot start before 9.30 am. A large number of the officers must travel very long distances, from the Erzgebirge, the Thuringian Forest or Mecklenburg-West Pomerania, in Wartburgs or Trabbis. Their journeys take between four and four-and-a-half hours in an unsettled weather situation, mostly in fog. So the length of the conference is restricted, to run from 9.30 am until 7 pm at the latest.

In an introduction I emphasise the special nature and the aim of this first conference:

> A week ago the unity of Germany was restored, in accordance with the will of the whole German people. Many of us will have greeted that moment with satisfaction, as the fulfilment of what caused us to join the forces. For many of us this is also the start of uncertainty.
>
> Today is also, one might say, an historic day. For the first time servicemen of the Bundeswehr and the former NVA come together in order to talk about the future common task. For all of us, this day will remain special in our memories as a milestone in our careers. This conference brings together officers of different backgrounds who are responsible in outstanding positions for the all-German Bundeswehr in the five new Länder.
>
> In order to underline the way ahead I don't want to deprive you of a quotation from the book *Soldiers of the People* which, until a short time ago used to be presented in the NVA for top achievement or as a gift. This is the quotation: 'Facing us stands the strongest imperialist military alliance, NATO, whose spearhead in Europe is FRG imperialism and the Bundeswehr, which has been educated in the spirit of militarism and anti-Communism. Within NATO the Bundeswehr plays a special role. Its nature and function are marked by the aggressive past of German imperialism, by the revanchist attitude of FRG imperialism and by the close alliance with the USA.'
>
> I remind you of this quotation in order to make it clear at the same time: I am the commanding officer of all the commanders present and have a commitment towards you according to the armed forces law. This

also means a commitment towards your welfare, and comradeship. You can expect from me: clear goals after we have taken stock, comradeship, a readiness to take up your problems and assist in your welfare. The aim of this conference is to inform about current developments, about the whole sphere of military policy as well as about future plans and the basic principles of personnel leadership and welfare, and to get to know each other and understand each other better. I expect you to be frank in discussion and to bring up problems and facts in order to improve the basis for making decisions.

We are talking as servicemen to servicemen, as Germans who have a common national interest in implementing in the armed forces the desire for a feeling of community, which exists in the democratic state based on the rule of law, and in reducing the size of the German armed forces according to the will of our people and the commitments we have entered into internationally. At the end of this process there should exist armed forces of our democratic state based on the rule of law – forces with no differences between East and West. Against this background I shall explain to you the task of the armed forces in united Germany and underline the room for manoeuvre in military policy, which will make it clear that the armed forces are a means of policy.

I then introduce the major-generals, the Chief of Staff and the departmental heads of the BKO and mention something of my career in the Bundeswehr from 1 April 1957 to 3 October 1990. These introductions and my few personal remarks are evidently unusual and cause some surprise.

The conference begins with an introduction on military policy entitled 'The Task of the Armed Forces in a United Germany', which is intended to make it clear that, in view of the upheaval in the international political situation, the armed forces in both Eastern and Western Germany must be drastically reduced. After this the deputy commanding officer, in his talk 'The Bundeswehr in the State and Society, and the Principles of *Innere Führung*', explains the most important differences between the Bundeswehr and the NVA, in order to demonstrate all of the challenges which face us. I then set out the basic ideas of Bundeswehr planning, in order to demonstrate the close connection between Bundeswehr planning, decisions on the budget and the involvement of the freely-elected parliament. In conclusion the deputy commanding officer speaks about 'Personnel Leadership and Welfare in the BKO'.

After each speech there is, after some hesitation, lively – and partly heated – discussion, which General von Scheven and I lead personally in order to underline our commitment. We repeatedly explain the link between our free, democratic state based on the rule of law, and NATO as an alliance of sovereign democratic states, but our argumentation is often not understood. Some officers find it hard to believe that the precept forbidding aggressive war, laid down in the Basic Law, really was a commitment, and that according to this Bundeswehr troops had no right to cross the inner-German frontier. It is equally difficult to make it understood that we are doing our duty to uphold the Basic Law, and promote human rights in the interest of peace and freedom.

During the discussion a colonel asks to speak. 'General,' he puts it to me,'we servicemen of the NVA have also served peace, according to our understanding and intent. Through our service we made a contribution to stability in Europe and we helped to support the peaceful change in the GDR. That was our joint interest.' With this a key issue in our dispute has been mentioned. There is quiet and a tense, attentive atmosphere as I answer:

> Colonel, in the Bundeswehr you are serving peace and freedom, and human rights, as laid down in the Basic Law. In the GDR on the other hand you were serving peace at the price of the freedom of the individual, a peace which many of our countrymen regarded as a 'peace of the graveyard.' That concept of peace, with no link to human rights and our Basic Law, is not enough for the future. It served the maintenance of the Communist system that was rejected by the majority of the people. You as commanding officers have a decisive role in the peaceful changeover from the NVA to the Bundeswehr. And I have heard from democratically elected representatives, that local NVA commanders had assured them that they would use no weapons against demonstrators. How things stood with the leaders of the NVA will have to be clarified. But if you want to stay in the Bundeswehr you must cast off the past of the Socialist armed forces without any ifs and buts!

In the break that follows this is the main topic of discussion. But many routine questions are also raised. One of the commanding officers, a colonel of the NVA, raised the problem of the missing official stamps for the free rail passes of the conscripts. The Reichsbahn would only accept stamped forms – orders are orders. Between 3 October 1990, when the NVA stamps became invalid, and 1 April 1991, when the stamps of the newly-formed units would become valid, a stamp vacuum had arisen. The Western commanding officers made do with the stamps they had brought from their old units, and shared them with the NVA commanders.

Military historians will probably find some mixed up stamp marks. Colonel Ocken, who was in charge of disbanding the frontier troops, used for 'correctly-stamped' dismissal papers and other official documents, stamps from the 16th Armoured Infantry Brigade – from which he was sent to the East for six months as a commanding officer.

Thursday, 11 October 1990

The Bundeswehr Chief of Staff visits the BKO. We report to him and have a discussion; afterwards he visits the troops. The great extent of the problems and tasks becomes clearer to him on the spot. He, too, begins to realise what an enormous task and challenge faces the command staff of the armed forces in exercising command over this large subordinated area and in co-ordinating the numerous tasks.

I tell him of my worries: due to lack of understanding and lack of knowledge about our special situation, the Federal Defence Ministry is making bureaucratic, ivory-tower decisions without consulting us in advance. I report that I have decided not to pass on certain orders and, if necessary, to submit them to the Federal Defence Ministry with the request that they be reconsidered. I also ask him to invite the media to visit our area so they can see how different conditions are from the West. The Chief of Staff shows understanding and promises us his support.

At midday I fly to Rostock to visit the navy, the service which will be facing the greatest difficulties. Out of 8,500 personnel, seven thousand must be dismissed. There is a depressed atmosphere among the men. It is clear to them that none of the ships will be taken over and the majority of the men have no chance of being kept in the service in the long term. However, they are still needed in order to hand over the ships in a technically flawless condition. The ships make a well-maintained impression.

The young petty officers are approachable and willing to discuss matters. Most of them want to leave the service as they see no career prospects here. But they want first of all to wait and see what the Bundeswehr will offer them. On the other hand many of the officers are very downcast, as they know how small their chances are. Most of them joined the navy only because they wanted to go to sea. We can already foresee the danger that in the end we shall have far too many officers and too few petty officers. We must make that clear, even though that will be unpleasant for many. Nothing is more depressing than lack of clarity.

I promise both the officers and the petty officers to do my best to make the decisions which are important for them, but I cannot promise them that I shall be able to do this in the next few weeks. They have to be informed definitely by 31 December 1990 at the latest, because then the temporarily increased retirement remuneration of the former NVA expires; this was introduced under the government of Hans Modrow to make it easier for servicemen to decide to leave the NVA. Compensation is paid according to length of service and rank. All servicemen aged over fifty could have a kind of early retirement arrangement giving them about two-thirds of their salary, which was a favourable offer. Servicemen who were younger received a single payment of up to 7,000 Deutschmarks, provided they were leaving by 31 December 1990. That was a particular incentive for those whose units were going to be disbanded anyway by 31 March 1991. I am therefore worried that even those servicemen of whom we are in need for the transitional period will leave. By law we cannot force any soldier to stay with us, anyone can leave immediately at their own request – without giving reasons.

This evening in Strausberg, I learn from a folder of press reports that a hundred pieces of land from our region are to be handed over to civilian users. This refers to territory part of which we are still using, and which we must now quit within a limited time which we can scarcely manage. However much the local authorities need to use this land, such decisions ought, in future, to be agreed with closer co-operation between us and the Federal Defence Ministry. Neither the branch office of the ministry, ourselves, or the military administration of VII Command have played a part in making these present decisions.

In the press folder I also find a short commentary in the *Süddeutsche Zeitung*, under the headline 'Tact'. In the article I am accused of opposing drastic reductions in personnel in my region. I had in no way discussed this question publicly, but had merely stated what had been agreed within the Federal Defence Ministry. The article goes on to claim that I am causing annoyance among my colleagues in the West, and it adds:

> Some are asking if it was really necessary to give one person command and disciplinary powers over three services, even if only for a year and in a limited territory. Chief of Staff Dieter Wellershof, the top soldier of the Bundeswehr, has on the other hand only limited command authority over the army, air force and navy. He is not their superior in the administrative chain of command, like Schönbohm. It will not reassure him much that Schönbohm was formally subordinate to his deputy. Friction losses are programmed. That could have been avoided if, from the start, structures had been created which were linked to the whole Bundeswehr. General Schönbohm calls for tact in dealing with his comrades from the former Volksarmee. This demand also applies to him in regard to his comrades from the previous Bundeswehr.

This short, poisonous article surprises me because nowhere had I discussed these questions publicly. It is a sign to me of personal sensitivities and possibly special factors relating to responsibilities in the Bonn sphere which cannot be seen from Strausberg. However, our task requires full commitment in my region of command – and not in Bonn.

Friday, 12 October 1990

Our weekly situation report deals mainly with the unguarded bases. The press has frequently reported break-ins in barracks we are no longer using and also break-ins in Soviet bases. There are headlines such as 'Soviet bases become death-traps'. A new sphere of problems is opening up here. This is not a Bundeswehr matter, but the police are not yet capable of acting and the Soviets have not handed over these bases in a correct manner. The procedure for hand-overs to the Federal Property Offices has only been clearly defined since 3 October. However, it is already evident that the bases which are no longer being used, and are being transferred to the general property holdings of the federal authorities are exposed to vandalism. Everything that is not firmly fixed down is being stolen. In view of our own burdens from guard duties it is impossible for us to take on these extra tasks. In any case it is only possible to ensure security in the whole Bundeswehr sphere by using officers up to the rank of captain as guards; in some cases even staff officers are being used as officers in charge of guards. The security situation continues to be tense and incalculable.

Monday, 15 October 1990

A flight to the former inner-German border to monitor the removal of the border installations, which is being carried out by former members of the frontier troops. In the barracks I am briefly informed about the course of the border and the security installations. The barracks has a neglected look; smashed windows, many vehicles are standing higgledy-piggledy on the base, ammunition is stored in ammunition bunkers which, however, are not fully secure. Similarly, small arms and grenades are not secure from thieves. The members of the former frontier troops are partly in civilian clothes and partly in black working uniforms without badges of rank – an unreal picture of a barracks. Are the former frontier troops reliable? I have doubts and order that all weapons and ammunition are removed from the barracks of the frontier troops as soon as possible. Supposedly this had been done a long time ago, or so it was reported to me – one of the unpleasant surprises that one has daily. Trust is good, checking is better – Lenin's motto applies here.

In a large storeroom at the barracks lie many uniforms of the frontier troops, all mixed up – it gives the impression that there has been looting. Four women, who have worked as civilian staff for the frontier troops for many years, are trying to bring order into this chaos and to sort out the uniforms. As it is still unclear what will then happen to the uniforms – whether they will be utilised or sold or whether they will land up on the rubbish heap – this work seems to me to terribly pointless. But the women are cheerful and happy that they have any work at all. They answer my questions in a friendly way. They say the clearing-up work will take a long time and after that things will somehow carry on.

In a frontier bunker outside the barracks I have a look at the old system for guarding the frontier. In this sphere there was no worry about cost, nothing was too expensive. The bunker is perfectly equipped, with a rest room, a medical ward, a small kitchen and the command centre. Plans and maps lie around and there are many telephones and signal lamps; on the wall is a sunny Mediterranean landscape.

The former frontier troops try, in spite of their civilian clothes, to behave in a strict military fashion. I feel uneasy in their presence. It would be interesting to hear something of their life stories. Why did they join the frontier troops? What was their attitude to the order to shoot at refugees? I have the feeling that such questions are being suppressed. Here, too, they are seeking to give the impression that they had only been doing their duty. I do not notice any conflicts of conscience.

Afterwards I fly by helicopter to the Harz mountains in order to see the working parties there. As the helicopter is landing, tourists come past. They want to know what a Bundeswehr general has to do with the former frontier troops. I explain my function as commanding officer of the BKO and tell them that the frontier troops have been disbanded and are now working in a civilian capacity, under our direction, to remove the inner-German frontier. The reaction shows hostility. 'It's good that that lot are themselves removing the frontier which they built and guarded. One should have no sympathy for them.'

Two to three men are working with each crane and truck. A sergeant-major works the crane, a lieutenant-colonel drags the wire fence from its fixture and a major assists. What is going on inside these men – are they coming to terms with their guilt? Do they feel guilty at all, or were they only 'organs' of the state?

We fly over the Brocken mountain, to see from the air what the possibilities are for removing the remains of the Wall in the difficult terrain. The expense and commitment devoted by the Communist regime to fencing itself off is unimaginable. Under the most difficult conditions hundreds of tons of concrete were brought up on to the Brocken in order to seal it off. From the helicopter the course of the frontier barrier-system can be clearly seen – the fence of metal mesh runs over all obstacles, no expense was spared. And we were on the way to accepting that as normality? Now we are faced with the difficulty of getting rid of it all. Nearby places have already lodged precautionary protests against the use of lorries and the construction of new roads. For this reason the repair of the old Brocken railway is being considered, for transporting the material away. That would certainly be in the interest of the places concerned. But who is going to pay for it all? After all, no one feels responsible; another 'brain-teaser' to be solved by agreement between the various authorities.

Late in the evening I receive a telephoned order from Bonn to report as soon as possible on the order in which we are disbanding the units and which units will be disbanded by 31 December 1990. Evidently the Budget Committee is pressing. It is assumed that the mass of the units can be disbanded by 31 March 1991. I state that I consider that this cannot be carried out. If disbandment takes place by 31 March 1991 we must expect that masses of officers and NCOs will leave on 31 December 1990, which will not only endanger the guarding of weapons and ammunition, but also the effectiveness of the command structure. In addition, the concept for utilisation of arms and equipment is still completely unclear. Every day we receive new reports and the situation is constantly changing. I consider it wrong and irresponsible in our difficult situation to take decisions without knowing all the facts and being able to assess the result.

Tuesday, 16 October 1990

Early in the morning in the headquarters, I discuss ideas for the utilisation or disposal of weapons, equipment and ammunition. The amounts involved can be seen in outline. We must disband units and do not yet know what to do with the equipment. There are no guidelines. This is not surprising, as the total amount of weapons and ammunition to be destroyed or made safe is only roughly known. However, we must first of all remove from the various barracks, all weapons and ammunition belonging to the units that are being disbanded and collect it together somewhere. It would make sense to do this at the place where the ammunition will later be made safe and the combat vehicles destroyed. But there is still no clarity about that. All the same, we can't wait for ministerial decisions because the pressure to disband units and to dismiss career and short-service men is great. So we are ourselves designating the camps where the weapons are to be collected together. For this purpose, we are at first using existing depots and then we must see what temporary solutions we can arrive at – in the hope that by then a concept for utilisation has been worked out.

Very few people have a clear idea of the immense difficulties involved in the disbandment of units. In the foreground are the servicemen and the civilian staff, but then we have to collect together in an orderly manner all the weapons, equipment and ammunition, all the wheeled vehicles, radio sets, uniforms, construction equipment and quartermaster stores, in short, everything that is in a barracks, so that it can later – according to the federal budgetary regulations – be utilised or disposed of with the prospect of making a profit. On top of all that it has yet to be decided with regard to some of the weapons systems whether they are classified as rejects and can therefore be destroyed, or whether they can still be used in the Bundeswehr or sold to allies. All of this is unclear and for this reason alone the pressure to disband the units quickly is irresponsible. I report this to the Federal Defence Ministry in order to make it clear that I would not carry out an order to disband the units by 31 March 1991.

Visit to the 9th Armoured Division at Eggesin in Mecklenburg-West Pomerania, an area which is very underdeveloped economically. In the situation report the usual problems come up, familiar now from all areas. The questions of keeping soldiers in the service, the selection of 'temporary soldiers' to serve for two years, as well as the social welfare questions, are ranked above all other problems.

Talking with the conscripts over lunch is hard work. They are taciturn and inhibited. In answer to my question they let me know that today the food is better because I am here. After lunch I follow the soldiers, taking my used plate, into an adjoining room and then down a staircase. We enter a room with a wide sink and six cold-water taps. The soldiers hold their plates under the taps and then dry them with a rag. There is no hot water, no washing-up liquid, nothing. I ask for an explanation from the Western commanding officer who has taken over this battalion. 'I have only just realised that that is not in order,' is all that he says.

The whole picture is terrible. In the kitchens there are no extractor fans, the floors are smeared with fat, plaster is falling from the walls. In the storerooms the walls are damp. There are no showers for the men so that only now do I understand what the word *Abschüsseln* means. After sports the soldiers had to wash themselves with water from bowls, that was the substitute for showers. Sometimes they took garden hoses and squirted each other with cold water. According to our standards such conditions are catastrophic but the NVA soldiers, who had lived this way for years, see nothing unusual in it. 'We knew nothing different, General,' said the former commander of the division, 'and we regarded it as normal. Moreover, we would have had no money for improvements. The money was just enough to improve the technical infrastructure and the storage of our main weapons systems. Everything else had to take a back seat.' When I asked him if he wanted his son to serve in the army under such conditions he reacted with surprise. He had not thought about that at all. It was not necessary, because his family, as well as himself, had privileges and had never been properly confronted with this reality.

In the evening I asked about 100-120 officers to dinner in a kind of rest-home belonging to the division outside Eggesin. It consists of simple huts built by the soldiers near the Baltic sea where they could get away from the daily routine of duty and refresh themselves when on leave. The evening has been prepared with great care and passes off in a pleasant atmosphere. The divisional band, which is shortly to be disbanded, plays some marches, and after the meal I give a short survey of the situation and the BKO's mission in the region. Afterwards I try to conduct a discussion with the officers. For the former members of the NVA it is a highly unusual situation, that such a high-ranking superior officer would come to them, make a speech and then want to discuss it with them. So it is not surprising that most of them are reserved and that the first contributions come from Western officers. I deal briefly with these remarks and then say to the former members of the NVA: 'I have come here to hear your problems but find that you evidently have none. So you already know how long you are going to stay in the Bundeswehr. You know when you will become "temporary soldiers" for two years, you know how much the pay-off will be and how the training for vocational qualifications functions. There are no problems, so we can get on with the social part of the evening. Or has anyone got questions?' With that I provoke a whole flood of questions and we talk for two hours about problems concerning the officers and their families. I cannot answer all the problems but I promise to send the answers to the division as soon as these points have been clarified.

Afterwards I move from table to table and talk to the officers over a glass of beer. The atmosphere loosens up and there is a lively exchange of views. On this evening for the first time, officers from the East and the West sit together in a relaxed atmosphere. There is a lot to discuss. The past and the Communist system are played down. One was in the party because that was the done thing – the convinced Communists were the others, the ones who have left the service. The main concern is their professional future – that dominates everything. Many wives of the servicemen are already unemployed, and in the Eggesin area there is scarcely any work except in the Bundeswehr. As a result of the drastic cuts many businesses have already closed. The Bundeswehr, it is true, is continuing kindergarten and school meals but the number of kindergarten places has been reduced and some kindergarten teachers have been dismissed.

There are, of course, many family concerns of the soldiers which I cannot solve. I can only listen and encourage them to stay in the army until the vocational training shows its first successes. I tell them that they can rely on local commanders developing initiatives to provide jobs and vocational qualifications – as is already being done successfully in the West by many commanders. And I can remove another important worry from the officers: they will not be evicted from their flats if they have been dismissed from the Bundeswehr. This rumour had been circulating throughout the whole BKO region. The men are visibly relieved.

Towards the end of the evening, around midnight, a lieutenant-colonel comes to me and says: 'I have been in the NVA for eighteen years and in all that time have never known a high-ranking general to visit the division, sit with us and talk over our problems. We notice how very different conditions in the Bundeswehr are from those in the NVA but we need time to get used to them.' But I, too, must get used to the new situation. Only two weeks after the unification of Germany and I am sitting together with men of a former NVA division and discussing their personal concerns and worries, for which I also bear responsibility. That still seems unreal to me.

Wednesday, 17 October 1990

It is foggy, not flying weather. I leave at 5.30 am on the bumpy, dark roads. In the morning talks are held at an air base with pilots from two units which are being disbanded by 31 March 1991. The young men make an excellent impression – they are lively and enthusiastic. The number of pilots to be kept on has still not been clarified. The air force command wanted to dismiss them all: not needed, retraining too expensive. I have pressed for at least some of the younger pilots to be kept on, in order that there is no basic ban on offering work to a particular group of officers. But so far nothing has been decided. So I must tell the pilots that scarcely one of them has a chance of being kept on. I appeal to their good sense and initiative. Then a young captain wants to speak:

> General, I am the spokesman of my comrades and would like to say the following: we became pilots because we wanted to fly, not for ideological reasons. But whoever wanted to go into the air force had to join the party. In the meantime it has become clear to us that we have scarcely any chance here. So we have been trying for weeks to obtain training in Hamburg as air traffic controllers. But for that we must do an English course and that costs money, namely 1,000 Deutschmarks per person. That is our main problem. We are thirty-five pilots, that means we need 35,000 Deutschmarks. Where can we get that sum from? We are not receiving any financial support, neither from the labour exchange nor from anywhere else. You have appealed to our initiative, so please help us!

I promise to obtain the money, without knowing what I am letting myself in for. In the opinion of our employment authorities and our vocational assistance service there was no need for additional English courses; there were enough applicants with knowledge of English. Pointing out the special situation of the pilots had no effect. Only after five weeks of discussions with all the responsible departments did a resourceful official of our vocational assistance service find a solution through a very loose interpretation of certain regulations. I am still thankful to this man. If the pilots had not received the money, further talk would not have helped, these young people would not have believed in anything any more. But that kind of reasoning could not, of course, be found in the regulations issued before unification.

In Strausberg this evening, I receive Directive No.1 with the instruction to disband the 519 units which are earmarked for disbandment, as soon as possible – by 31 March 1991 at the latest – and to work out a plan within a week for carrying this out; those servicemen who are not to be dismissed are to be transferred into newly formed units. So my protest of a few days ago, that such a directive could not be carried out, has had no effect.

In relation to the third supplementary budget for 1990, the Budgetary Committee of the Bundestag has laid down that next year, the number of longer-service personnel in the BKO region must not exceed 25,000 and the total number of servicemen must be not more than 50,000. That is, for the time being, only a recommendation, but it is being accepted by sections of the Defence Ministry as binding – without explaining to the committee the difficulties of putting it into effect. They seem to want to take a risk, the extent of which no one in Bonn can estimate.

In discussion with my headquarters staff it is confirmed that I must not carry out this directive. An over-hasty disbandment of units will cause a loss of credibility and of the feeling of community, and could lead to incalculable difficulties, particularly in the sphere of security and reliability. We still have no place to collect together the weapons and ammunition of the units that are being disbanded; our ammunition depots are chock-full. I shall therefore have to ask the Federal Minister to either give me more room for manoeuvre, or to personally take on the responsibility which I, as his commanding officer, cannot accept.

In addition, we have received an instruction to the effect that, together with the military administration, we must dismiss 10,000 civilian staff by 31 December 1990 – that is, in just over two months. As every garrison administration has several hundred civilian staff, dismissals will in part affect those whom we still urgently need for the future, for instance foremen in the boiler-houses, nurses and telecommunications technicians.

However, it later turns out that dismissals have been made partly with the involvement of cadres of the old regime and without the participation of the staff representatives and have therefore to be rescinded. Moreover many employees, under old GDR law, must be given notice of up to a year or even more – although no one really knew this when notice was given. As a result the whole dismissal business has been a washout. All of us have squandered trust and sown insecurity, the worst thing that could happen in this tense situation.

Thursday, 18 October 1990

In the afternoon in Berlin to a jubilee function – '40 Years of the *Berliner Pressekonferenz*'. For the first time a German general in uniform is taking part in such an event. I am pleased, and moved by the strong approval and encouragement that I receive from many people I do not know.

We take a night flight by helicopter to Erfurt and drive to Bad Salzungen. Shortly before midnight final discussions are held with the commanding officer in preparation for the first public oath-taking ceremony in the BKO region. I overnight in the so-called 'general's room' which at least has what was known in GDR days as a 'wet cell' – a shower cubicle. A few thin jets run from the shower nozzle. Everything is tatty, as usual it smells of disinfectant, the linoleum flooring has blisters.

Friday, 19 October 1990

The oath-taking ceremony in the marketplace takes place according to Bundeswehr tradition. The small square is well filled. Several thousand people are there and they even applaud as the soldiers march in. For me too, it is a happy, inspiring moment as the soldiers swear publicly to serve the Federal Republic of Germany faithfully and to defend the law and the freedom of the German people. The oath-taking has an additional, special importance: the Germans are united in a democratic state based on the rule of law – there can no longer be a civil war. In spite of this, a small group of people with three banners demonstrate against our ceremony; this evening on television the protest is depicted as an 'important message'.

Before the start of the oath-taking ceremony I entered into conversation with a Protestant pastor whom I had asked to take part in the event with me. He had declined, saying that it did not fit in with his ideas, he did not like military spectacles. I had tried unsuccessfully to explain that according to our concept in the Federal Republic of Germany – to which, after all, we now all belonged – the solemn commitment of citizens to their state was in no way a military spectacle, but rather an important event for the young soldiers and their relatives. However, the pastor could not be persuaded to come on to the stand. But he did promise to join the spectators and watch the proceedings.

Later, at the reception in the town hall, he comes spontaneously towards me and admits that the oath-taking ceremony was quite different from what he had imagined. He says he must reconsider his attitude, the event has pleased him. 'Perhaps,' he concedes, 'in all these matters we must move much closer together.' I find this is an encouraging experience.

After the reception the Defence Minister invites conscripts and their relatives to lunch. I discuss with some of the conscripts the pastoral lecture which had prepared them for their oath-taking. I learn that out of 250 soldiers about 180 had voluntarily attended the lecture. Although they had not been christened, the conscripts said, they had been interested by the lecture and would like to attend one again if they had the chance. Issues had been raised which they could not really discuss properly elsewhere.

Parents told me that they had taken an extra day's holiday to attend the oath-taking, which they had enjoyed. They spoke about the fear of threatened unemployment, but also about their happiness at being united in freedom and being able to visit their relatives in the West. 'General, the best thing is that we don't have to live in fear any longer.'

Saturday, 20 October 1990

On the way to Hamburg I visited a motorised infantry regiment. The regimental commander and one of his deputies, both from the Western Bundeswehr, are quite optimistic about the future. But here, too, is that same miserable sight in the barrack-rooms, in the shower block and in the kitchen. The kitchen is unbelievably dirty. The kitchen sergeant is smeared in almost as much fat as the greasy, brown plastic beakers standing in the cupboards. There must be some decisive changes here.

At lunch in the commanding officer's dining-room, with artificial flowers and oilcloth on our table, a former member of the NVA tells me that an inspection visit to the troops on a Saturday, with only two days' notice, would have been unthinkable in the NVA era. As a rule several weeks' notice were given of visits by high-ranking generals. Before their arrival the programme for the visit was reviewed and was subject to acceptance by an inspection team. The general had only moved about in a prepared area, on freshly swept or raked paths, past whitewashed pavement edges. Even treetops had been rearranged to give the visitor a better view of the parade ground from the commander's room. The former members of the NVA have still a lot to learn – they are up against a great deal.

In the evening a talk with the Minister, in part about the timing for the disbandment of units. I am given more room for manoeuvre: the disbandment of the units can be carried out according to the situation and in a flexible way, but with the instruction that the vast majority of the units are to be disbanded by mid-1991. This is the minimum amount of time that I need.

Sunday, 21 October 1990

Midday visit to an ammunition depot in Mecklenburg-West Pomerania, which is one of our large installations. There is still some storage capacity available. The soldiers on guard come from a garrison 150 kilometres away and have been sent here for a week. Their living quarters are better than in previous depots. To my surprise, however, the commanding officer, a lieutenant-colonel from the former NVA, tells me that he and his two deputies have decided to leave the service on 31 December, as they see good opportunities in industry. When I point out that there are promising opportunities for them in the Bundeswehr, as we need specialists for the organisation of the depots, they respond with the question: 'General, can you guarantee that?' I have to admit that I cannot, so they will probably leave. This example indicates something I have also discovered in other spheres: more specialists will probably leave at the year-end than we can cope with. We shall have difficulties retaining enough specialists, particularly for the storage of ammunition. So we must take action in advance by giving officers clear promises about their employment, at least as temporary servicemen for two years.

Afterwards, I visit the Rheinsberg Palace. It looks neglected and cannot yet be visited. The palace and the park have nevertheless kept their charm – Socialism has not destroyed everything. As I walk around in my green NATO uniform I am greeted by people whom I do not know, from Eastern and Western Germany. They wish us all the best.

Monday, 22 October 1990

Visit to the air force group headquarters, the MiG-29 wing and the combat helicopter wing. Everywhere the same questions seeking clarity. The MiG-29 pilots and technicians can see that they may still have a chance, and they hope that their aircraft will continue to be used in the long term. Now that decisions have been made, they know that they can undergo tests and, after those, can stay in the service at least for the next two years. Originally the military leadership wanted to scrap the MiG-29s because they were not needed and the technology was too expensive. The minister then ordered tests with the aim of keeping them in service, because the scrapping of these most modern fighters would doubtless have been met with incomprehension and considerable public disquiet.

Tuesday, 23 October 1990

Office work. I realise that I need more time in the headquarters because the late evening hours are not enough. Although I read all my papers in the car or helicopter, and give written orders, I have too little time for discussions on basic principles in the headquarters. However, in this phase, visits to the units and discussions with the officers have priority. My Chief of Staff works excellently and takes over important tasks from me. The same applies to my deputy and old friend, General von Scheven.

Wednesday, 24 October 1990

From 5 pm until 11.30 pm I attend a commanding officers' meeting with the directly subordinate commanding officers of the army, air force and navy, together with my deputy, the Chief of Staff and the departmental heads. We unanimously reach the view that the situation as a whole has stabilised. We must continue with the policy of reductions and disbandment, even though it is quite clear that the reductions cannot be made without first knowing the future plans for the stationing and structure of Bundeswehr units.

The headquarters staff has, with extraordinary commitment, worked out a three-stage plan for the disbanding of units in an orderly fashion and for harmonising this process with the formation of new units. We put this plan to our commanders and come to the joint decision that it should form the basis for our further planning. I want to announce the decisions as soon as possible, so that the units are not kept in the dark about their fate for long. Those officers and NCOs who cannot be kept on as temporary servicemen for two years should, as far as possible, be told personally how long they can stay in the Bundeswehr on special terms of service.

A new problem is emerging: the staff of the former 'financial and economic organs' of the NVA, both officers and NCOs who have been responsible for the whole financial sphere and for the payment of wages and pensions in the armed forces, will on the whole probably leave. They are being sought by banks, insurance companies and the new inland revenue offices which are being set up, because they have qualifications and a good reputation. We, on the other hand, cannot make any firm promises and the current surprising wave of dismissals of civilian staff, ordered at short notice, does not make it any easier to present our arguments. We let the officers know that in any case we will need them to fulfil our task. However, we are unable to give details of future salaries. A fairly large section at least, will stay on for some time, in order to guarantee that their comrades are paid. They are not doing it on account of their own salaries but out of commitment to their comrades, who would otherwise receive no money. How long they will keep their word no one knows.

Of course, just a short time later I receive a report that in one of our areas it has not been possible to pay the men as the finance staff have left the service; it would only be possible to issue pay with a few days delay. In another case I am told that a battalion commander from the Western Bundeswehr has borrowed 100,000 Deutschmarks for a few days from a well-known German bank in order to hand out pay.

Those few examples show our new difficulties which have primarily been caused by lack of clarity. If conscripts were to demonstrate in public because they are not getting paid, it could have terrible effects on discipline and trust, and could lead to further demonstrations. So the situation is extraordinarily precarious. The crucial mistake was that some of the unit administrative officials were sent to the East too late.

As a result we are still without senior administrative officials in the headquarters who are directly responsible in this sphere. They will only start their duties on 29 October. Fortunately, in my command headquarters there is a small department in existence, which is working with great commitment.

During discussions about administrative matters a further problem emerges: the newly formed garrison administrations, headed by a few Western officials, are at present unable to take over bases which we have vacated or which will be vacated shortly. According to the system which has been established, the garrison administration must take over the bases and then hand them over to the Federal Property Office. However, the branches of the Federal Property Office dealing with Eastern Germany do not yet exist. This is causing ridiculous results here and there: we quit bases under high pressure, partly because of demands from the local authorities which are already waiting for the sites. But then we cannot hand over the bases because the garrison administrations and the local Federal Property Offices are not yet ready to accept them. The by-product is that we still have to go on guarding the bases.

Thursday, 25 October 1990

In the afternoon I pay a formal first visit to Army General Boris Snetkov, the Commander-in-Chief of the Western Group of Soviet Armed Forces at his headquarters in Wünsdorf just outside Berlin. With the take-over of the BKO, the newly formed liaison group to the Western Group of the Soviet forces, headed by Major-General Foertsch, was placed under my command. The liaison group is responsible for all matters relating to the temporary stationing of the Soviet troops and their withdrawal. Initial contacts with the Soviet commanders have gone smoothly; the constant dialogue makes it possible for the Soviets to grasp the new situation and to accept that they are now stationed in a sovereign country. For the commanders of a former occupation army, this is not easy.

In this respect, too, our discussions are contributing to a change in attitude and we are managing to bring about contact between the Soviet troops and the local authorities. It is often the locally responsible Bundeswehr commanders who take the initiative in arranging the first meetings, in order to overcome the failure of both sides to talk.

The meeting with Snetkov is a special experience for me. For the first time since my Moscow visit accompanying Federal Minister Scholz, I meet – now as a German commanding officer and representative of the sovereign, free Germany – a Soviet general who, with his troops, is still our guest. I land at the base in my Soviet-made helicopter at the base and am met by the Chief of Staff and driven to the headquarters building. The barracks is very large. The roads are swept, soldiers directing the traffic stand at all the crossings; evidently they are intending to put on a big show of protocol. In front of the headquarters building there is a guard of honour of young soldiers with pleasant faces. Army General Snetkov – small and wiry – awaits me in his large room.

He tells me about the history of the Western Group of Forces from the Second World War up until the present. It was, he says, a successful and proud formation. I reply:

> General, when you, as a young lieutenant, stormed into Brandenburg in 1945, I was fleeing to the West with my mother and four brothers and sisters; my father was still at the front. I am happy that today, as the representative of sovereign Germany, I can speak with you and that we can discuss questions which have arisen from the happy and peaceful developments of recent years. They include the temporary stationing of your troops and their withdrawal by the end of 1994. We want to help you to leave Germany with dignity. I assure you that we shall do all we can to ensure we become good neighbours.

Our discussion lasts not for forty-five minutes – as originally planned – but for ninety. We cover all the questions which can be dealt with at a first meeting. Snetkov states that he, of course, intends to keep to the withdrawal date and says that he will work closely with the state governments, and above all with us and our liaison group attached to the Soviet forces. My suggestion that he could underline his support for the withdrawal process by visiting the Premiers of the Eastern German states, who have just been democratically elected, got a reserved reception.

Evidently he is more interested in intensive co-operation with the Bundeswehr. He would like to have a direct telephone line to me, so that we can talk to each other at any time; he says he always has an interpreter in his room. He is primarily interested in leaving Germany in an honourable and dignified way. His forces should not get the feeling that they have retrospectively lost the Second World War. I promise him close co-operation but make it clear that we must speak frankly about differing interests and standpoints, as that, too, is part of a good neighbourly relationship.

This discussion can provide a good start for our further co-operation. I ask Snetkov to receive the head of our liaison group, Major-General Foertsch, as he is the representative of the Federal Government in all military questions. Snetkov will consider it, but makes no firm promise.

A visit to the Berlin Bundeswehr hospital, the former hospital of the GDR People's Police, which stands right next to the Charité Hospital. By GDR standards it is a fairly modern hospital, but now modernisation up to Western standards is unavoidable. Nurses and doctors make a positive and motivated impression – they have prospects.

In the evening I fly to Bonn. Home again for the first time.

Monday, 29 October 1990

I hold talks all day in the Federal Defence Ministry about the current situation with the chiefs of the three services, departmental heads and permanent secretaries. Everywhere there is strong commitment and readiness to help but not enough knowledge of the real situation on the ground.

In the evening I hold a detailed discussion with a group of journalists whose questions and comments make it clear that the extent and the problems of our mission have not yet been fully recognised. I decide to pay more attention to the media.

Wednesday, 31 October 1990

I visit the frontier troops who are removing the Wall in Berlin. An officer of the former frontier troops explains the system to me with all of its refinements and subtleties. The whole system of frontier security was of such perfection and technical intelligence that in retrospect it is still frightening. The smallest escape route was blocked: every watercourse, every canal, every ditch. The officer shows me everything without betraying any emotion: the sealing-off fence, the ditch obstacle, the Wall. I am reminded of a diary entry by Ernst Jünger written during the war, in which he notes that the SS thugs were shooting holes in the backs of people's heads with the same precision shown by train guards in punching tickets. Has it been like that here?

The former frontier troops are now working to remove the Wall without any contract or decision about their pay or social security. They are working with their heavy equipment. The drivers of excavators and bulldozers, who had been trained earlier, have in the meantime gone off to work in the secure building trade. Thus, time and again we train new drivers, who then leave after a short period. This is also a contribution to vocational training. Admittedly we are pleased for anyone who has found a secure workplace. However, the person in charge on the ground never knows how many workers he will have the next day – and we are supposed, and want, to remove the Wall by the beginning of December.

Afterwards I visit the mayor of East Berlin and the woman speaker of the city parliament. They show lively interest in the Bundeswehr and the future stationing of units in Berlin. But at the forefront is the demand that the Wall be gone by the beginning of December! If we want to manage this we shall have to use additional engineer units as well as the frontier forces.

Thursday, 1 November 1990

In the afternoon I hold talks with the commander of the 5th air force group, Major-General Mende. The same problems exist in his area too. There is no strategy for the utilisation of ammunition and equipment, additional guards are needed to make up for disbanded units. The pilots have their licences only until mid-December. By then nearly four hundred jet fighters, in the main the older models MiG-21, MiG-23 and SU-22, must be concentrated on four bases. But until now agreement has not been reached in the ministry as to where this is to happen. In addition, it is not clear in what technical state the aircraft are to be kept. Are some to remain airworthy so they can be flown to wherever they can still be used? We have no longer the time for such considerations. As soon as the planes are taken out of the maintenance cycle, technically they are no longer safe. Either we fly them within the next fortnight to their destinations or about three hundred aircraft must be transported by road through the five new Länder, which does not seem acceptable to me. Even so, the technical regulations and flying instructions must be adhered to exactly, to avoid the risk of crashes. That means that a decision must be made now.

Friday 2 November 1990

Up to now, none of the problems which face us and which are being added to daily has really been solved. Because we are being forced to reduce personnel quickly, the situation is becoming even more complicated and more difficult to assess. The flood of letters that are reaching us shows how dissatisfied people are – and the expectations they have of us. Each day I receive between thirty and fifty letters from former members of the NVA, their relatives, or from civilian and military personnel who have left the services. These letters in part show helplessness, an inability to take decisions, desperation – but the tone is becoming ruder and more demanding. It is not very encouraging.

I visit the so-called 'medal cellar' where the NVA's stock of war medals is stored. Medals for 'courage in the face of the enemy' are kept there in cardboard boxes. They were intended to be awarded after the outbreak of war. They bear the significant name 'Blücher Medal' and exist in different classes. There are also field-marshal's epaulettes for the former Defence Minister of the GDR, Army General Heinz Hoffmann, who in case of war would evidently have been promoted. Would anyone have believed all this before the political changeover?

As here, it can be seen throughout the NVA how seriously the possibility of a war was treated. They were ready for action at all times. The forces were at eighty-five per cent readiness, the armoured combat vehicles, the main weapon systems of the army, were waiting at their depots, fully loaded with ammunition, and when the alarm was given the crews had to be ready to move off between half an hour to two hours, according to the specific situation. For this reason there was such a severe restriction on the movements of officers and NCOs, particularly at weekends. They were allowed out of their bases on only one evening in the week. An officer who lived by the Baltic told me that he even had to leave a sketch map of his location at the base if he went to the beach with his family at the weekend.

The camps, where the vehicles and equipment for the five divisions which were to be mobilised, were excellently equipped and organised with German perfection and at considerable expense. Mobilisation could be carried out very quickly: all the mobile weapons systems were filled with fuel and ammunition and ready to – when the alarm was sounded the reservists could retrieve their equipment and weapons from designated buildings and leave immediately, ready for action.

Consideration had also been given to civil defence, which had a staff of about half a million. Millions of ABC-masks (atomic, bacteriological and chemical) were in readiness to protect the population. In addition there were hospital ships, hospital trains and reserve hospitals which were kept ready in the regional capitals. Even 'war money' had been prepared since 1980 just in case. It comprised old banknotes from the 1955 issue, which had originally been earmarked for destruction in 1970, but which had been overprinted with the words 'military money'. The military money was to be used during 'operations on the territory of the adversary' as a second currency for financing the expenses of the NVA. Similar arrangements by the Polish and Czechoslovak People's Armies have also become known. Akin to the preparation of military money was the production of about two-hundred thousand identity cards for the civilian staff who were to follow the forces. This figure indicates how many non-military personnel they had planned to use for supervision and administration in occupied territory. Preparations to counter internal disturbances were also made, by means of a bundle of measures which were individually tested in manoeuvres. A threatened shortage of personnel in case of war was to be overcome by putting to work students, or schoolchildren from the ninth and tenth classes (aged 15 and 16) or students. The education minister, Margot Honecker is said to have been responsible for this as the authorised representative, in the spheres of education and culture, of the Chairman of the National Defence Council, that is Honecker himself.

Finally, the political leadership had also prepared itself by constructing a system of bunkers and command posts so that the party leadership and government, as well as the fifteen regional party secretaries with their appropriate staff, could take over command from bunker installations in case of war. Everything was consistently arranged to ensure they could go into action in the most effective way. Evidently they had seriously expected war against the 'imperialist class enemy' and drew extreme consequences from this. In addition this perfectly organised and secure system broke down within a few days; I found very few officers who still spoke in favour of the past.

Wednesday, 7 November 1990

The rapporteur group of the Bundestag Defence Committee – including a member of the Party of Democratic Socialism – visits the BKO. We explain our difficulties and the need for more time for restructuring and disbandment. The understanding for our concerns is great, as is the readiness to help.

Afterwards we fly to Staaken, in order to demonstrate the removal of the frontier installations, and then to the 1st Motorised Infantry Division in Potsdam-Eiche. Here we are able to give the Bundestag members a very vivid demonstration of some of our difficulties. A central heating installation – built at the end of the 1930s – is coke-fired and supplies part of the barracks with hot water. As in the pre-industrial age several workers shovel coke onto barrows which they push into the boiler-room and empty above the boilers. The coke is laboriously shovelled into the furnaces. Two workers then loosen it so that the glowing ash falls down to the storey below. There it is sprayed with water by a worker and then loaded into a coke barrow, pushed to a refuse dump and from there it is taken away. I think it better not to ask where it goes. This is the way jobs were created under Socialism. However, in the new personnel estimates the stokers and all the other personnel needed for this work have not been taken into account.

A walk through the kitchen and the living quarters is equally depressing. The kitchen is dirty, there are no fat extractors, it is impossible to clean the floor. The kitchen and a nearby building are heated from their own boilerhouse which sends stinking clouds of smoke into the sky. In the living quarters plaster is flaking off the walls, there is no decent furniture and the showers don't work.

In discussions with men of all ranks personal problems, too, are mentioned. A colonel and a major tell us that they can understand the need for reductions, but they call for the offer of vocational re-training if they have to leave the service. There are complaints about the different social welfare arrangements between East and West. The conscripts do not understand why they receive smaller payments for Christmas, leave, and at the end of their service than their comrades in the West, and less remuneration for overtime work undertaken in more difficult conditions. This is really not fair compensation. In view of the conditions would a special bonus not be appropriate?

I explain to the Bundestag members my view that the conscripts, as citizens of the Federal Republic, are serving the same state, and that the wages and pay-offs of the conscripts should not be fixed according to the economic strength of the individual federal states – this is not the case in the West either. I explain that the call for equal treatment is made particularly understandable in view of the fact that a large number of the conscripts leaving the service would be unemployed and were in need of the usual pay-off in the West, 2,500 Deutschmarks. Against this background it was indefensible to pay only five hundred Deutschmarks in the East.

The understanding shown by the rapporteurs for our difficulties makes me feel confident. It seems to me decisive that the responsible people in parliament and the government should experience on the spot, that all the difficulties we face cannot be compared with normal conditions in the old Federal Republic, and therefore these problems are difficult to communicate. Experience cannot be gained by reading.

In the evening I have invited the commanders of the Western Allies' Berlin brigades to dinner, to thank them for the help they have given us in the setting-up of the Regional Defence Command 100 in Berlin. They show great interest in our work, and are fascinated at the way two previously hostile armies are now getting on with each other. They had not believed that it could go so smoothly. They seem to forget what it means to belong to the same people and to speak the same language.

Chapter 8

First Decisions on
Disbanding Units

Thursday, 8 November 1990

I visit the army headquarters for eastern Germany in Potsdam. Flying over the Brandenburg countryside and lakeland moves me again and again. Potsdam, then Sanssouci Palace amid the lakes, so beautiful. That I can see all this from the air, that I am flying over a united Germany, still seems like a miracle. The briefing at the army headquarters produces the usual worries: we need more time and the men need more clarity about their prospects.

Next we visit to a former elite regiment of the NVA. Up until two years ago, in the case of war it would have been ordered to attack West Berlin. A smart commanding officer reports to me. Now a major, he is proud to have become – in 1989 – commanding officer of this regiment, which he joined twenty years earlier. The soldiers demonstrate their special abilities in single combat and as infantry. The training facilities are excellent, ours could be no better.

However, my sudden wish to see the kitchens and living quarters causes consternation, and the result is as I expected: the kitchen in a disgusting condition, the plaster flaking off, the floor smeared with fat; the rooms sparsely furnished like everywhere else, and the showers are not working even though the unit does a lot of sport.

At lunch I talk with the commander and a few officers about their reactions at the time of the political changeover. The commander talks readily.

He admits to me:

General, when I became a soldier I was sure I was doing the right thing and I was proud to serve in this elite regiment. When I became the commanding officer in September 1989 it was the peak of my career. Our regiment led all the parades, we always marched at the head. But in October and November 1989 the first feelings of uncertainty arose. We were given completely unclear, sometimes contrasting, orders. We were ordered to go to Leipzig to do police duties, at first with arms and then only with truncheons. During one of the demonstrations we found five conscripts from our regiment among the demonstrators. That really made us think. But the changeover came so quickly, General, that I still have not quite come to terms with it. Above all I have no idea what I should do in future. In the Bundeswehr there is probably no future for me.

Another officer also talks readily about his past:

My parents were teachers, both in the SED. I was brought up in the spirit of the party and I believed I was serving peace. It was not always easy for me. As an officer I was always subject to the eighty-five per cent state of readiness, I never had time for family and friends. I saw my brother, who lives here in the GDR, only twice a year. We were cut off from the population, lived on our own housing estate and there wasn't even the opportunity for the barracks sports club to get together with other clubs. Anyone who became an officer was completely occupied. He had no time to think, he went along with it all. Not until October and November 1989, General, did I start posing critical questions. Earlier perhaps, we had some small doubts and we discussed this and that, but we basically thought everything was in order. But in July this year – as an officer of the NVA in uniform – I took part for the first time in the Nijmegen March in Holland. There I experienced real comradeship, friendship and openness between soldiers of different nationalities, and I realised how we had been deceived, how dreary was the world in which we had been living. We had none of the warmheartedness that I found in Nijmegen. We had no comradely contacts with other armed forces, and even friendship with the Soviets existed only in regulations and slogans.

This lieutenant-colonel had tears in his eyes.

In the evening I hold talks with Dr Carl, permanent secretary in the Federal Defence Ministry. He agrees that we can immediately take on 1,500 officers as short-service personnel for a period of two years. This has been a controversial question until now, as it had not been clear whether the proposed personnel structure made this necessary. I decided to pose the question against the background of the unlimited numbers of personnel leaving, and the danger that in some areas the whole system could not be kept going. Until now this proposal had been rejected, but tonight it was finally approved. Afterwards, from 6 pm until midnight, a meeting was held with the three service chiefs of the BKO, with the main theme being: disbanding the units and creating the necessary pre-conditions in the personnel and material spheres. In order to speed up the disposal of weapon systems and vehicles I decide, after consultation with the commanding officers and the headquarters staff, that the weapons systems should be taken to designated places and rendered unusable. So-called peripheral gear and other items of equipment will be packed together in storerooms and these will be locked; disposal can be carried out later from these storerooms. We report that this is our intention and so we put pressure on other bodies to take action.

I tell the three service chiefs that it will now be possible to take on 1,500 short-service servicemen for two years as key personnel, and I determine how that shall be done. I say that the chiefs can make firm promises in their services according to set quotas. As a result of this promise I expect an overall stabilising effect because at last the many words are being followed by deeds. At this meeting we solve further problems but we once more encounter some new ones, for example the lack of clarity about setting off transitional pay against unemployment benefit, the taking over of guard duties by civilians in the particularly critical areas and the whole question of the soldiers who will be taken on for two years.

Finally, one of the service chiefs reads out a teleprinter message, which demands from all units and offices the following:

> In accordance with the Treaty on the Establishment of German Unity, Chapter Six, Paragraph Three, Number Fifteen, the Decree of 6 June 1974, on keeping dogs outside, comes into force in the aforementioned area on 1 July 1991. With regard to the animals owned by the Bundeswehr, the appropriate Bundeswehr departments are responsible for upholding the law on the protection of animals and the decree issued on the basis of that law giving them legal protection. The Bundeswehr Kommando is therefore requested to register all service dogs, according to a system, and to report the result. Among other things, the following are to be reported: the size of kennels with six square metres of running space, kennels which have less running space, the type of dog food, the planned siting of the dogs, details on ending their service owing to unfitness, statement of reasons etc.

One service chief rightly asks whether the questions concerning the dogs are not a little more exacting than those concerning the conscripts.

At the close of the lively discussion, shortly before midnight – we are now really dog-tired – it is obvious that many of us are exhausted and that some of us are at the limit of psychological and physical stress. We are all worn out and fatigued. Nevertheless it is imperative that those in charge radiate calmness, composure and even humour. In spite of all the stress we are a harmonious team.

Friday, 9 November 1990

The main problem is becoming more and more obvious: German unity has come too quickly for everyone, new priorities must be set. This also applies to the Bundeswehr. It seems that in the West it has not yet been realised that sacrifices and new focuses of attention are needed to master the changeover here in the East. Owing to the overall economic situation and the psychological situation, the East is the much weaker partner. The Bundeswehr in the West will be reduced by about four per cent of career and short-service soldiers in 1991. Here, on the other hand, it will be forty per cent – and for some that is still not fast enough.

Tuesday, 13 November 1990

The first regional conference of commanding officers, in Delitzsch, with more than two hundred participants, with whom I want to improve the exchange of information and views. Because of their deep feeling of insecurity the servicemen believe all kinds of rumours which I must counter with facts, personal discussions and trust. The armed forces ombudsman of the Bundestag participates as a guest. His presence underlines his personal commitment regarding our problems.

Wednesday, 14 November 1990

I take a flight to Peenemünde to visit the navy with Permanent Secretary Dr Carl. On board one of the modern, but no longer needed, ships crew members and civilian staff explain their problems: absence of information on social welfare questions, unclear division of responsibilities between the Federal Defence Ministry, the Federal Minister for Labour and Social Affairs, and other departments. The problems are most acute in the navy, because it is being cut from 8,500 to 1,500 servicemen, as none of the ships is staying in service and the number of civilian staff is also being drastically cut. They also mention the surprising, and partly incorrectly conducted, dismissal of civilian staff, which has led to considerable annoyance and to a loss of trust; this will not be restored quickly even though some of the dismissal notices have been rescinded. It once again becomes clear to the delegation from the ministry that the problems are much more complicated than they had assumed from a distance.

Chapter 9

AN INTERIM BALANCE SHEET – BETWEEN HOPE AND RESIGNATION

Thursday, 15 November 1990

At a meeting of commanding officers in Basepol, north of Berlin, the atmosphere is tense, questions are aggressive, particularly those on social security. When I say that officers whose units are to be disbanded on 31 March are still needed after 31 December, I'm faced with the following question: 'General, why should I stay until 31 March to disband my unit? If I leave already on 31 December I get an additional 7,000 Deutschmarks thanks to the increased remuneration which is valid only until then!' My attempt at a counter-argument which is perhaps mathematically correct hardly convinces anyone. Some officers prefer to receive the 7,000 Deutschmarks even if they then become unemployed. 'Why should we go on making an effort,' they add, 'when we're going to be dismissed soon anyway?' Now that they don't know what they are serving for, money is becoming the decisive factor.

In the break several commanders, who have been transferred from the West, talk to me. They fear that they alone will have to ensure the functioning of their units from 1 January as it is totally uncertain which of the former NVA officers will still be there. More and more want to leave on 31 December, although I find considerable readiness to continue. It appears imperative that we superiors talk to the men concerned, direct their attention to their future chances and underline our joint responsibility for the future. Some worries come from lack of knowledge and faulty or belated information, or even false information. It is difficult to estimate how many officers deliberately start rumours or intentionally give false information. To inform correctly is a leadership task. We must talk to each other a great deal, only in this way can mutual trust be won.

Although the very tense and lively discussion ends with the majority of the officers seeing the need for the reductions, as regards their personal futures most are really uncertain and sceptical, some bitter – who couldn't understand that? At present we are asking for their co-operation because we need them, but in a few months we must dismiss many of them. This is the real difficulty: to ask for co-operation and reliability and, at the same time, to have to tell most of them that in the long term they have no chance.

In the light of this meeting and the previous situation reports I write a report to the ministry about the state of the BKO six weeks after the take-over of command by the Federal Minister of Defence. It reads in part:

1. The take-over of the former NVA into the Bundeswehr has gone remarkably smoothly. This is due in the main to the fact that the former officers of the NVA were ready to co-operate. There has been no apparent resistance to a common way forward. Mistakes noted so far stem from the differences in mentality and training. The Bundeswehr officers have tackled their tasks with tact and the necessary clarity. They have begun to help in introducing a new style of leadership into the former NVA.

2. The officers of the former NVA continue to feel insecure. Some of them have formally carried out the changeover to our system of training and command but internally they have, to a large extent, not yet been able to cope with the rapid turn of events. In addition, the situation concerning their future careers is unclear, as are the economic developments in the country, in case they have to seek work outside of the armed forces. As a whole these officers have become more positive towards us. They are developing more confidence and are beginning to pose more questions.

3. At two regional meetings of commanding officers with commanders up to the regimental level and the level of independent battalions, the following was shown: There is a realisation that the reduction, the reform and the reconstruction of new units is necessary. Some officers hope that they will not be affected by the reduction.

   In the sphere of social welfare a great deal is still unclear, for instance: the application and putting into effect of the Employment Promotion Law and the possibilities of the Vocational Assistance Service, the calculations of pension claims and transitional payments in the future pay structure, and all questions concerned with remuneration.

   All commanders share the same concern about the heavy burden of guard duties with its effect on training and on the mood of the men. One commanding officer reported to me that his conscripts had got together and complained that they had to do a lot more guard duty than their friends in the West and did not even have the same pay, particularly Christmas pay and redundancy money. As far as I can determine this is an individual case but it indicates the trend.

4. Co-operation with the Federal Defence Ministry is basically good; here it must be borne in mind that there is a complicated problem to be solved, which requires the co-operation of many headquarters branches and other offices. It can be seen from everyday events that this co-operation must be further improved. Sometimes directives from the ministry must be co-ordinated by the Bundeswehr-Kommando Ost in such a way that some of them must be added to or rescinded. The responsible persons in the Federal Defence Ministry frequently lack understanding of the particular local working conditions here, and of the links between the various spheres which impinge to a considerable extent on civilian life. The following shortcomings will decide the course of future work:

   a. The units have at present about fifty per cent of their normal personnel. But they still have a full complement of weapons and ammunition, and in some cases even additional *weapons* and ammunition from other units which did not belong to the NVA. To disband the units and, at the same time, reduce personnel will be possible only if a decision is made on where the equipment and ammunition is to go. Otherwise the disbandment of a unit means that the detachment that takes over to carry out the closing-down and guard duties will have to be as large as the previous unit. This is the limiting factor for future cuts.

   b. There is a lack of ideas for the utilisation or disposal of the equipment and ammunition which is being weeded out, so it has not been possible to designate depot sites for the weapons systems.

   c. Decisions made at high levels in the ministry which affect the Bundeswehr-Kommando Ost are being communicated to the Kommando very late, with a three to four week delay, even though these decisions have important implications for our work.

Friday, 16 November 1990

The commanding officer's situation report shows that in many areas we are still marking time. When I report to Bonn that the aircraft must be flown to four air bases in order to collect them together, I receive a message saying: 'Keep to official channels and collect the aircraft together in such a way that they remain operational but can, if necessary, be destroyed without moving them again.' This order leaves everything open and decides nothing, even though we urgently need instructions! So General Mende and I decide what we think is right, and report this. We hear nothing. But six months later it turns out that our quick decision was right: without it the aircraft would have had to be transported at great expense by land – and then no one would have understood why.

Sunday, 18 November 1990, Remembrance Day

Breakfast with an acquaintance from the Federal Ministry of Defence. He tells me that he is under the impression that our task is being dealt with in the ministry in too routine a way. The extent of the challenge, he says, has apparently not yet been perceived; only the min-

ister, several permanent secretaries and departmental chiefs are
really actively involved. Most people can hardly imagine how things
really look in the East. During this discussion I recall that most of my
visitors from Bonn only come to Strausberg and don't travel to the
'provinces', where the real difficulties lie. And not one of the civil
and military departmental heads ever comes to the BKO to hear of
our experiences and ideas.

At 10.30 am a remembrance service is held in the large military
cemetery in Halbe, south of Berlin, in memory of those who fell
after being surrounded by the Soviets in 1945. For the first time
since the war a Protestant pastor preaches. In the cemetery lie
40,000 dead: victims of the war and of the concentration camp of
Ketschendorf which, after the war, was kept going first by the Soviets and then by the SED. For a short time in 1945, my father-in-law
was among the internees there – then he was transported as a 'capitalist' to Karaganda in Siberia.

At lunch one of the participants tells me of the difficulties in taking
over and restructuring a *Landratsamt,* an area administrative authority, which has only nine employees out of 238 with democratic cre-
dentials. The old Communist cliques, he says, are still powerful, and
the officials – so it seems to the general population who have applications to lodge – have not changed. For this reason too, there are
psychological barriers which people in the West can only partly
understand. He explains that in the view of the general population
things will have changed only when *those* officials who used to bully
them have finally disappeared. He then tells me that Western German firms – particularly insurance companies and banks – are taking
on former SED officials, without considering their past, because they
are 'efficient'. New cliques out of the old cadres? My informant was
himself not in the SED and as a result was not promoted above
deputy departmental head at Interflug, the GDR state airline.

Monday, 19 November 1990

A day spent in the office. The telephone to the Western Group of the
Soviet Troops works, and is regularly checked. The Commander-in-
Chief is still refusing to receive Major-General Foertsch, saying he
has 'no time-window open'. I instruct the deputy head of our liaison
group to pass on my comment: a Commander-in-Chief decides for
himself when he wants to open this or that window; evidently Snetkov
does not want to open the window for us. I hope that this will do the
trick at last.

Retired Lieutenant-General Baarss tells me about the disciplinary
system in the former NVA. Even the NCOs had disciplinary powers.
The link with the SED was particularly oppressive. Every disciplinary

procedure resulted in a party hearing; the tie was perfect. In personnel management the party played the decisive role; here everything was subordinated to the discipline and the direction of the party.

In the NVA, commendations, bonuses or benefits in kind were not only used to increase efficiency but also to make personnel more submissive. The central figure in this system was the regimental commander, who had between 80,000 and 250,000 Ostmarks available each year for awards to outstanding soldiers. These awards were made for good performance while on duty, for instance in training or in marksmanship, but also for socio-political commitment or exceeding the expected norms. Benefits in kind included electric drills, coffee services, boxes of cutlery and other articles for daily use which couldn't be bought in the shops. Bonuses from three hundred Ostmarks upwards were paid. For example, a departmental head in the Defence Ministry, with a staff of seventeen, could pay out up to 8,500 Ostmarks annually in bonus awards. As a rule commendations were made several times a year. It was important for the regimental commander to make awards regularly, because that would underline the fact that his regiment was a particularly good one and had efficient officers. One officer, for example, received 53 commendations in 26 years of service, another 93 in 31 years and a third 114 in 34 years.

As well as praise there was, of course, also criticism and punishment – ranging from simple fines and confinement to barracks, up to disciplinary imprisonment or demotion. Many of these measures could be imposed by a superior responsible for discipline, with no judge involved – an inconceivable and arbitrary method according to our view of law. Reasons for punishment could be ridiculous. For instance, an officer was given a disciplinary punishment because, after a traffic accident in Czechoslovakia, he allowed his car to be towed by a West German.

So, it is all the more important now to give the disciplinary superiors quick and thorough legal instruction about our disciplinary system. Unfortunately, right from the start we did not get enough legal advisers. Here, too, we need more staff; this is a 'gap in the market' which cannot be filled by volunteers. The legally trained officials don't move to the places where there is a particular need from a legal point of view, but stay where they are. However, they cannot be transferred against their will – what is the law must remain the law.

Tuesday, 20 November 1990

Visit to the Information Centre for Intelligence which, with a staff of several hundred, was at the heart of the NVA's military intelligence. At the time of my visit it is being disbanded by a former NVA colonel under the supervision of a West German colonel. The former

NVA colonel does not hide his professional pride regarding the detailed knowledge the NVA had about the Bundeswehr. I have the opportunity to convince myself that they really did have a clear picture. Information about specific people as well as general military knowledge, is available; as an example they show us material about the tank training brigade in Munster, north of Hanover, which includes detailed information about the command post, technical equipment and similar things. The greatest concern of the officer who is reporting to me is regards his former spies – he fears they might be unmasked. I hope they have the same fear.

After the colonel's report, I provoke him by saying:

> Colonel, on one decisive point you seem not to have had a clear picture at all. During all of my visits to the troops I have found out that the NVA units assumed that the Bundeswehr and our NATO allies were at a high state of readiness on weekends. I am told in the units that the West could have attacked the states of the Warsaw Pact at any time. Shouldn't a really well-informed NVA intelligence service have told them that at weekends the Bundeswehr had only a low state of readiness with only firemen on duty?

He replied:

> We knew all that and reported it to the chief of the NVA. The leadership knew very well that in fact the Bundeswehr and the NATO alliance were not capable of a surprise attack and that at weekends they had only a low state of readiness. Yet the political and military leadership had decided that the NVA must maintain an eighty-five per cent state of readiness around the clock. This was based on the imperialists' constant readiness for aggression and on the presence of chemical and nuclear weapons; but from the point of view of the military intelligence service we could find no proof of readiness for aggression – at least at weekends.

In response to my query about whether such political manipulation hadn't made him doubtful, he said only: 'General, the leadership of the party and state regarded these measures as right and necessary, and we followed them.' How fully the party and state leaders kept themselves informed and how un-informed they kept their servicemen and the population – information and disinformation complemented each other in a fatal manner. The colonel had not grasped the mechanism of this system of repression and manipulation, or did not want to grasp it, and it had never entered his head to question the reason for a state of readiness which was a burden to all servicemen. 'Always prepared' was also the motto of the *Freie Deutsche Jugend* (FDJ), the Communist youth organisation.

As the staff of the military intelligence service were specially selected and ideologically convinced men, I am interested to find out when they first started to have doubts. My informant concedes that the break did not happen until the party congress of the SED in

November 1989, when it had become obvious that the ideology had collapsed and the party was faced with the shattered remains of its history. Only then, he says, was every convinced supporter of the SED faced with the need to find a new orientation. The colonel himself has evidently quickly adapted to the new situation. He tells me that he is leaving the service at the end of the year in order to work as an estate agent. A vocation or just a job? I imagine he has become a successful estate agent.

We walk through long corridors to the new building. On the locked doors I read nameplates and job descriptions which are no longer valid. In this enormous office block there are no sounds to be heard apart from our echoing footsteps – a ghostly emptiness, everyone has been dismissed. It's like a horror story that is now over.

I visit the new, unfinished building in which the military intelligence apparatus was to be housed; from the outside it is a tall, ordinary five or six-storey office block, which only from the inside is revealed to be a multi-storey concrete bunker. After being under construction for eighteen months it is almost finished. The equipment, including the computer installations, is of a modern technical standard; on the top floor there is a gym and sports hall with parquet floor, where the soldiers who worked shifts would have been able to do physical exercise. The whole bunker is constructed in such a way that it would have withstood air attacks in case of war and would have remained operational.

Asked how the local population reacted to the construction of the bunker, our guide replied: 'No questions were asked here and no explanations given. The population had no idea of what was happening. The time taken to build it was noticeably long but everyone in the GDR was used to that. Moreover, we first built up the facade and then constructed the bunker inside. It was all secret.' One can hardly believe that this perfect system collapsed like a house of cards and that now only buildings, like mute witnesses of a disastrous past, serve to remind us of it.

Wednesday, 21 November 1990

Late in the morning joined the minister at Tegel airport in West Berlin and drove with him and the accompanying journalists to Prenden, north of Berlin, to visit the GDR government bunker. This was built at the cost of about 500 million Ostmarks close to the leadership's living quarters in Wandlitz and could be quickly reached from there by autobahn. In a time of crisis or tension it was intended to accommodate the entire party and state leadership of the GDR. Here, too, from the outside one sees only an especially well protected barracks complex. Only by going through a normal barracks block does one reach the interior of the bunker, which also includes radio stations and reserve bunkers. Everything was organised so as to camouflage the building. The personnel were checked and selected by the Stasi and in an emergency they had planned to use a special guard regiment 'to guarantee security'. With telecommunications secure from outside access or interference, this installation was part of a system of command bunkers which extended to the regional capitals of the former GDR. From here the party and state leadership would have been able to continue to govern even under war conditions, as the installation was organised in such a way that they would have been able to survive for two weeks independently of the outside world.

It is noteworthy that the command and telecommunications links to the Warsaw Pact states and, above all, to the Soviet Union, were in the hands of the Stasi, not the NVA. The partial situation reports, which were switched through to the top leadership, were selected and transmitted by the Stasi and not by the NVA. Whoever prepared and selected information had a decisive influence on leadership decisions – that applies here too.

The bunker rooms for the top leaders – for Honecker, Mielke and comrades – are evidently equipped just to their taste. From plastic slippers, heavy plushy dressing-gowns with stripes, and underwear, to porcelain pottery with flower designs, everything is there that was needed for survival. Synthetic wood and artificial flowers in the living quarters create socialist *Gemütlichkeit* [comfort]. But, after all, the bunker and the technology were no substitute for inner stability and the support of the population. The people lost their fear and freed themselves from the state and the party.

In the evening I again discussed with headquarters staff the order for the disbandment of Category 'B' units – those being disbanded by 30 June 1991 – and then signed it. It is probably the most important order that I shall sign during my time in Strausberg. It must now be obvious that we are disbanding units but also that we shall start the reconstruction of new ones. However, we are still facing great difficulties because there is no concept for utilisation or disposal of the materiel. What is to be done with the materiel afterwards? Where is it to be collected together, how to destroy it and dispose of it?

At least, knowledge in the ministry of our difficulties is growing from day to day. Even so, co-operation between the ministry departments and my headquarters is still unsure and patchy. Every directive which is issued in one sphere also has effects on other spheres. For instance, the Bonn headquarters department responsible for supplies requests that we take on more personnel, while the department in charge of personnel planning demands that we dismiss as many servicemen as possible, and does not take notice of the reasoning of the supply people.

After issuing the order, I talked until well after midnight with the Chief of Staff about the future course of the BKO. We are agreed that we must get our way vis-à-vis the individual sub-departments and headquarters departments of the Federal Defence Ministry, even though it is clear to us that we shan't make new friends that way.

Thursday, 22 November 1990

The Chief of Staff of the army invited me to give a situation report on the BKO to the army leadership, down to the divisional commanders, and to make it clear where we need further support. This talk takes place in Koblenz and is extremely encouraging. The desire for a truly united army can be felt, but the overall problems and the large number of tasks we face in the region of the BKO, surprises many of the Western commanders; some of them have not yet been in the BKO region long enough to gain a personal impression. It is once again shown that the decisive motto 'one unit helps another' and the links made through twinnings are really achieving something.

Monday, 26 November 1990

Talks with a Soviet general, who visits me on the order of the Soviet General Staff. He brings a letter from Army General Moiseyev, which refers to some particular aspects of the hand-over and take-over of bases. He would like the hand-over to be speeded up, and he reminds me that in this respect we Germans have treaty commitments. I point out to the general that this is a matter for the Federal Finance Minister who, until now, has not been able to make very rapid progress in establishing the overall organisation of the Federal Property Offices, or get them operating fully. I ask them to show understanding for this. However, it is difficult to make the general understand that, for such questions, the Finance Minister and not the Defence Minister is responsible.

In addition, a further dilemma becomes clear: the Soviet troops are vacating about a thousand sites in four years. That means the hand-over, almost daily, of a training area, a hospital or a barracks area of whatever size. The pre-condition for an orderly hand-over would be functioning Federal Property Offices which, however, cannot be established so quickly because it is difficult to find enough officials willing to volunteer.

In the afternoon I discuss with my headquarters staff a problem that, in all probability, will hit us when the first cold weather starts. Until now industry in the GDR has been dependent on help from the NVA in the winter – so what is to happen this winter? In previous years the NVA had provided up to 55,000 servicemen for all sections of the economy. They worked under extremely difficult conditions, particularly in open-cast mining and in the chemical industry, as well as on the railways and other forms of transport. Serviceman sometimes had to do work which normal workers refused to do. In freezing temperatures they had to re-lay and maintain railway lines in brown-coal mining areas and on the state railways, and they had to work in the chemical combines in unhealthy conditions. Whole formations were moved into the brown-coal areas. Some of them had to sleep in schools and gymnasia and 'sweat away normally' during the day. In some towns they kept the whole haulage sector going, cleared the roads of snow and ice and contributed decisively to supplying the population. Would that be necessary once again? Anyway, we are not ready for it, we have no 'skilled workers' and not the slightest experience in that sphere. We also lack the equipment needed for work in the economy, as well as drivers and trained servicemen who could be used under such difficult conditions.

According to the regulations now in force throughout the whole of the Federal Republic, it is possible to use the Bundeswehr only in case of a catastrophe. However, if there were no more brown coal and, as a result, no heating, then that would probably be the case. I discuss this with the territorial commanders and ask them to look at the documents of past years in their headquarters and to determine what requests might be made to us.

Tuesday, 27 November 1990

A visit to the 8th Motorised Infantry Division in Schwerin, Mecklenburg-West Pomerania, and the 27th Motorised Infantry Regiment in nearby Stern-Buchholz. The programme of the visit is well organised and I get a picture of the state of training and the situation of the personnel: there is the same high level of uncertainty everywhere and a trend towards dissolution. Thanks to the order on disbandment of units there is now clarity regarding future prospects, but only a few officers have so far applied to become 'temporary servicemen for two years'. Evidently they have not received precise information, and they believe rumours, for instance, that officers over thirty had no chance of being taken on as temporary servicemen. Certainly, my statement at the commanding officers' conference is well known: that all officers up to the age of forty-five could stay in the forces for a further two years and that a small number could remain after that. The rumours, though, are apparently more convincing. This indicates that credibility will remain one of our major problems.

At an advanced training session for NCOs I ask one of the new staff sergeants, who has taken part in a Bundeswehr leadership course, to explain to his comrades in a few words the principle of *Innere Führung*. The staff sergeant mentions several articles of the

Basic Law and paragraphs of the *Soldatengesetz* but is not yet able to explain the fundamentals of *Innere Führung* and the essential difference between the former NVA and the Bundeswehr. I ask a captain who is present to take over the task for his staff sergeant and notice that there are some gaps in his knowledge too. 'Citizens in Uniform' cannot be created overnight. The desire for togetherness and readiness to learn cannot make up for knowledge and for common experience of democracy.

Later, dinner and talks with about fifty officers from the division and the motorised infantry regiment. The officers talk about the high state of readiness in the NVA. They had been convinced that this was necessary because of the threat posed by NATO. And now? I tell them about my conversation with the colonel of the military intelligence centre and say that the state and party leadership knew very well that the Bundeswehr was not ready to attack. They believe me. 'But how could we have known that then?' they ask.

Evidently, doubts had only arisen when the officers, with sections of their units, had been drafted to work in the Bitterfeld area. For the division this meant that about thirty per cent of the soldiers were working in the general economy while the remaining soldiers were in the unchanged high state of readiness. It slowly dawned on the responsible commanders that, under these conditions, the state of readiness had actually made no sense militarily, although it had done ideologically. At that time, in the winter of 1987/1988, the first critical discussions evidently began about the credibility of the system – but only in tiny groups, very privately and always at considerable risk.

I mention that in 1988, as commanding officer of the 3rd Armoured Division in Buxtehude, near Hamburg, I was, as it were, just over the frontier and often thought about the plans of the 8th Motorised Infantry Division. The officers all said that they themselves had not had any knowledge at all of the plans. Only the divisional commander, his deputy and the Chief of Staff had been told. They had to go to meetings at the regional military headquarters in Neubrandenburg, where the operational plans were decided on.

A colonel who is leaving tells me about his son, who is serving as an NCO in the Bundeswehr, but wants to leave as soon as possible because he had volunteered for the NVA only so he could get a university place afterwards. 'General,' he says, 'we got our junior NCOs by forcing those who wanted to go to college to enter the NVA first. You can imagine that such people didn't make very good NCOs. In the end we officers had to deal with everything, including the lowest of the low.' Another officer admits to me that only now had he realised the extent to which he and his comrades had been deceived by the party and state leadership. And what sacrifices had been

The roughly 2,300 tanks and 7,800 armoured personnel carriers that were taken over from the People's Army were collected in several depots and subsequently wrecked in line with CFE treaty rules. In this photograph, the depot at Bantzen is shown.
Photo by Detmar Modes.

Tanks awaiting haulage for scrapping.
Photo by Detmar Modes.

Some 100,000 trucks were taken over from the Volksarmee;
they were sent in by tens of thousands to the Peenemünde Depot.
Photo by Detmar Modes.

Armoured personnel carriers and spare parts before being turned into scrap.

Federal President von Weizsäcker talking with conscripts in East Germany on the occasion of his last troop visit on 29 April 1991.

Photo by Walter Jeromin.

Federal Defence Minister Dr. Stoltenberg (centre), the Minister for Disarmament and Defence of the former GDR Eppelmann (on the left) and Lieutenant-General Schönbohm (on the right) on 3 October 1990 following the ceremony on the occasion of the assumption of the supreme command of the Volksarmee.

Photo by Tessmer FOTAG-GmbH.

Lieutenant-General Schönbohm talking to conscripts during one of his numerous inspection tours. Only by talking to these soldiers directly during his many visits was it possible to get to know former NVA soldiers and to gain their confidence.

Photo by Walter Jeromin.

Colonel-General Burlakov, the Commander-in-Chief of Soviet troops in Germany, talking, through an interpreter, with Lieutenant-General Schönbohm and Major-General Foertsch in February 1991 on the occasion of the signing of an agreement to cooperate in German air space.

caused by the permanent state of readiness and giving up of family life! Having realised they had been cheated, they are unable to believe anything any more, he says. All of them can hardly believe that the change has taken place. They are depressed because of the uncertainty surrounding their personal careers and the question of the consequences arising from the past. They now have a very low opinion of their former army leadership, they mistrust their own institutions and their former superiors and are very sceptical about the future. Shall we succeed in making a new start with them?

Two years earlier, with my officers in Buxtehude, I had worked out a new defence plan and, wearing civilian clothes, had looked along the River Elbe at possible crossing places for the 8th Motorised Infantry Division, directed towards our left flank. Today I am the superior officer of this division and am thinking about the job prospects of its career and short-service soldiers. What an irony of fate! The officers concede that if things had gone the other way they would not have treated us like this. They would have been true to the concept of man and the ideology they had been taught – just as we feel committed to our Basic Law and the idea of the citizen in uniform.

On the next morning, a walk through Schwerin – a strong smell of brown coal. The old town is run down but the houses have survived. I am sure that the city will become beautiful again. A woman comes out of a house, sees me in my battledress, sticks her tongue out at me and turns her back. I am surprised and say: 'Have you burnt your tongue?' She turns round and shout: 'Shame on you, you've only changed your shirt!' She took me for a former NVA officer and expressed the feeling one comes across everywhere: the population mistrusts the 'turncoats of the NVA' and shows it openly. On the other hand they are friendly towards 'original members of the Bundeswehr' in spite of all the former propaganda. Our commanders are being asked for advice in all kinds of non-military matters. For instance, a commander who was formerly active in local politics in the West has become an adviser of the mayor of a small town. Western officers and NCOs are on hand in the new states and are putting their experience at the disposal of the local population. For this they are winning thanks and recognition.

A visit of a West German acquaintance, who has become an unpaid adviser to the newly formed state government of Mecklenburg-West Pomerania in Schwerin. He is an experienced and professionally successful administrative official, who explains to me the difficulties in setting up the ministries and the middle-level institutions. He says that many qualified administrative officials need to be transferred to the East in order to reconstruct an effective administration based on the rule of law, but not enough experts are volunteering. I learn that the trend is that, for the high-level official posts, the volunteers are either older officials who have little chance of promotion in the West or young, capable colleagues who jump several grades in one go – but have little administrative experience. In one office the letters are 'filed' in a cardboard box; even office routine seems to be difficult at the start! Will these civil servants who have no immediate chance of promotion come to the East – as is possible in the case of servicemen and Bundeswehr officials?

Wednesday, 28 November 1990

Meeting with the three service chiefs of the BKO region. Problems are becoming more complicated. In various spheres we are getting less and less room for manoeuvre because of more directives, and the pressure to act is growing. For instance, within the units it is generally known that servicemen who leave by 31 December 1990 receive extra payments as part of the additional remuneration which has a time limit. However, it has now become known that a serviceman who leaves under these conditions at the year end, but at the same time applies to become a temporary serviceman for two years, can be taken on later without losing his pay-off. There is a danger that many officers will try to exploit this legal loophole by leaving on 31 December and then rejoining as temporary servicemen. We are worried about maintaining command capability and fear there will be chaotic conditions, particularly in telecommunications, logistics and security. Because of this, in taking on men for two years, we shall give preference to those who stay with us beyond 31 December 1990.

On top of everything the Federal Government has proposed that Western officers who have been promoted while serving in the East should receive only one-third of the increase in their pay. Well then, does this mean a salary cut for 'inferior' work? That would be unacceptable. In addition there is agitation about the higher remuneration being received for service in the new Länder. Thus a member of the German Bundestag, under the heading 'bush money for Western officials in the former GDR must be cut very quickly', writes that West German officials – that is, officers too – are being paid much too well and are thus not contributing towards a feeling of unity. 'What is happening,' he says polemically, 'takes on the flat after-taste of highly-paid colonial officials, who have to instruct the dummies from the East, and for that they even get something added to their high salaries.'

However, this polemic is inappropriate. Many of the officers and NCOs from the West are having to live in military living-quarters, provided officially, of a kind which we would not expect anyone in the West to accept. At weekends they often cannot go home, as the distances are too great and the shuttle service organised with transport planes operates only with delays and considerable problems. Officers who want to move house can get no flats or houses because there is not yet a functioning housing market. So they are unable to live with their wives, have no social life and scarcely any contact with the population. I hear that workers of a Munich building firm can regularly fly home, by Lufthansa, at weekends from Leipzig at the firm's expense. However, the nearby officer or NCO is flown to his family by Bundeswehr shuttle – often by roundabout routes taking several hours, as further servicemen have to be collected from other garrisons. To say that we live in 'the style of colonial masters', is an unjustified accusation from a man who lives a long way from our daily life. Such an attitude is hardly helpful for us or for the unity of the Germans.

There are also special difficulties in the administration of the forces, as pensions and wages have still to be paid according to the former NVA law. The federal budgetary system will be in force only from January 1991. The staff of the financial and economic departments are supposed, as it were, by means of 'private study', to adapt themselves to our federal budgetary system and our law on remuneration and, with a small number of personnel, to work out the pensions of the large number of officers who are leaving. A smaller staff, more work and on top of that getting used to a new administrative practice – it is all too much, it cannot work. Who in the West would even work under such conditions? In addition, there is the lack of clarity about future pay, as the officers of this branch can continue in the service only with reduced pay.

The atmosphere among the commanding officers and the unit commanders is quite tense. Some feel they have been left on their own, because support is lacking, particularly as regards the forces' administration. A situation is developing in which things are unclear and further uncertainty is spreading. Even so, everyone hopes that we shall somehow muddle through. We have managed until now and have always been given help in time.

Thursday, 29 November 1990

I visit the 1st Motorised Infantry Division in Potsdam and the artillery regiment. Here I feel optimism. As well as the disbandment of the units, the planning for the establishment of new units is clearly evident. The commanders have already been instructed about the tasks they will face from 1 April; the recruits make a lively and open impression. They still don't understand though, why they, as citizens of the Federal Republic of Germany, should get smaller pay-offs and Christmas bonuses than their comrades from the West. I agree with them.

At lunch with the recruits there are white tablecloths, and at the end of my short talk, I comment: 'I assume that there are white tablecloths every day, not just because I'm here.' Laughter releases the tension and a lively discussion follows. I advise the battery chief either not to make that kind of preparation or, better still, to do it every day. This kind of thing, too, is a leftover from the old time.

When – as Army Chief of Staff – I visit the battalion a year later almost to the day, the re-organisation has been finished and the training improved and 'western equipment' has been supplied. The living quarters are being refurbished or rebuilt, one can see improvements everywhere – the men, too, have become freer and more natural. The unit had even taken an 'exam', and was now authorised to fire a salute for a state visit.

During the commanding officer's situation report in Strausberg a fatal accident in a guardroom is reported to me – a soldier has been shot in the stomach by his comrade who was 'playing' with his weapon. There have been a number of accidents in guard detachments, and during one of my surprise visits to units I had discovered, in checking the above guard, at an ammunition depot, that the young soldiers had not been properly trained in the use of their weapons and were handling them carelessly. I had ordered the commander to supervise the training personally and to give his company commander (a former NVA man) a similar order. In spite of this order, this fatal accident happens two weeks later due to an infringement of all security regulations, and a lack of ability in the man in charge of the guard. No criticism can be made of the superior responsible for disciplinary matters, the prosecutor's investigations do not result in any charge – but all of us who have responsibility are reproaching ourselves. Now we must, in some cases, assign officers or older sergeants as guard commanders in order to avoid danger to life and limb while ensuring that the guard is secure.

Friday, 30 November 1990

Today the first fourteen former NVA sergeants in the BKO receive their appointments as short-service soldiers for two years and then take the oath of loyalty to the Federal Republic of Germany. The take-over and oath-taking are seen in the headquarters as an important signal.

Monday, 3 December 1990

Visit to Bishop Christoph Demke, Chairman of the Federation of Evangelical Churches in Eastern Germany. I had preceded my visit with a letter to all bishops of the Evangelical and Catholic churches in the new Länder, in which I had explained the task of the BKO and expressed our wish for pastoral care of our servicemen. My letters were all answered positively and my offer of discussions accepted. The discussion with Bishop Demke was intended to be the starting point for further talks between the church and the Bundeswehr.

The bishop set out the church's reservations regarding the use of military chaplains, explaining that worries about being subordinated to the state were very great. Because of this, he said, the state should not impose itself on the church. The individual serviceman should turn to the church, there must be no religious instruction ordered from above. Bishop Demke is concerned that military chaplains could become subject to orders from the state, the military command, or some less clearly defined political authority because they would be paid by the state. Military chaplains already existed in Western Germany. My references to the theological independence of the military chaplains, and their freedom in teaching, did not help. Mistrust against the state is deep rooted, along with the fear of once again becoming dependent in new and unknown ways. In the new Länder the church intends merely to appoint representatives to the armed services and to authorise ministers to carry out part-time pastoral work among servicemen. It seems that the church is reacting with so much reserve because it fears that we soldiers will choose local pastors whom we like, who could then put pressure on the church to approve them. However, in the BKO region only ten to fifteen per cent of the servicemen have been christened, so the church has a great chance of coming into contact with young people who are not only materially in need, but also in great spiritual and psychological need. Does that not create a greater duty of care – more so in the East than in the West? So I urgently request that the conscripts and the longer-serving personnel be given at least some possibility of getting to know the church and the pastors.

While Bishop Demke agrees with me that members of the forces should have pastoral care – also during manoeuvres and in troop training areas – he does not accept the need for organisational measures and voluntary participation in religious education. My description of the thoroughly positive reaction of the young recruits in Bad Salzungen to the pastoral lecture, before the oath-taking ceremony there, does not help my case, but merely provokes the question of why a military chaplain from the West had given the pastoral talk. The after-effects of the Communist system are showing themselves – mistrust of the state runs deep.

I remember meeting a pastor of the regional Protestant Church of Berlin-Brandenburg, in Berlin in early February 1990. We were both taking part in a conference, 'Forum Deutschland'. Sitting, by chance, next to each other in a bus on the way to a reception, we discussed the economic situation in the GDR, people's fear of the 'efficient West', the forthcoming revisions of property ownership and about new wrongs. My fellow passenger spoke of his experiences as a pastor in the GDR, of harassment by the authorities, dirty tricks by the

Volkspolizei and oppression by the SED party secretaries. His children had not been allowed to go to university, they had to learn manual skills; only his youngest child had been able to go university, thanks to the recent changes.

When he heard what my profession was, he expressed surprise: 'Goodness me, is this what a Bundeswehr general looks like? I had a completely different idea.' Then we talked about NATO, which he imagined consisted only of a U.S. troop presence and nuclear weapons – the result of Socialist indoctrination and 'public service' television reports? I became conscious, on that evening in February, of the importance of conversation and a sympathetic exchange of views. I have never forgotten one sentence from that evening talk: 'You know, I have fought against the state all of my life and my family have had to pay bitterly for it – but they always backed me – and now, all of a sudden, I'm supposed to support a state which I don't know at all; we need time, try to understand that!'

On one of my later visits a bishop asks me what it is that I want from him and why I had come. My spontaneous answer is: 'Bishop, I am the commander of atheist armed forces. I am offering you the chance of evangelising these armed forces and you ask me what I want from you!' That surprises him and we get into a lively and interesting conversation. Another bishop welcomes me in his office quite differently: 'General, I didn't think that ever again during my working life, a German general would visit me to discuss pastoral work among the servicemen – until just over a year ago that was still unimaginable. I thank you from the bottom of my heart that you have come!' Even so, finally he, too, said: 'I'll help as much as I can. But I fear that I have not enough pastors to take on the work of military chaplains.' I point out to him that at the local level, in some places, there is a greater readiness for co-operation than is possibly known to the church leadership – or desired by it? I offer to give a talk to the bishops' assembly about Bundeswehr matters, and our view of military chaplaincy, to contribute to a better understanding. The offer is welcomed but is not taken up anywhere, neither now nor later.

Tuesday, 4 December 1990

Visit to the 11th Motorised Infantry Division and also to the 17th Motorised Infantry Regiment, which is being disbanded. I ask the commander, an officer from the Western Bundeswehr, to provide a report on how he is tackling things. He has started, with considerable success, a local initiative to find jobs for soldiers who are leaving, and is working closely with the employment office and all authorities and firms in the Halle region. A former member of the NVA is obtaining the necessary information and is available for questions. In addition, all of the regional and national newspapers are studied in a central office, and the officers and NCOs are told about all job vacancies. With help from the Vocational Assistance Service, advice on applying for jobs is being given. In this way it is ensured that the majority of the officers who are leaving either obtain further professional training, or can take up a job straight away. The overwhelming majority know what they will be doing when they leave on 31 December. The local initiative of this commander has shown that we are taking seriously the commitment to care for our men, and are doing all in our power to help. This creates trust and credibility! I find this exemplary co-operation in many other places.

Discussion with the officers at lunch is, understandably, relaxed and open. Once again they tell me what a burden the use of soldiers in the economy used to be:

> General, the soldiers did the dirty work everywhere – work that no one else wanted to do: in aluminium and carbide production, at the Leuna chemical combine and in coal mining, sometimes in temperatures of minus ten Celsius. We were billeted in mass living quarters, in gymnasia – with worse hygienic conditions than in the barracks and with miserable, mostly cold food. We were maids of all work. And none of the soldiers who were drafted into the chemical or aluminium plants had any idea what the health risks were. The conscripts were only used for short periods but career and short-service soldiers had to do that work regularly. At least in this respect the efforts of the NVA ought to be recognised.

Afterwards, I visit the Regional Military Command. The commander has already disbanded the former NVA headquarters, which were placed under his command, and has created an effective command structure in his whole region. Here, too, excellent work has been done, co-operation with the city and other public bodies is good. Moreover, contact has been made with the Soviet forces and a sensible, business-like relationship has been established.

Wednesday, 5 December 1990

In the evening I hold talks with General Foertsch, head of the liaison team to the Soviet forces in Eastern Germany, about his visit to Czechoslovakia. There he inspected barracks which have been vacated by Soviet troops and are no longer usable: almost everything if not immovable has been dismantled from the living quarters and removed; even some electric wiring has been ripped out of the walls.

The environmental damage, too, is considerable. At an airfield a test boring revealed kerosene three metres down. We therefore decide to make early contact with the Soviet forces stationed in Germany – 'prevention is better than cure.' In Germany, too, the environmental damage will probably be very serious and it is of absolutely decisive importance to talk to the Soviets about this. If we do not insist on compliance with our directives in this matter right from the first take-over of a former Soviet base, the example of Czechoslovakia could be repeated here and we then we could hardly expect to solve the problem of environmental damage. We don't want to take over the Finance Minister's responsibilities but do want to help him.

Thursday, 6 December 1990

Visit to the commander of Military Region Seventy-One in Erfurt, the capital of Thuringia, where good work is being done. A former NVA colonel, who is leaving on 31 December, has even offered to assist voluntarily and without pay until the end of the re-structuring. Here, too, contact has been made with the Soviet forces with whom many questions of interpretation have to be clarified.

Afterwards I visit men of a signals unit, part of a Western formation, who are camped in a forest above Erfurt. They are working on the incorporation of the NVA telecommunications network into that of the Bundeswehr. They are friendly young men with impressive chiefs. One notices a good spirit permeating this group. Using this example, I try to make clear to journalists, who have joined us, how young people, servicemen, are contributing through their personal efforts to the growing together of Germany. It has got cold, there is snow on the ground and I have brought Nikolaus parcels for the soldiers. Asked how things are going, one of the young conscripts says: 'General, through our work we are ensuring that you, your comrades and your superiors can telephone throughout the Federal Republic of Germany. And when I tell my girlfriend that, she understands why I'm here. What is more, the work is something special under "battlefield" conditions! Things are fine with us!'

Monday, 10 December 1990

In the evening I attend the year-end dinner of the Berlin Press Club. During the dinner an East Berlin politician tells me how he sees developments. He feels that West German bureaucracy is getting more and more out of hand. From his own experience he can confirm that so far as lawyers and notaries are concerned. As well as necessary changes, it seems to him and his colleagues that additional bureaucratic demands have been piled up to prevent East German notaries from having an equal share in the documentation – and earnings – stemming from the expected boom in the purchase of houses and land in the East. There is no equality before the law. The law of the stronger is evidently depriving the weaker of their rights. The situation is similar with the doctors. His wife, an internist, had worked for many years voluntarily treating accident victims. Now, however, she must learn, in evening courses and at weekends, how a first-aid kit is packed, how a death certificate is made out, and how many other such bureaucratic difficulties can be dealt with. She and her colleagues feel themselves, thanks to this kind of 'further education', to be humiliated, deprived of their rights and professionally disqualified.

This is precisely the approach which, because of its rigid methods, leads to considerable misunderstandings. There must be conformity with our regulations. Once again it is a question of 'qualification', a much-used term in the Communist era but now meant differently! We should not operate by means of regimentation. In that way we are blocking much goodwill. I make a strong resolution to watch that this does not happen in the Bundeswehr.

Tuesday, 11 December 1990

Drove with my two brothers to Bad Saarow, our birthplace. Living in the house where we grew up is a former NVA captain, who bought it from a master chimney sweep. My parents, who had lived there during the Second World War, had not been able to exercise their option to buy the house, because of the war. Memories come to mind as we look at the house.

Afterwards, we visit the nearby small manor house where my mother spent her childhood and which was sold by my grandfather in the 1920s. It has just been renovated. As I'm in uniform I am welcomed particularly warmly by the custodian: 'General,' he reports in an almost military tone, 'I thought you would come here. I know that the manor house once belonged to your family.' He shows us the rooms, offers us coffee and tells about the time prior to 3 October, and about all the earlier shortages. However, he can no longer remember that he chased my mother off the property two years ago, when she wanted to see her childhood home once again. Now the atmosphere is no longer so relaxed, as our host refers to the former situation and his duties. We take our leave.

Wednesday, 12 December 1990

The press trip I had planned for journalists from the five new Länder is cancelled due to bad weather. I had wanted to give them a picture of the changes which have taken place so far in the region covered by the BKO. Instead I hold a press conference. My purpose, as part of our press and publicity work, is to describe the difficulties we are struggling with and to seek understanding among the public for the new armed forces. The old NVA and its representatives were rejected lock, stock and barrel by the population as mainstays of the SED regime; no one wanted to have anything to do with the officers. The privileged, sealed-off life that the NVA personnel and their families led, the compulsion and arbitrariness which were dominant both internally and in relations with the outside world, and the use of conscripts to do work which lay beyond their duties – all that had caused the NVA to be hated among the public. It must now be made clear to the population that we shall disband the NVA, so that we can reconstruct completely different armed forces, fundamentally unlike the former NVA, even though former members of the NVA serve in them. To achieve this we must inform people and let them take part in our life, we must open the barracks and explain which units are stationed in them, what goes on in the barracks and how things are changing.

In addition, it should be made clear that, in seeking to master the tasks facing us, we wish to do so together with the former members of the NVA who are still insecure and have little trust in their new superiors. The former NVA men should realise that I, as their responsible commander, will back them up. It is therefore necessary to offset rumours about the hopelessness of their situation and, by means of an active press policy, to show them possible prospects for their personal futures, so that the planned possibilities for vocational training and other measures are taken up. I base my hopes on the principle of the 'self-fulfilling prophecy' when I emphasise to the journalists: 'Things are really moving, the first signs are there.' Those who are hesitant can gather hope if the situation improves as a whole. That, too, is an aspect of our press work. Information in the press is often believed more than official announcements. The very open and critical discussion has an extraordinarily positive echo in the days that follow. It is recognised that we servicemen have by now achieved a great deal and that we are tackling the tasks which lie before us with energy and clear goals.

In the evening I get a phone call from the Permanent Secretary in charge of administration, who tells me that my wife is not allowed to fly in an air force plane to Berlin at the weekend as there must be no 'Lex Schönbohm'. He says that as a matter of principle it is not permitted for the wives of servicemen or officials to be carried in Bundeswehr aircraft. I reply that I consider this order not to be very sensible, as a large proportion of the commanders stay in their garrisons at the weekends and it is therefore desirable for their wives to be able to visit, to get to know their husbands' workplaces and living conditions and to help in building up social contacts. In this respect, I point out, the wives and families are making an important contribution to the development of the inner unity of Germany, even though this is not taken into account in the regulations. I draw attention to the time-consuming transport conditions which, particularly at weekends, make train or car journeys practically impossible. But the Permanent Secretary shows little understanding. Several months pass before wives are allowed to fly on the Bundeswehr shuttle or with regular airlines at the expense of the Bundeswehr.

The same sort of thing occurs with a teleprinter message, circulated down to battalion level, which restricts the use of official phones to official purposes only; for private calls the nearest public telephone must be used. This 'nearest public telephone' exists in the Federal Republic, according to the regulations of 1978, but not in the five new Länder. Up until now, after making some technical adjustments, we could telephone, although in a somewhat complicated way, by way of the Bundeswehr network to Western garrisons and then, through the exchange, make a call on the post office network, with the cost of the call paid by the servicemen. This enabled personnel stationed in the new Länder to call home, at least from time to time. The new order would ruin all of our efforts. Fortunately, at my request, the order was withdrawn, but it showed us once again how divorced from reality some staff are.

Thursday, 13 December 1990

Headquarters work and meetings. Disquiet in the units because, once again, contradictory teleprinter messages about the payment of wages and pensions were sent directly to units. Again we lose trust because an order has to be rescinded as it is impracticable. I shall have to prevent this continued sending of orders into my command region from all kinds of departments.

In the evening one of my commanders tells me about the following occurrence: an officer from his headquarters, a lieutenant-colonel, had been to him and had withdrawn his application to become a 'temporary soldier for two years'. Asked for his reasons, he said he had received an anonymous phone call that morning in which he was reminded about a commitment he had made to work for the Stasi, which he had signed as an NVA lieutenant. The caller told him that although he had never been used by the Stasi, his commitment was still valid as long as he remained an officer – that is, in the future too. The lieutenant-colonel felt that he could be blackmailed and so withdrew his application. I fear that the Stasi will be with us for a long time.

Late in the evening I read a letter from a former NVA soldier who is applying to be rehabilitated and appointed a staff sergeant in the reserve. After eight years as a staff sergeant in the NVA, he was demoted to private and dismissed with no pay-off, because he had infringed Service Regulation 10/9. The accusations made at that time can be clearly seen from extracts of an assessment:

Assessment of Staff Sergeant N.N.

Comrade N.N. possesses no firm class standpoint. He only studies documents and decisions of our party and state leadership to show the required knowledge during further education in social science. It is evi-

dent from discussions that he has no firm knowledge of Marxism-Lenin-
ism and is therefore not able to understand current affairs correctly. He
draws insufficient conclusions for his duties as a superior. He does not
fully realise and apply the demands of the 1980s.

His infringement of Service Regulation 10/9 must be seen in this context. Because of his negative political attitude he allowed his wife to have
direct contact with people from the FRG, and he receives Western mass
media [television]. The reasons for this lie in his inconsistency and his
superficial attitude towards military regulations. In talks with him so far,
the political importance has not become clear to him.

Staff Sergeant N.N. does good and exemplary work in the technical
sphere. It is marked by great technical knowledge and commitment. In
organisation and supervision there are no shortcomings. As a superior he
tries to achieve military discipline and order, and the fulfilment of the
unit's duties. In so doing it is not easy for him to behave consistently as a
superior, in view of his character. The discipline of Staff Sergeant N.N. in
the face of his superiors does not always accord with regulations. He
forms personal opinions and standpoints, states these openly and is not
able to subordinate himself to the collective. When he receives orders he
does not understand, they are met with rejection or contradiction.

Comrade N.N. can bear physical stress. Psychologically he is somewhat unstable; this often shows itself when he becomes excited without
cause. He reacts unreasonably and argumentatively to criticism. He exercises self-criticism only to a minor extent. He does not always fit in with
the collective. He puts his personal interests above those of society. This
is partly due to his character, as he is very tight-lipped and does not
always act honestly. As for societal activity, he acts as the leader of a
study group, where he does a good job. In relations with superiors he is
very much influenced by personal differences.

Lieutenant,	Lieutenant-Colonel,
Company Commander	Commanding Officer

Obviously this was intended to set an example: the soldier received
a punishment which endangered his whole existence. Are the superiors who drew up such an assessment still amongst us, still in the service? Or have they drawn their own personal conclusions and left
voluntarily, because they can no longer look a soldier in the eye?

Friday, 14 December 1990

Early in the morning, I fly in the Antonov, a Soviet-made transport
aircraft, to Bonn, to take part in a meeting of departmental chiefs. At
the meeting, amongst other things, the infrastructure programme for
the region of the BKO is discussed. For the renovation and construction of living-quarters, kitchens and sanitary installations alone,
investments totalling about 16,000 million Deutschmarks are needed.
To carry out this work the planners are proposing expenditure of
about 350 million Deutschmarks annually. In the discussion I point
out that if we adopt this proposal the programme for bringing things
up to Western standards would take at least forty to fifty years, which,

after all, scarcely anyone would want. If Germany is to grow together, this must happen more quickly. It is necessary, I say, to show clear signs of change. We must differ from the previous system, not only through our conception of humanity and the principle of the citizen in uniform, but also in the infrastructure; after all, I add, the conception of humanity determines the infrastructure.

My views are agreed with and support is promised, even including the sending of furniture from the West to the East. Finally, the minister decides to set new emphases for work in the BKO region, to the detriment of the West. We are soon to receive a sum of twenty million Deutschmarks, which is to be used within two months through a so-called 'commanders' programme', with close co-operation between the local commanders and the garrison administrations. The new programme will lead to serious cuts in Western infrastructure planning – but now things are really being shared.

Taken as a whole, the programme later proved itself, and a great deal of inventiveness helped us to make rapid improvements: through the purchase of large dishwashing machines, self-contained kitchens and showers, and also by painting and installation work inside the buildings, which was carried out in part by the servicemen themselves. In the awarding of work contracts, it has been shown that there are not enough efficient firms of craftsmen able to take over such work at short notice. By the end of January, thanks to a large number of measures, with local initiatives and the ideas and suggestions of all concerned, improvements can be seen in some barracks and progress is being made. Every sign of change is important – we are taking this seriously.

During the general discussion at the conference, I report, giving concrete examples, on our annoyance over the many directives from the ministry, distributed to the lowest command levels, which have widespread and unforeseen effects. I ask that there should be prior consultation and refer once again to the instability of the psychological situation. Furthermore, I say, the uniformity of command must be ensured. At the end of the debate the minister states that, in future, Defence Ministry directives – including those concerned with administrative matters – should not be sent direct to the units but only to the commanding officer of the BKO, who will then pass them on. This decision improved cooperation and understanding and prevented the repetition of previous slip-ups.

In the evening, for the first time since 3 October, we have guests at home – officers from my headquarters. A relaxed and stimulating evening. We are all concerned with the question of how we can achieve the unification of Germany. How many people in the West know what a great challenge we face? Some of my guests have the impression that only a few people are seriously getting to grips with this question, and that the majority of West Germans feel it has nothing to do with them. This serves only to increase the responsibility of those who can see what needs to be done.

Tuesday, 18 December 1990

A visit to the 2nd Engineer Regiment, at a former NVA training area for chemical warfare troops. Once again everything indicates how seriously the threat of war was viewed. Here, defence against chemical weapons was tested by the army, air force and navy; the appropriate mock-ups, used to stage exercises under realistic conditions, are still in place. The area, which covers about nine square kilometres, is equipped with all sorts of specialist equipment, including a section for infantry anti-tank combat, and another for flame-thrower exercises, where a special company of the 1st Motorised Infantry Division was trained for attacking West Berlin through the city's sewers. For exercises in detecting radiation, radioactive sources are dotted around to create realistic training conditions and to obtain verifiable results. There was also instruction in the use of napalm. The international laws of war were evidently of just as little concern as the poisoning of the environment which, it is true, we have not yet assessed, but which undoubtedly exists.

In the nearby barracks the usual sight: wretched shower rooms and scruffy kitchens – mould everywhere. Surprisingly, near one of the shower rooms there is a very comfortable sauna, including a solarium. The tiles and fittings in the showers came from the West. The sauna was intended for the higher-ranking officers of the engineer unit; here the general of the unit 'ruled'. A former employee spoke of regular drinking sessions held in the sauna; they were undisturbed and among themselves. Close by are the unacceptable shower rooms with rusty shower nozzles and dirty floors. The contrast depresses – how power and authority were misused in this state.

This evening my deputy, the Chief of Staff and I invited the whole headquarters to a year-end drink after the Chief of Staff had held a retirement ceremony for 210 former NVA officers. We thank them and present them with certificates, which we have designed and had printed, for their service with us in the last three months. This gesture is met with thanks. In many conversations with civilian and military staff I hear that they are facing the common future with confidence, even though some difficulties still await us. Above all, I am pleased to hear again and again that the former NVA personnel feel they are being treated fairly; the officers and NCOs of the Bundeswehr, they say, are quite different from what they had expected. A new start has been made, the effort is worth it.

Late in the evening I visit our acquaintances near Strausberg. I take them some school books from my wife's school for the primary school there. The wife, a former primary-school teacher in the GDR, who was dismissed for political reasons, tells me that she has applied to be reinstated because she was dismissed for reasons which can no longer be valid. At the local education office she found that the secretary in the front office of the personnel department was the same one as before – probably someone who worked for the Stasi. In the department concerned she spoke to the same woman who had handed over her dismissal papers five years previously. She says that those who had belonged to the SED cadres are once again doing well – floating on top of the soup like specks of fat. The schools, especially, are a big problem as little has changed in them. For instance, she adds, the teachers and headmaster at her school were dismissed after the political changeover, but then reinstated. So nothing has changed: those who used to praise Socialism are now trying to explain democracy.

In addition, her one-time headmistress had even made the surprising statement that the current phase of capitalism was, according to Marx, only transitory and would lead to its own collapse – and then Socialism, the true form of Communism, would be finally victorious.

Wednesday, 19 December 1990

Talks with Bishop Forck and Provost Furian from the Evangelical Church of Berlin-Brandenburg. Once again, the difficulties which the Protestant Church has in its relations with servicemen, become clear. They say that they see themselves as critical partners of the democratic state based on the rule of law; pastors cannot be military chaplains because then, as federal employees, they would get into a situation of dependency on the state. When I point out that military chaplains serving in the Western Bundeswehr are not subject to orders from the military or the state, it does not alter the church's refusal. Are pastors really dependent on whoever pays them? Instead, shouldn't this statement by the church cause people to have doubts?

In the afternoon we hold an Advent concert in our conference rooms, with the Bundeswehr band which plays Christmas carols and choral music for the first time. We have invited the Strausberg district council, several teachers, the mayor and the district administrative chief. They are probably all in this conference centre for the first time; it has existed since 1985, but was closed to the public during the Socialist era. After the concert we put on a buffet and there is much animated discussion. For many of our guests it may be a completely new experience to talk to servicemen about common concerns and needs. Discussion groups are formed, which are later continued between Strausberg citizens and servicemen of the BKO. A reflective and hopeful evening for us all.

Thursday, 20 December 1990

At 8 am I take part in a religious service in the conference room of the former GDR Ministry of Disarmament and Defence. I visited it for the first time at the end of May with Gerhard Stoltenberg when we held talks with Minister Eppelmann and Admiral Hoffmann. On the far wall of the room the state emblems of the GDR were resplendent. Admiral Hoffmann, then the head of the NVA, underlined almost provocatively the independence of the GDR and explained the function of the NVA in view of that. This officer, who had reached a high rank in the SED state, self-confidently explained to us the principles of the NVA military reform, which had already begun, and the change in the NVA from being the armed forces of the SED to being the armed forces of a democracy. From this he drew the conclusion that there was no longer any reason for desertions – and therefore servicemen who had fled into the Federal Republic must be returned. All of that is fortunately in the past, overtaken by events. What a change in seven months! The Socialist emblems are shrouded and an ecumenical service with Christian Christmas carols takes place, and we join in with all our hearts.

A local Catholic priest conducts the service, assisted by one of our officers who is an authorised preacher. Although the overwhelming majority of officers in the BKO are Protestant, we could find no Protestant pastor who was ready to conduct a service for members of the armed forces. Even after the fall of the Wall the Protestant church has erected unexpected barriers. In the Prussian heartland of Protestantism there is no Protestant military chaplain, but there is a Catholic military dean.

Afterwards I attend the inaugural meeting of the newly elected Bundestag in the Reichstag building. In the break, I speak with various members who are interested in our work and progress. They want to visit the 'East' more often in future and to contribute to the common task. My reference to the costs of German unity – in the armed forces too – is listened to attentively but without comment. Would it perhaps help to rattle a collecting box?

Talk with Lothar de Maizière who, in spite of his resignation as Deputy Chairman of the Christian Democratic Union and Vice-Chancellor, makes a composed and calm impression. What this man did for Germany and all Germans has been so quickly forgotten.

After my return, a visit to the operational training centre in Strausberg, a training centre for the higher command of the NVA. Regular exercises took place here, based on an attack reaching as far as the

Rhine. As detailed information about the Bundeswehr was stored electronically, they were able to call up details of which units – and in which formation – were stationed in any garrison in the West. On a large relief map an advance to far beyond the Rhine was simulated, and 'defence on the territory of the enemy' was rehearsed. This training centre was maintained in the most up-to-date state with much hard work and attention to detail – both as regards technology and information.

In the evening I receive a letter from Colonel-General Burlakov, the new Commander-in-Chief of the Soviet forces in Eastern Germany. He hopes for good co-operation and sends me best Christmas wishes – a positive sign.

Friday, 21 December 1990

In the morning, talk with Colonel Ocken, head of the central disbandment headquarters of the former frontier troops. This comprised more than 40,000 soldiers and civilian staff, and its task was to keep the GDR frontier secure by military means – that is, the inner-German border of 1,378 kilometres and the border around West Berlin of 161 kilometres. To 'secure the state frontier' the following wasteful construction was carried out: 1,476 km of forward barriers, 1,410 km of rear barriers (frontier fences and hinterland walls), 845 km of ditches to stop motor vehicles, 715 watchtowers, 4,507 km of cable lines, 6,637 km of telephone wires and 19,930 communication posts along the frontier.

The labour detachment of the frontier troops still has 4,900 former soldiers employed under special conditions; they can apply to leave or can be given notice at any time. Assisted by engineer troops of the Bundeswehr, they have removed the Wall in Berlin on time: one year after the opening of the Wall this shameful object has finally disappeared. However, during the work there was a lot of friction. Part of the wall top was made of material polluted with asbestos, which had to be specially made safe. There was also controversy about how to dispose of the Wall. Towards the end of the GDR era a foundation had already been set up to sell parts of the Wall and use the proceeds for cultural purposes. We, on the other hand, were ordered to sell the Wall and other parts of the frontier barriers and transfer the money into the federal budget, to pay for at least part of the costs of the demolition. However, the foundation, headed by a senior official of the Protestant Church, protested about this and accused us of 'illegally cashing-in' together with the former frontier troops. This was an effective accusation which won considerable play in the press, and which we were able to deny only by means of a factual clarification of our task.

Now that the frontier troops have fulfilled their duties they are to be disbanded as soon as possible. They can no longer be paid any longer from the limited Bundeswehr budget, and because of their past they are widely hated. On the other hand we have, in them, effective and cheap labour, who could demolish the inner-German frontier and – above all – remove the mines.

Afterwards, for the last time this year, the commanding officer's situation report with my headquarters staff. It becomes clear to us that, from the number of applications being made to become 'temporary servicemen', we shall not reach our goal of retaining 25,000 servicemen for the coming two years. Although we can meet our needs for officers, there will be a large shortage of junior NCOs. We shall also be short of sergeants, and the great need to catch up on training will, in addition, cause long absences. As a result, the personnel question is becoming the decisive problem. Not until the end of January will we have a clear idea of how many officers and NCOs we shall have, to begin the formation of our new units.

For the coming year the emphasis lies on the reconstruction of new units – we must not be diverted from this by the many other difficulties. The reconstruction, the new start, has priority. In the Federal Defence Ministry one often hears the view can often be heard that disbandment should be fully completed before the reconstruction begins – one thing after the other. However, an army can not only be winding up and disbanding. We must show the soldiers goals if we want to maintain and exploit the initial impetus.

In our last year-end report we sum up our assessment:

> At the year-end more than 25 per cent of the long-service servicemen of the Bundeswehr-Kommando Ost will be dismissed. Command effectiveness and security in the region of the Bundeswehr-Kommando Ost will nevertheless continue to be assured. It has been possible to prevent vital breakdowns in day-to-day duties through organisational measures taken on our own responsibility. However, the loss of knowledgeable personnel and specialists in large numbers cannot be without effect on the further disbandment of units. Moreover, it cannot be ruled out that there will be an effect on the setting up of units and offices within the planned Bundeswehr structure. If we do not succeed, in the coming year, in assuring day-to-day disbursements of allowances and pay, the consequences for the inner structure and on public opinion will be significant. Until the second half of January 1991 we will not be able to fully assess the concrete effects of the considerable loss of personnel at the year-end on the fulfilment of our mission. At present the fulfilment of the mission as a whole is assured, with some reservations.

For most of us, Christmas leave now begins at last. I spend a few more days in the new Länder with my wife and children. We want to get an impression of this sometimes still alien country. We attend opera performances, go to concerts and visit Wittenberg, Leipzig and Weimar. In spite of the high prices, people are buying, every-where there are pre-Christmas crowds.

After a short Christmas stay in the West I drive back to Strausberg on 30 December, with my wife, in order to be on the spot in case there are any problems after the large wave of dismissals of officers. Fortunately it turns out that this worry is unfounded. The situation remains stable and the command capacity assured.

At the year end I thank the units in an Order of the Day for their joint efforts and formulate the goals for the New Year:

> Servicemen, Civilian Staff,
> Since 3 October we have been working together to build up the Bundeswehr in our command region. We have all been given a task which is being watched very closely by our people and our neighbours. In the Bundeswehr – the armed forces of our democratic state based on the rule of law – the unification of Germany is given visible expression. That must be both a stimulus and commitment for us.
>
> I thank all those who, since 3 October, have helped to guarantee the effectiveness of command control, the ability to function, security, the reduction of the former forces, the restructuring of the units and preparation for the re-building of new units. We can be proud of this joint achievement.
>
> I particularly thank those servicemen and civilian staff who, in spite of their imminent departure and pressing worries about their personal futures, are continuing to do their duty.
>
> In 1991 we shall all be faced with special challenges. The size of the Bundeswehr must be further reduced, the principles of *Innere Führung* must be applied and new units built up. That will only be possible if we all make a strong effort.
>
> Our common future is at stake and, in particular, that of the armed forces in united Germany. The inequalities between East and West – in social welfare and, above all, in the financial sphere – cannot be removed in the short term, neither for the population nor for the servicemen. However, we can be confident that the differences will be quickly removed. For us, serving in armed forces based on conscription, it is decisive that in our thoughts and actions we behave as servicemen in armed forces which have a democratic mandate – that must apply to all personnel in the region of the Bundeswehr-Kommando Ost.
>
> Until now we have successfully made our way together, and together we shall master the tasks which lie before us.
>
> I wish you and your families a happy Christmas and a happy New Year in 1991.
>
> Schönbohm, Lieutenant-General

Chapter 10

OPTIMISM SPREADS

Monday, 7 January 1991

I spend the day on headquarters work. Both officers and NCOs have returned from leave rested and refreshed. New optimism is spreading, and the conviction is growing that together we shall be able to fulfil our tasks. Let us hope that this will prove right.

Burlakov submitted by 31 December – on time – the plan for the withdrawal of Soviet forces. The Soviet officers worked over Christmas; the Christian Christmas holidays are not kept by them.

Tuesday, 8 January 1991

I visit to the 2nd Missile Technology Base in Brück, a supply depot about seventy kilometres south-west of Berlin, where all army missiles of the former NVA are stored, including twenty-four Soviet-made SS-23 missiles. At present the question of their destruction and disposal is being clarified at the political level. In accordance with the Treaty on Intermediate-Range Nuclear Forces (INF), all Soviet SS-23 missiles have been destroyed. That the NVA retained its missiles is an extremely explosive political issue. The GDR had brought these INF missiles to Brück in a top-secret manner. At the 2nd Missile Technology Base only five officers knew of the existence of these missiles. The warheads have been removed, only the missile propulsion units are still lying there.

After the political changeover all kinds of small arms were sent to the base. The commandant, formerly a lieutenant-colonel of the NVA and now a Bundeswehr captain, tells me how – particularly in the spring of 1990 during the round-table talks in the GDR between various political groups – small arms were delivered in railway waggons, in trucks, wicker baskets, fruit crates and all sorts of containers.

The weapons were taken from the Stasi, the factory fighting groups or the Society for Sport and Technology, packed up and sent to Brück. Now they are kept in storerooms which can be securely locked. The number of weapons, of all sorts, which are piled up there is unimaginable – sub-machine-guns, pistols and rifles. They are now being counted again, packed up and then transferred to one of the underground depots. In an arms store the special weapons of the Stasi are shown to me: pistols hidden in camera cases, rifles camouflaged as walking-sticks and so on. The sort of thing one usually hears about only from spy films.

Afterwards, I visit the 3rd Engineer Pontoon Regiment in Dessau. The recruits, who have started service at the beginning of January, are pleasantly open and keen. Some of them took part in the demonstrations in Leipzig against the old regime, and most of them accept the Bundeswehr because they see in it the expression of the sovereignty of the democratic state based on the rule of law. Even so, after a short while our talk here, too, moves over to the question of the different pay and leave regulations for conscripts in East and West.

The company commander is a former member of the NVA, who has carefully prepared himself for his duties. He sees his appointment as chief of the basic training company as a special sign of trust. He tells me that he wants to do all he can to justify this trust. A good sign. Some of his section leaders are second lieutenants or lieutenants; this is the only way that we can compensate for the lack of NCOs.

At lunch I speak with the officers about their situation and learn that most of them have applied to become temporary soldiers for two years, but have so far received no reply. They are disappointed, but are still hopeful. Some point out that they did not seek the additional remuneration given to those who left by 31 December, in the hope that they would at least be allowed to stay in the Bundeswehr during 1991 – as a reward for their loyalty. We must make and communicate our personnel decisions more quickly; although that will hardly make things easier for us.

A visit to the radio technology service, a department of telecommunications intelligence, whose work was directed against the Bundeswehr in particular. As a part of the NVA intelligence service this department was excellently equipped technically, was able to participate in satellite intelligence and to monitor radio messages and telephone calls. The information gathered here was of special importance to the NVA command, as it gave a comprehensive, differentiated picture of the situation. The officers were well trained and subject to special security regulations. They feel that the Bundeswehr is discriminating against them because, in a questionnaire we sent out, respondents were asked if they had belonged to the Stasi or to the radio technology service. They strongly emphasise the difference between these two institutions, and declare that they had nothing to do with the Stasi.

I tell them that, regardless, we cannot take any of them on, as we have no use for them. I learn that they are not being employed in industry either, in spite of their qualifications, because the fact that they have been in the radio technology service for years is enough to lead to the rejection of a job application. I understand their problems, but cannot help them to avoid their past. They feel that they are being unfairly treated, and consider themselves to be indispensable because they are specialists. Yet we can only offer them vocational training – in common with the other servicemen and employees who are being dismissed because of shortage of jobs.

Later, I visit the deputy mayor, whom I knew earlier in the West. A retired judge, he returned to his hometown with his wife immediately after the political changeover, joined a political party and took part in the election campaign. Now he is wrestling with the problems of a large city which is in upheaval, trying to achieve progress in city planning and the establishment of new industry, and re-organise the administration. His wife has moved with him. They live in a small two-room flat heated by brown coal. A pioneering spirit is not limited by age.

Wednesday, 9 January 1991

We visit to the armed forces sports club *Vorwärts* in Potsdam, the training ground for Olympic champions into which immense sums of money were invested during the GDR era. Even children were put into the hands of the NVA if they had distinguished themselves at sport. They lived in a home attached to the sports club, went to school in the morning and trained in the afternoon. 'If a child is not world class at fifteen or sixteen,' a trainer told me, 'then we have no new blood.' The children made big sacrifices, but when they won events they were given medals, and large financial and material rewards. These incentives have now disappeared, and fewer and fewer parents are ready for their children to accept such stress.

Later, in Berlin, I hold talks with the Protestant Bishop of Berlin-Brandenburg, Martin Kruse, who, as Chairman of the Evangelical Church in Germany (EKD), a Western body, is the only EKD bishop who is also a member of the Federation of Evangelical Churches of the former GDR, as part of his diocese is in Eastern Germany. We are agreed on the need for pastoral work among the military, but also on the need for patience and perseverance; we must not hurry things. We must prevent the existing agreement with the state, on pastoral care in the armed forces, from being harmed due to previous experiences and strains in the East.

In the evening, a discussion on the Deutscher Fernsehfunk television network about the BKO. In the break, during the adverts, viewers can ask questions. The telephones get overheated; there is a great desire for information in every sphere, from the problem of social security to questions about the possibility of volunteering. Once again we are shown the great importance of keeping the public informed.

Chapter 11

QUESTIONS OF
SOCIAL WELFARE

Thursday, 10 January 1991

Early in the morning there is another discussion about the frontier troops. In the Federal Defence Ministry a directive is being prepared to ensure, by 30 June 1991, the complete dismissal of the frontier troops and the removal of all mines from the former inner-German border. This directive cannot be carried out because, judging by current progress, we shall be involved with mine-clearing at least until 1993 at least. After assessing all of the available information it emerges that, in some sections of the frontier installations, there must still be a great number of mines lying in the ground. Of the mines laid on GDR orders, roughly thirty thousand could not be removed as they could not be found. Thus, it is possible that in some sections there are still from five to five hundred mines lying in a mine belt. These areas must be ploughed, harrowed and very carefully searched. The large number of personnel and the great deal of time required for this task cannot be reduced, even by giving orders. Anyway, a sufficient number of members of the former frontier troops are prepared to take on this less than safe job.

Afterwards, a flight to Drewitz airfield, near Görlitz in Saxony, to which we have flown about 150 MiG-21 and MiG-23 aircraft. These planes are being kept there until a final decision has been made about their destruction. The storage arrangements are in order but, because we do not yet know what is to happen to them, for technical reasons all the planes are fuelled. If they are to be destroyed later – which is to be expected – the fuel must be removed once again. For this we require specialised personnel and special equipment, of which there are only limited numbers available. Decisions which are still to be made are leading to more work, higher costs and a greater need for personnel.

The officers make a conscientious, but very downcast impression. Many of them have applied for the temporary commissions, but have received no reply. So they expect to be dismissed from the Bundeswehr with two months' notice. I can only listen to their questions without being able to answer them all.

This is followed by a visit to a tank regiment which used to be one of the elite regiments and is equipped with the most modern, Soviet-made tank, the T-72. The regiment is being disbanded, the tanks collected together and then taken away. In one company, basic training is still going on. The recruits here, as at other places, make an open and energetic impression. The officers and the NCOs – almost all former members of the NVA – are ready to work and learn. They are enjoying the new basic training for the conscripts. When the regiment has finally been disbanded, by 30 June this year, some of them will be able to go on serving, on temporary commissions, in other garrisons and units.

I return to Strausberg for a meeting with the BKO service chiefs. It is the first such meeting of the New Year, one hundred days since we took over our joint responsibility. I start by saying that the transition from the NVA to the Bundeswehr has, as a whole, succeeded remarkably well and the BKO need fear no comparison with other military regions. The previously expressed worries about desertions, mutinies and the use of firearms have all fortunately proved to be unfounded. For this we must thank not only the officers and NCOs who came from the West, but also, in particular, the members of the former NVA who from the start have joined in the common task. The BKO has coped quite well with the large departure of personnel at the year end. Command-control effectiveness and security were constantly assured. Our need for officers is being met by a sufficient number of applicants who wish to become temporary soldiers, whereas there is a shortage of from sixty to seventy per cent of junior NCOs, and fifteen to twenty per cent of sergeants. We can view the future with confidence even though all difficulties have by no means been overcome.

Monday, 14 January 1991

A discussion with a former colonel of the NVA, who was Eppelmann's adjutant for a few days. In February 1990, together with two comrades, he had written a letter to Minister Stoltenberg suggesting that the NVA and the Bundeswehr should be unified. The letter never reached Bonn. It was evidently intercepted and it first became public in April 1990. The military commanders of the NVA had pressed for the dismissal of the writers and Eppelmann had to give in. The colonel then lived in hiding for seven months in Goslar, Western Germany, as he thought he was being hunted. Now he is living in Strausberg once again and has found civilian work. As a witness of the events, he describes to me the critical period of political upheaval, when the 1st Division in Potsdam had been given orders which laid down the action to be taken in case of an attempt to storm the Wall. Thanks to a merciful fate it did not come to that. My informant is optimistic that we shall succeed in forging joint forces but, at the same time, he warns of turncoats. Unfortunately, though, he is unable to tell me how to recognise them.

Tuesday, 15 January 1991

I attend a conference in Dresden of the Bundeswehr's commanding generals, with the Bundeswehr Chief of Staff presiding. The supreme military leadership unanimously recognises the level of reconstruction achieved in the East, and promises continued support. I ask for direct, unbureaucratic help in accordance with the motto 'one unit helps another'. Only this form of assistance, I say, will make it possible for us to fulfil our mission.

Afterwards I talk with the Catholic bishop of Dresden, whom I thank for the fact that we now have a Catholic military dean in our military region, who is overseeing and co-ordinating pastoral care of the military. I hear at the same time of the difficulties being encountered by the church in its efforts to find a building for a Catholic school. Evidently the old Communist cliques want to stop this project. How far can the Bundeswehr help in this?

The situation in the Gulf has become even more serious. Our command region must also give some help. The servicemen have contributed to this by working under great pressure and with great personal commitment. Officers and NCOs have voluntarily worked over Christmas – and that even though some of them were then to leave the service on 31 December. They wanted to show their goodwill and capacity for work. The conscript drivers have reliably carried out the deliveries to Bremerhaven port. As a result six thousand hospital beds have been despatched within a week.

I am in agreement with my deputy and the Chief of Staff that from now on there must be one general in readiness at Strausberg at the weekends. We must maintain command readiness around the clock and, above all, always have experts always available for logistical and medical questions. Often, requests come in at very short notice, and we are only able to fulfil our many supply commitments because everyone wants to get down to it and help.

Thursday, 17 January 1991

A speech and discussion in Gütersloh, west of Hanover, at the Bertelsmann Forum, about the tasks of the BKO, an event overshadowed by the outbreak of the Gulf War, which has made us realise some of our shortcomings. It had almost been forgotten that servicemen must be trained so that they can fight – and manoeuvres and low-level flights are part of that! In the near future it will be appropriate to have a discussion about the armed forces as a means of policy and about the tasks of the Bundeswehr; primarily because it affects the Bundeswehr of a united Germany.

At dinner, there is talk about developments in the new Länder. I ask a leading official of a Western local authority what effects he sees in his sphere of responsibility. He tells me about the twinning of his town with an Eastern German town and the resulting demands in both the personnel and material sectors. For instance, the local authority has sent officials to give assistance to the Eastern town for short periods; personnel levels are not high enough for longer term transfers. In the Western town a multi-cultural cinema centre was to be built, with aid from the Land concerned. The official had proposed postponing construction, and the transfer to the East the money – or at least, that part of the money which was to come from the town – to fund urgently needed building works. The discussion on this proposal is continuing, he says.

Involuntarily I make comparisons: in the West we are constructing traffic-calming zones, laying pavements and cycle tracks, constructing traffic islands and splashing fountains, while our countrymen in the East literally have rain coming through the roof and public transport is on the brink of collapse.

Monday, 21 January 1991

Yesterday, a few hundred people demonstrated against the Gulf War in front of our headquarters in Strausberg, they daubed walls and facades, climbed over the fence and roamed around our grounds. A serious infringement, at the least trespass, for which our sentries were not sufficiently prepared. The police, who were warned in good time, also proved themselves incapable of acting against the demonstrators. It turns out that our extensive grounds are not sufficiently secured against such infringements, as the NVA had no need to fear that sort of thing.

What do my servicemen think about the demonstration? How can I expect an independent view, free of Marxist thinking, from people who have been kept politically dependent for forty years? How far does the anti-Gulf War agitation in Western Germany reach? Anyway, a demonstration has taken place, and against the

BKO. It was, of course, also directed against the Americans. It is not understood that the Americans are only doing what was planned by the United Nations.

Today, it is being said that everything was quite peaceful; the infringements were not meant to be serious. Nevertheless, the incident concerns me a great deal. I see it as an attack on the Bundeswehr, which must not be repeated. In future we must be better equipped against such surprise moves and better prepared for 'peaceful demonstrators'.

Later, I visit the central disbandment staff of the frontier troops. We are sitting in the room of the former commanding general of the frontier troops. I feel embarrassed. It is a more than uneasy thought that murders were both ordered and monitored from this room. The room is depressing, the colours do not match, the walls are panelled with dark wood to cover up the bugging devices, and the heavy furniture seems oppressive. Eight men in civilian clothes, former officers of the frontier troops, report on the situation in a factual, clear and self-confident way. They consider themselves competent and they explain the technical aspects of the removal of the frontier installations. Did they use these tones to discuss the construction of the lethal apparatus? These men are now – as before – doing 'good' work. They are probably normal fathers of families, who have made a 'contribution to securing the frontier'. It is hard to imagine that they were the ones who issued the orders to shoot on the frontier, that they served this murderous frontier system. Can one understand them at all? When are we being fair to them, and when unfair? We must be considered and balanced in our judgements, in order not to condemn them wholesale. However, I myself will probably never make peace with the members of the frontier forces.

Tuesday, 22 January 1991

I visit the Chamber of Trade in Frankfurt/Oder, as I want to support co-operation between the Chambers of Trade and parts of the Bundeswehr. The President and Manager explain their many difficulties. Numerous new regulations are coming from the West, but there is not only a shortage of experienced professionals who could apply them, but also of training facilities and instructors in the firms. A lot of paper is coming from the West, but little practical help. By now they are determined to deal with things by themselves. They are optimistic and think this is the only way to make progress. 'We are too far in the East here, General,' they tell me, 'scarcely anyone would come here voluntarily. So we must help ourselves!' I remember the words of my father-in-law, a genuine Brandenburger and Berliner: 'God helps those who help themselves.'

Afterwards, a visit to the *Vorwärts* sports club in Frankfurt/Oder. This, too, was a club of medal hunters: a hundred medals won in the Olympic Games, world championships and European championships over the past eight years. The commitment is admirable but if the sportsmen are to succeed in the 1992 Olympic Games there are still some bureaucratic obstacles to be overcome.

Wednesday, 23 January 1991

I fly to Hamburg, to the Bundeswehr staff college. In the evening, after working hours, I make a speech about the work of the BKO, followed by a discussion, to five hundred course participants and staff. I am impressed by the eager attention, the high level of interest and the varied questions. Once again it is made clear that many servicemen are following our work with intense interest. Some of these men would be ready to come voluntarily to the new Länder to make a contribution to the unity of Germany. Naturally this motivated basic attitude particularly pleases me. A year later I come across one of the participants, who has reported in the East for his first post in the General Staff, and is now living with his wife and child in a pre-fabricated housing estate.

Afterwards more discussions are held in the 'working group for peace and security' led by Christoph Bertram, in which journalists, professors and other interested people participate. I try to set out the overall problems of our mission in twenty minutes and to explain them further in the following discussion. Some listeners are surprised at the dimensions of the problems and the varied nature of our task. Until now it has not been so well known. Only slowly is it becoming accepted that the armed forces are playing an important role in overcoming the division of Germany, particularly as armed forces composed of conscripts. It continually surprises me how few people are concerning themselves with the inner unity of Germany.

Thursday, 24 January 1991

Flight back to Strausberg, and meeting with the three service chiefs of the BKO region. As before, there are differing views about the number of officers to be taken over as temporary soldiers. We are requested to give a detailed explanation for all posts in our budget – and this at a time when everything is constantly changing and we still have no proposals for the disposal of materiel. We do not know how quickly we can hand over the bases, who will take over all the extra tasks which we are carrying out at present, and when this will happen – everything is unclear. We can only work by rule of thumb – and then a detailed explanation is expected of us! Under these conditions the reconstruction phase is being made more difficult; not everyone has grasped this yet.

Out of the original 32,000 officers available, 22,000 have already left between September and January. Now we have to build up a new personnel structure. More officers and NCOs must be transferred from the West into the units which are to be newly set up. For this we must at least create a financial stimulus through appropriate remuneration, as the other living conditions – housing, school facilities and social life – are hard to bear.

Monday, 28 January 1991

A flight to Marienberg in the Erzgebirge mountains. Sudden fog forces an emergency landing at a Bundeswehr depot which happens to lie on our flight path. The commander is surprised, recognises me – which pleases me – reacts very quickly and obtains a bus for us so that I can go on to Löbau to the former officers' training college.

It is being disbanded and the property is to be handed over, with part of it being used to park more than two thousand tanks. In talks with the commander of the college, the local area administrative official participates, and expresses particular thanks for the good co-operation and initiative shown by the commander in creating training facilities for the servicemen. In spite of this, here, too, some servicemen and civilian staff have questions about their own futures. It is extremely difficult to give generally binding answers. It is not always understood that the future also depends on one's personal initiative.

Of the planned two thousand tanks about one thousand have been collected together and they must be made safe. The necessary technical work – removal of batteries, draining radiators and much more – is considerable but is being done reliably; at least there is something meaningful to do.

By car on to the motorised infantry regiment at Marienberg, a two-and-a-half hour drive through hilly, partly wooded countryside. The roads are narrow, with many curves, and full of potholes. The towns and villages have a depressing look. Everything is rundown, decayed. The Socialist planned economy has not yet destroyed the countryside but the fabric of many buildings is rickety. The recruits on the garrison training area appear confident when talking to me. When I question them about the situation regarding unemployment, one of them answers: 'General, it is difficult. If we find no work here, we shall have to go to the West, whether we want to or not.' And another one adds: 'Before, we *had* to live here, now we *want* to live here, General.' It is a young man's expression of faith in our country.

At dinner with officers of the regiment I make another short speech, and afterwards we discuss questions which are concerning the soldiers. They cannot believe that at weekends the Bundeswehr was only in a minimum state of readiness, while they were at an eighty-five per cent state. They cannot understand why it had to be that way. A young officer says finally: 'General, then with a brief attack at the weekend we could have advanced to the Rhine and occupied everything. I ask myself today, why didn't we actually do it?' This spontaneous remark elicits startled shock and some embarrassed laughter. It is a good opportunity, so I answer: 'Now one of you has said what many of you think. Isn't it true? But would you really have dared to attack the Federal Republic and actually advance to the Rhine?'

In discussing this question from a strategic point of view it emerges that the problem of a civil war – Germans fighting Germans – evidently played no role in the concepts of the NVA officers. We Germans in the West were, for them, 'the others'. True, we spoke the same language, but were no longer felt to be part of the same people. Were they basically any different from their countrymen of a similar age in the West?

Tuesday, 29 January 1991

A visit to the Military Regional Command in Leipzig. Here, too, the transition since October has succeeded quite well: all subordinate command bodies have been disbanded and the new Military Sub-regional Commands are being set up. Liaison with the Soviets has been successful – contacts have also been made at the local level. As a result, our liaison organisation accredited to the Soviet forces in Germany is of increasing importance. In the Corps and Territorial Commands, in the Military District Commands, the Military Regional Commands down to the Sub-regions we have appointed former NVA officers with Russian-language knowledge in order to ease understanding and to solve common problems.

For the local population, the Soviet armed forces have been occupation forces since 1945. The expression, by order, of friendship towards the Soviet Union changed nothing in that respect. Now both sides must get used to behaving differently towards one another. Locally, our commanders have ensured that, as regards both the civilian population and the Soviet forces, a large number of common problems have been discussed: we can help to organise waste collection and disposal, to settle traffic regulation questions and to arrange many other matters which make living alongside each other more bearable, and accord with our attitude towards the environment. The Soviet commanders are surprised at the openness with which we from the Bundeswehr approach them. Often, our commanders make it possible for responsible Soviet officers and representatives of the local authorities to start talking to each other at local level. The changeover from occupation forces to forces which are enjoying hospitality is obviously not quite so simple.

For the first time, the commanding officer in Leipzig invited the members of the former NVA Military Regional Command for an early evening drink – out of forty-six officers invited, forty-three came. They have left the service. Some have taken early retirement, others are looking for work. In general, both in the Bundeswehr and among the former NVA members, there is a strong desire for a sensible relationship with each other. It is a complete novelty for the former NVA officers that the commander's room, which used to be occupied only by the five top officers of the former Military Regional Command, is now open to all of the other officers and that even the commander himself mixes with them. They are beginning to see the new style of leadership and are reacting with approval. Gradually change is making itself felt.

Afterwards I visit two large depots. One is commanded by an officer from the Western Bundeswehr and the other by a former NVA officer. The officer from the West only arrived a short time ago and he complains about the many problems he is encountering which he never had in the West. I surprise him with the remark: 'You should not run things right away according to Western standards, but rather work under the existing conditions and ensure security.' I tell him that he should not talk about his problems, but should tell me which tasks he is able to solve himself and where he needs my help; general discussion of problems is not much help. I then receive a precise, business-like report. I am sure that here, too, things will progress. The commander of the other depot, the former NVA officer, then a lieutenant-colonel and now a captain, has made the best of the conditions under which he has to work and is applying Bundeswehr regulations step-by-step, without much discussion, consistently and clearly. A pleasing picture.

Thursday, 31 January 1991

Permanent Secretary Dr Carl, along with some of the departmental heads, visits the BKO. At last some urgent outstanding decisions are made: among other things we can take over about seven-thousand officers as temporary soldiers for two years. This is the number for which I have been fighting for months. The next day I learn, during a talk in the ministry, that the decision had been made fourteen days previously by the minister, but we were not told. There are times when it is better to get a move on.

Monday, 4 February 1991

In the afternoon talks are held with Provost Dr Furian of the Evangelical Church of Berlin-Brandenburg. We have now moved closer to each other and want to appoint pastors at garrison level to hold services, give the servicemen ethical teaching and be ready to have pastoral discussions with them. This is a hopeful start.

In the evening, there are drinks with colonels from the Western Bundeswehr who were promoted to the rank on 1 February, and who will now serve long-term in the BKO region. They describe to me the difficulties in their various posts, up to the level of deputy brigade commander, but they are confident. The only ones who are moving their homes are those who no longer have children at school and whose wives do not have a job. However, even these people, in spite of all of their efforts, have so far found no flats or houses. The chances are very slim; until now nothing has been done in this respect – neither here nor in the West. Two of the servicemen want to put up a prefabricated house.

Tuesday, 5 February 1991

In the morning, I travel once again in the Antonov to Bonn, to take part in a meeting about our personnel policy. The result is as we wish, the numbers for the temporary soldiers are now finally fixed, I can inform the units and we have firm plans. I obtain agreement that servicemen and officials from the West will be paid for moving their homes near to the former inner-German border, if in this way they reduce the travelling distance to their place of duty.

Wednesday, 6 February 1991

A visit to the Parliamentary Commissioner for the Armed Forces. I have an exchange of views with him and his senior staff about our work. There is much commitment, and a lot of interest in what is happening in our region. The Commissioner wants to help us and to tackle tasks as they arise. He confirms that it is necessary to transfer more NCOs from the West to the East, supports equal pay for conscripts in East and West and a reduction in the burden of guard duties.

In spite of the predominantly smooth co-operation between officers of two formerly hostile armed forces, there are occasional complaints from both sides. For instance, a former NVA second lieutenant reports to me that a lieutenant from the West had ordered a soldier to immediately remove an NVA belt which he had put on after losing his Bundeswehr belt; the lieutenant had said that, after all, the soldier would not come on duty wearing an SS belt. This second lieutenant also complains that the same lieutenant and the company commander, who is also from the West, had tried to make him look ridiculous in front of the soldiers, and advised him to resign straight away because he was no use. The company commander had also recommended that a young soldier remove the inner lining from his sleeping-bag, as it was intended only for 'dirty NVA officers'. Furthermore, the two Western officers had been drinking unduly, the lieutenant said.

Fortunately these are only individual cases – I know of only this one complaint about Western officers. However, it does point to possible tensions and to the need for supervision, particularly by the commanders. The fact that disappointments cannot be avoided, I learn from a commander from the West who had been involved in a lively argument about *Innere Führung* with his former NVA officers. While on the toilet he hears – unintentionally – the summing-up of two participants: 'We really fooled that *Wessi!*'

In the afternoon I take part in talks in Bonn between the minister and Colonel-General Burlakov with his delegation. Burlakov is a turbulent sort who takes the offensive in talks. One would not like to have a dispute with him. He appears not to like lack of clarity, so it seemed to me right to put our position consistently and absolutely clearly. He refers to the difficulties regarding transport through Poland in relation to the withdrawal of Soviet forces. He does, however, make it clear that he is committed to fulfilling the treaty – even if it leads to additional costs. In addition, he complains that after the withdrawal from Germany two- hundred thousand servicemen will have to live in tents in the Soviet Union; the flats built with money from the Federal Republic are not sufficient. The situation is not manageable for him, he says, and we ought to continue our help and build an additional 19,000 flats. Finally, Burlakov refers to crimes committed by Soviet deserters who had escaped to the West: a regimental commander had fled with a secret weapon, another soldier, suspected of murder, had broken out of investigative arrest. Both had applied for asylum and are now subject to German law but, he says, they must be handed over. Almost all the problems mentioned by Burlakov are outside the responsibility of the Federal Defence Ministry. One can understand some of his worries, but we are unable to solve them. Even so, the meeting has contributed to mutual trust and Burlakov wants to visit me soon.

Friday, 15 February 1991

Again a flight in the Antonov to Bonn, in order to report, with my senior staff, on our concept for the disbandments by 30 June. A difficult question is: who is to take over the tasks, outside of the sphere of the three services, which will have to be solved in the transitional phase after the disbandment of the BKO? This refers in the main to the depots of equipment and munition, for which there is no longer any use in the Bundeswehr. As we see it, the main ministry department 'armaments' must take over the materiel and dispose of it, but the department is not prepared for this and has no money. Decisions are pressing, but we must wait.

Return flight in the evening, work in the headquarters, and talks with the executive committee of the Association of Bundeswehr Reservists. They want to admit former NVA reservists into their association. I point out that such persons can only become 'Bundeswehr reservists' if they have served in the Bundeswehr and have knowledge of it. The association cannot take in everyone who wants to join, merely to increase its numbers.

Monday 18 February 1991

In the morning I have a ninety-minute talk with Colonel-General Burlakov and Major-General Foertsch. Thanks to the personal relationship that we have built up in the meantime, we are able to discuss difficult problems, such as desertions, housing construction, transport costs. Burlakov is seeking contact with us and would like to hold discussions with people who show understanding for his difficulties, communicate them to Bonn and, if possible, solve them. During the talks it becomes evident that there is great willingness to co-operate in all aspects of the withdrawal from Germany, and we confirm the need for our direct telephone link.

Afterwards, the agreement on the use of the airspace over eastern Germany is signed by a representative of the Federal Minister of Transport and the Air Force Chief of Staff. A further step in attaining our sovereignty.

Tuesday, 19 February 1991

We visit to the missile fuel base, a central fuel depot for the anti-aircraft missiles. The depot is chock-full and disposal measures are urgently required so that we can disband further units. We are disbanding anti-aircraft units and handing over the weapons systems, but we have nowhere to put the fuel and oxidators. This cannot be done until new depot capacity has been created or the missile fuel has been disposed of. Until then the barracks must be strictly guarded in order to prevent fuel from falling into unauthorised hands.

The missile-fuel base lies well hidden in a forest – with no signpost. Although the local population knows that something is there, no one knows what it is. Here, for the first time, I come across an officer who, when he makes his report, I am unsure whether he is from the Western Bundeswehr or is a former member of the NVA. Not until five minutes later, does it become clear from various phrases he uses, that he is a former member of the NVA: 'We are carrying out the following measures.' 'The object on the territory of the local authority XY is being specially protected by the organs.' 'Allow me to continue.' 'Lieutenant-General, the end of my information report.' In the NVA a certain form of speech had developed that would be worth investigating more deeply. 'Lieutenant-General, allow us to begin with the measure ...' was the most frequent cliché. A general 'allowed', and the term 'measure' was used to describe everything from an evening invitation, or a manoeuvre, to a meeting – also the work of the cadres in the collectives.

Afterwards, we visit a battalion used for defence against atomic, biological and chemical warfare. The materiel that we have taken over shows that the NVA expected to have to protect itself against chemical weapons. They thought, and acted, much more consistently than we in the Bundeswehr! The Western commander, who has been appointed to serve for six months, has also arranged a twinning with his old unit in the West. From there he is getting a lot of practical help which he urgently needs.

Chapter 12

THE NEW ERA BECOMES APPARENT

Wednesday, 20 February 1991

Along with invited journalists from East and West, we fly to Eggesin, to start our press trip intended to show them, by use of concrete examples, our working conditions, the state of the infrastructure we have taken over, and what has already changed between October and February. I notice considerable progress in all spheres since my last visit in mid-October. Craftsmen are refurbishing the barrack blocks and the kitchens are being renovated, large dishwashers are being unpacked and installed. Training is beginning to fall into a normal routine – with active help from the West. The enormous quantities of superfluous military equipment are being collected together and the burden of guard duties can at least be somewhat reduced. Some of the officers and NCOs have already been taken on as temporary soldiers – actions are following words. However, our 'own goals' are also concerning us. For instance, a commander who was transferred from the West to the East and rented a two-room flat through the garrison administration, was immediately given notice to quit by the same administration which claimed he was not really ready to move house, and as a result his right to a flat was cancelled. According to the regulations on the allocation of flats, only those who move with their families are classed as ready to move. However, when the regulations on living accommodation were drawn up in the West, who thought about the future living conditions in the East? In Eggesin there is neither a functioning housing market nor an officers' hostel. I take up this point at further meetings.

The journalists discover that East and West are working together and growing closer. The 'new' officers confirm that they, too, want a common future, and they explain how the Western officers are helping them in this. The officers who come from the West have, in this respect, a mission which clearly goes beyond the daily service routine in the West. Special demands are being made of us in public. Our officers represent the Western part of the Federal Republic – as citizens in uniform.

The divisional commander has made contact with area administrative officials, schools and churches, and has ensured through numerous initiatives that in his area at least, the Bundeswehr is seen as a different sort of army and that the eastern part of our country accepts us. Together with the employment office and local industry he has been helping his soldiers to obtain vocational qualifications and to find jobs. For instance, he has succeeded, through co-operation with a Chamber of Industry and Commerce, to organise courses for further training and, after that, to find jobs for soldiers in civilian professions; actions which create credibility and trust. In the ministry, so I hear, his enthusiasm has already led to the feeling that he is overstepping the bounds of his responsibilities; I support him.

During an evening reception, the journalists have an opportunity to talk to officers, NCOs and men from the Eggesin area. The journalists from the East are amazed at the frankness of the discussions. 'Doesn't it cause you trouble, General?' I am asked.

Thursday, 21 February 1991

The press trip takes us to an air force radar battalion in Trollenhagen, about eighty miles north of Berlin. We are shown the completely new responsibilities which have arisen from the attainment of national air sovereignty. The journalists are surprised at how much eastern equipment has had to be utilised to carry out this task, and how few officers and NCOs from the West are needed to ensure command and control.

The result has been a worthwhile trip under the headline: 'BKO on the way to the Bundeswehr and to normality in training.' True, there is still rather a long way to go, but we shall master it. The journalists from the five new Länder have discovered in their talks with the servicemen and at the evening reception in Eggesin, what distinguishes the Bundeswehr from the NVA. I have no need to add much myself.

Monday, 25 February 1991

I fly to Lüneburg, in Western Germany, to the 8th Tank Brigade, to see conscripts from the East and West being trained together. The 8th Brigade is particularly active in co-operating with the 9th Tank Division in Eggesin. A good number of the officers and NCOs are on duty in the East, but some have already returned. The soldiers tell me of their experiences in the East. Doing duty there has evidently led to much thought about the conditions there, and has also led to identification with the Eastern Bundeswehr. However, they also expect from the former members of the NVA – both officers and NCOs – honest and straightforward behaviour.

A staff sergeant tells me that he went to Eggesin because he was ordered to. However, after he had experienced the conditions in the East, and seen how much needed to be done there, he was considering whether to ask for a transfer for a longer time. A young NCO from Lüneburg describes his experiences in an Eastern barracks in a written report. As it is representative of the impressions and experiences of many others, here are some extracts:

> The period dealt with in this report is the first seven weeks of general basic training in the 4th Company of the 9th Motorised Infantry Regiment, from 1 January until 15 February 1991.
>
> The reception in the 4th Company on 2 January 1991 was very friendly and there was no sign of negative attitudes among the NCOs of the Eastern and Western Bundeswehr. They soon started to talk to each other, although at first a certain amount of reserve could be felt.
>
> Problems are arising in training duties and from the differing degrees of interest being shown by the NCOs of the Eastern Bundeswehr in their own further professional training. For instance, I often have the impression that many NCOs of the Eastern Bundeswehr lack the motivation to learn new ways or to learn more, so they can keep all the more to the former 'NVA training methods'.
>
> This lack of motivation among the NCOs of the Eastern Bundeswehr has been considerably worsened because of the waiting time before receipt of employment contracts as temporary soldiers. The result for us NCOs of the Western Bundeswehr is that we must try to compensate for the lack of commitment of the NCOs of the Eastern Bundeswehr. This is only possible through additional stress as a result of, for example, extra personal study and the preparation of several training courses at the same time.
>
> It can, however, be clearly seen that some of the NCOs of the Eastern Bundeswehr are really trying, by their behaviour as well as the preparation and conduct of training, to meet the standards of the Western Bundeswehr.
>
> In comparing the junior NCOs of the Eastern and Western Bundeswehr, problems of a quite different sort are evident regarding barracks duties. The NCOs of the Eastern Bundeswehr are unable to independently carry out the tasks of the duty NCO. They cannot assert their authority over their subordinates at all. As a result, we NCOs of the Western Bundeswehr act as supporters of the duty NCO, in order that the duties of the duty NCO in our company are carried out at all. (...)
>
> In the barracks incidents often occur during which soldiers of other companies try to make me look ridiculous when I am leading a platoon, by shouting out, for example: 'Section halt, left turn, quick march, attention.' The platoon, too, is affected by shouts. When this happens I have no way of taking action against this behaviour, as, in the case of someone

being temporarily detained, there is not even a detention cell in the barracks, and the soldiers of the other companies ignore all orders. The cause of this behaviour clearly lies in the leadership of the companies. For instance, the high standard of our company can be attributed only to the large proportion of Western Bundeswehr NCOs in the individual platoons and a company sergeant-major in the company command. (...)

As regards cleaning, it should be said that the NCOs of the Eastern Bundeswehr have scarcely any conception for hygiene and cleanliness. Only through 'instructional demonstrations' by superiors from the Western Bundeswehr on how to clean quarters, was it shown how the living quarters could be brought up to a hygienic standard. In spite of all this it must be said that, particularly in the sphere of toilets and washrooms, it is not possible to achieve a somewhat clean area. (...)

The supply of warm water is also not satisfactorily arranged. The cause lies in the defective electric boilers, which can no longer be repaired. The installation of new electric boilers is being organised by NCOs of the Western Bundeswehr on their own initiative. However, it is not only the sanitary installations which are sub-standard, but also the whole of the living quarters. Hygienic conditions cannot be achieved at all, if only because of the coal stoves and the coal cellar which create so much dirt that the desired level of cleanliness, which is supposed to be created by cleaning the quarters and the barrack rooms, does not last for long. Thorough cleaning of the corridors is made even harder in this season because of the low external temperatures which cause the cleaning water to freeze. Conditions in the barrack rooms are also unsatisfactory. Wallpaper is peeling from the walls and ceilings, and the walls are starting to crumble so it is virtually impossible to keep the rooms in a reasonably decent state and fit to live in. The only thing which at present makes this situation still bearable, is that the soldiers are evidently used to such conditions and do not complain. (...)

The Western instructors have, without exception, had good results with the recruits from the five new Länder. Within a short time *Ossis* and *Wessis* could no longer be distinguished from each other except for their differing dialects. The young soldiers from the East turn out to be extraordinarily enthusiastic, and because of their paramilitary training they are also better prepared for military service than their comrades in the West.

They have lost their shyness and insecurity but at the end of their three months' basic training they go back to their Eastern home areas with mixed feelings. They are naturally looking forward to being with their friends and families, in places that they know, and they are not depressed about returning to the poor conditions back home. They are ready to help in reconstructing the exploited and run-down region. Some of them fear, however, that they will fall into the hands of former NVA soldiers and be maltreated by them or again become subject to them. They have hopes about the effects of *Innere Führung* and the selection of personnel in the Bundeswehr, but they are still sceptical and want to wait and see. Can one criticise them for that? I explain once more their rights as soldiers and what we are doing to achieve orderly training. We superiors – particularly those from the West – have our duties in this sphere too.

In my presence the recruits discuss whether any permanent achievements remain from the GDR era. A heated, very emotional debate. 'You really can't say that it was all in vain,' a recruit from Frankfurt/Oder says to his Western comrade. 'My father was just as hard-working as yours, but you just had the good luck to be living in the West.' In saying that the young man was expressing something which concerns many: was everything that was done to no avail? Has a whole generation been cheated of their lives?

Tuesday, 26 February 1991

Visit to the Motorised Infantry Regiment in Mühlhausen, western Thuringia, a unit that is being disbanded. During the drive through places close to the former inner-German border I see building and renovation work everywhere. Everything is becoming more colourful, including the villages.

I hold talks with the officers. They are waiting to be taken on as temporary soldiers and for a decision about their future garrison, once this unit has been disbanded. They are confident that they will soon be in a united army.

I ask to be shown the whole materiel section and the depots shown to me and determine that the enormous quantities of arms and spare parts, apparatus and additional equipment cannot – under normal routine – either be 'processed' or dealt with according to our regulations. For instance, in a storeroom of about five hundred square metres, two staff sergeants and a depot worker are sorting the spare parts and equipment to prepare them for disposal. The storeroom is packed with shelves, which are filled up to the ceiling. The men stand on ladders and throw parts from above into large containers – an almost surreal sight. When I ask them how long their work is expected to take, they say that they will need months to assess the amount of materiel in just one depot. But in every motorised infantry regiment there are between seven and ten such depots. Here the German love of orderliness is leading to a senseless 'work creation programme' – first expending much effort in cataloguing the equipment in detail, and then scrapping it. Due to this I later have the cataloguing stopped and have the materiel belonging to the weapons systems assessed only by weight, which is contrary to regulations.

There is an increasing shortage of drivers to transport heavy equipment to collection points and to the railways. It is foreseeable that we shall soon only have officers as drivers. The collecting together of the 2,500 tanks, 2,350 artillery pieces and the more than seven-thousand armoured infantry combat vehicles, in the newly established assembly depots is taking place by rail through the Reichsbahn. We cannot keep to our planned timings because the traffic management and the transport capacity are not yet effectively co-ordinated. Nevertheless, we must move at speed in the whole command region because the personnel strength in the units is falling further and further, and we can only set up the new units once the old materiel has gone.

Afterwards, we visit an underground installation which is perfectly equipped technically and still being used. It can be supplied underground by two goods trains, is specially protected and has thirty-thousand square metres of ventilated storage space; there we can store most of the 1.2 million small arms.

Wednesday, 27 February 1991

I hold morning talks with the Catholic Bishop of Berlin, Georg Sterzinsky. He is very sympathetic, is positive towards the Bundeswehr and supports military chaplaincies. We have a lively exchange of views and I am able to answer many questions in detail. The Catholic Church is dealing with us in a very frank way.

From late afternoon until well into the night, another meeting with the three service chiefs. The taking over of the temporary servicemen has been finally approved and can be carried out quickly. Unfortunately, we still have considerable problems in some areas: in the forces' administration, in matters of pay and in the entire take-over of the former financial sections. Considerable difficulties with pay are evident in the forces' administration, which has to be newly established and which, below the level of corps and territorial commands, consists entirely of former staff of the NVA 'financial and economic organs'. For instance, the departmental heads who have been appointed are earning less than some of their subordinates who used to be staff officers. The former NVA staff officers have special service contracts. In the long term they can only be taken on as employees or civil servants in the forces' administration sector. However, if they now, in February, change over to a civilian contract of service they can be paid only according to the framework wage agreement of the GDR and, at their grade, they would receive less than unemployment benefit. So we are keeping these officers on for the time being as forces' administration officials for, if they were to leave soon, wages, conscripts' pay, and pensions could not be paid.

An improvement in the financial situation, and pay which accords with the work carried out, will be possible only when the pay scales for federal employees and the position of *Beamter* have been introduced. No one knows exactly when this will happen; it is hoped to be on 1 July. In one of the command areas there are, for instance, twenty-two heads of forces' administration offices who have pay grades lower than some of the servicemen subordinate to them. In another divisional area, out of twenty-eight former heads of forces' administration offices only thirteen are still there. The others have chosen civilian jobs in preference to the unclear financial situation. These difficulties have direct effects on the forces' daily routine. The Western servicemen, who are often transferred to one garrison after another, are not receiving, for weeks or months, the payments due to them for separation from their families or travel costs. Likewise, there are many errors in payment of pensions and wages which, in view of all the unavoidable difficulties, are an additional annoyance. (It later emerges that until the end of 1991 the wages for thousands of personnel were calculated wrongly.)

The real problem though is, as before, the collecting up of arms and ammunition. In this respect we are in a difficult situation. If, within the foreseeable future, the special Western regulations on storing ammunition were to be introduced, a completely new depot concept would have to be developed. This would mean that we would no longer be able to store at least thirty per cent of the unneeded ammunition (about thirty thousand tonnes) and would have to take it to the West and dispose of it there later. The fact that this transport to the West – quite apart from the high costs – would be bound to face strong resistance among the public is obvious. It would probably not make any difference that, because of the strict ammunition regulations which also existed in the GDR era, there had been no accidents since the foundation of the NVA. It remains to be stated that these former depot regulations, although different from ours, were evidently safe. For us it is thus very important that units are not finally disbanded until we are able to remove the ammunition from the garrisons. So the facts compel an extension of the exceptional authorization to continue using the GDR regulations.

Thursday, 28 February 1991

In the morning discussions are held with two dismissed NVA generals who are employed as advisers in the BKO region. We have already spoken a number of times about the current situation and can speak frankly to each other. Is there a tendency towards disquiet, or a rebellious atmosphere, among the former NVA officers which could lead to unpleasant surprises? I have repeatedly heard rumours that disgruntled officers could make common cause with other dissatisfied groups in society and threaten the new authorities. However, my informants describe the atmosphere to me as being, although tense, under control on the whole. They say that the former members of the NVA definitely appreciate our efforts – such as the various initiatives of local commanders and regular information for the members of the forces. They add that thanks to the temporary soldiers' being taken over an important step has been taken – actions have finally followed words, and this is decisive.

There is, however, no general solution to the individual problems of officers who have left. Those over fifty have their early retirement settlement and can live on that. Those aged between forty and fifty are taking up vocational training and hope to get a job afterwards, perhaps a profession. They have the greatest worries as to whether, in view of their age, they will get work again. The younger officers, if they leave, in any case want to make a real new start – but they must first learn where and how that can be done. Things are certainly not so easy for the individuals – but there are some opportunities.

My advisers report to me about the potential for conflict which exists in the former NVA housing estates in Strausberg. Living in a block with eight to ten flats, for example, there are only two or three officers who are still serving in the Bundeswehr. The other tenants – all former servicemen – have either left the Bundeswehr at their own request or have been dismissed by us. Now opinions are clashing: 'One takes an oath only once in life,' is the accusatory line taken by the incorrigible or disappointed people to those who want to take advantage of their chances in the Bundeswehr. Some find it an outrageous idea to go on serving in the Bundeswehr after being demoted by two ranks.

Disputes are unavoidable, as many generals and admirals live in Strausberg who were kept in important posts after the democratic changeover in the NVA. For some officers who are now doing their duty with us, tensions arise from the old relationship of loyalty to former superiors whom they still have to get along with as neighbours. It is unavoidable that the families, including children, cannot remain untouched by this. So everyone must be in control of *themselves*, but fortunately now, not of *others* – as in former days.

The two NVA generals recommend that I invite all NVA generals and admirals who were still in the services in 1990 to a briefing talk about the tasks and work of the Bundeswehr. After a lively debate in the headquarters about the pros and cons, I later turn down this proposal. A single malicious headline in *Neues Deutschland* or another newspaper could call in question the honesty of our efforts and destroy much goodwill overnight. Among the general population an impression of a suspicious new chumminess between the generals of the East and West could arise. We agree that all of our efforts are, for the time being, concerned with the present and that the wounds of the past are too fresh for us to view history with the necessary distance.

There was considerable commotion among the former officers – particularly the generals – when, in November and December of last year, 8,500 official telephones in their flats were disconnected on my orders. In the NVA many officers had official telephones in their homes and could telephone around the former GDR through the NVA headquarters network. After the political changeover they were also able, via this network, to contact all the offices of the Bundeswehr and could thus maintain an efficient information system. In addition, there was above all no longer any service necessity for the privilege of a special telephone connection, and we wanted neither to hand out new privileges nor to confirm old ones. Indeed, telephone lines were – a new experience for us West Germans in the East – a particularly valuable possession after 3 October because they were so rare. After discussions with our legal advisers and experts I had therefore decided that the official telephones in the flats should be removed after individual checks carried out by the responsible local commander. Only special social welfare considerations justified a line, for example, the serious illness of a family member for whom a doctor must be reachable at all times. Telephones were also permitted in remote areas with a poor infrastructure if they were essential for work. All other lines were, however, consistently disconnected, while those concerned were free to apply for a telephone – just like any other citizen in the new Länder who wanted a telephone. Not surprisingly, we had many complaints about these 'drastic' measures, from the generals in particular. I doubt whether a discussion with those concerned would have had any results.

After the meeting I visit the most modern anti-aircraft missile unit of the former NVA air force, which is equipped with a missile system that was only introduced in 1985 under strict secrecy. The electronics are evidently out of date – large and expensive but very effective. The fifty plus missiles, propelled by liquid fuel, are kept in an enormous installation which has much technical equipment, a large number of personnel and high running costs. They are sited in concrete bunkers. When the alarm is given they are moved outside on rails and made ready to fire. The young officers – most of them have studied for several years in the Soviet Union and are masters of their profession – demonstrate the system to me with pride.

Until the political changeover extreme secrecy was imposed here, which is why strong rumours circulated locally that nuclear missiles were stationed in the barracks area and that Soviet soldiers were hidden there. In order to end this suspicion I invite journalists from the surrounding area to a press briefing. The commanding officer explains the function of his unit. For the journalists it is a completely novel experience to view the military 'object' from the inside and to have the weapon system with which the unit was equipped demonstrated to them. It once again becomes clear to me that not only must we give information frankly but we must also literally open the doors. Only in this way can we reveal things and show that there is nothing to conceal or hide.

The young officers make an attentive impression during our discussions; they are still somewhat intimidated but ready to learn. They want to show their capabilities and goodwill and are proud that I praise their commitment. One of the officers was elected mayor of a small local community after the political changeover, which shows an unusual closeness to the population. All of the other officers live in their housing estate – away from the local community and the nearby town and without any contact to the people. The consistent separation was evidently planned, right until the political changeover. In any case it was intended to prevent officers or family members from giving information to the public about the weapon system which was hidden here. And it really is amazing how well this secret was kept.

In the afternoon, talks with the member of the Brandenburg state parliament representing Strausberg. In Strausberg we have 'inherited', from the NVA, a cultural and sports centre which had formerly kept the whole of the cultural and sports activity in Strausberg going, and possessed the only covered swimming pool in a large area. Owing to our tight financial situation, I have been given an order to close the centre by 31 March, but my staff and I are agreed that we shall not do this under any circumstances. We cannot explain to the public that, after the peaceful changeover, because of a gap in 'competences' the children can no longer go to the swimming pool or take part in sports. Transitional arrangements must be found, as the town of Strausberg and the state of Brandenburg are not yet able to pay. So we reach agreement on a compromise with both the Federal Forces Administration and the town. According to this, Strausberg will not take over the centre until 30 June, so we shall only hand it over once the BKO is disbanded on 1 July – this, too, adds to our credibility.

Monday, 4 March 1991

The Federal Defence Minister visits Strausberg. We tell him of our problems which, in the main, are known or are routine. On all concrete questions he promises support and quick decisions. In the evening I have invited the generals who have just been promoted. At last, the budgetary posts which are necessary for this have been established, so the two commanders of the Regional Commands, after carrying out their duties excellently for five months, can at last be promoted to the correct rank – along with some of the deputies and brigade commanders. It is a jolly evening. We all know that we have been struggling together and have covered a good deal of the way, even though many tasks lie before us.

Monday, 11 March 1991

At a conference of Bundeswehr commanders, I give an overall review of the work in the BKO:

Development and Situation of the Bundeswehr-Kommando Ost.

More than five months after the unification of Germany it can be said that the transition from the NVA to the Bundeswehr has succeeded remarkably well, in spite of all the difficulties. This is a joint achievement. All servicemen and civilian staff, who came from the West to take responsibility in the region of the Bundeswehr-Kommando Ost, have contributed to it, as have all those who came from the former NVA and were ready to serve the common cause. And this is the achievement of the whole Bundeswehr, East and West, because it is only thanks to the energetic and unbureaucratic support from the Western Bundeswehr that it has been possible to carry out the transition so smoothly, and to achieve what now gives me the basis for this favourable assessment of the situation.

The Bundeswehr has – with a relatively short preparation period – faced a difficult task: to take over a previously hostile army, to disband it and at the same time to incorporate part of its personnel in its own ranks. In so doing, it has been necessary at all times to ensure security, as well as command and operating effectiveness.

The way in which the Bundeswehr has tackled this task is also an impressive confirmation of the success in educating and training our servicemen. It is also a good start for mastering the problems during the growing together of Germany: tackling tasks together, during which each one contributes what he can, the stronger more than the weaker. The transition has succeeded, but the road to united democratic armed forces is still a long one. The need for togetherness in reaching this goal will accompany us in the coming years. (...)

The name 'Bundeswehr-Kommando Ost' is actually a wrong choice, for the region of the Bundeswehr-Kommando Ost has, for the time being, very little to do with the 'Bundeswehr'. It is not the Bundeswehr that we encounter in the new Länder. Not yet. Those who came from the West had to learn this very quickly. And the Bundeswehr as a whole had to realise that the mechanisms which had been developed optimally down the years, were not, as a rule, suitable for the conditions found in the region of the Bundeswehr-Kommando Ost. Initiative and flexibility appropriate to the current situation were, therefore, usually more helpful than a decree gazette issued in 1974. Also, it has not always been easy to demonstrate this to the originators of regulations which had proved themselves in the Western Bundeswehr.

The Bundeswehr-Kommando Ost is starting to conduct training according to the principles of the *Innere Führung* and is creating the conditions for the transition to the decentralised command structures of the separate services. This mission is determined by the values of the Basic Law and by the treaty commitments entered into by the Federal Republic of Germany.

To realise the idea of the citizen in uniform means, above all, to complete a process of changing consciousness. It must be made clear that the

Bundeswehr, with its democratic mandate, its constitutional basis and its internal order stemming from the principles of the freedom-loving state founded on the rule of law, is a radically different kind of armed force from the NVA. Our values must be underlined: that the individual is central and not the collective, and that the freedom of the individual also means behaving responsibly and showing individual initiative. The readiness to co-operate is there. There is often an impressive sense of duty to be seen, in spite of the difficult conditions.

Social welfare questions as well as pay matters are coming more and more to the fore. Financial differences between East and West are still understandable to the temporary servicemen, but cannot be explained to the conscripts who are fulfilling the same commitment according to the Basic Law as those in the West. Because of these different financial arrangements in particular, the personnel of the Eastern Bundeswehr often feel that they are second-class servicemen. We have about two-thousand officers and NCOs from the Western Bundeswehr on duty. They have tackled their task and have started to introduce a new leadership style into the armed forces. It is not least through them, that the young conscripts are experiencing the change, as I am told again and again. (...)

The reduction of the armed forces while they were still subject to the NVA, from 170,000 to about 100,000 servicemen was already a considerable cut. Under the responsibility of the Bundeswehr-Kommando Ost the number of personnel was further reduced. We now have about seventy thousand servicemen. Within four months about seventy per cent of the officers were dismissed, the older ones in particular – and that under the most difficult of social and economic conditions.

As of January of this year we have about forty-thousand conscripts, about 10,500, mainly young, officers and about nineteen-thousand NCOs and temporary servicemen. The junior NCOs are simply experts without leadership competence. The officers are behaving loyally and are ready to learn, but because of their completely different training they have a great handicap when compared with their Western comrades. We have therefore introduced a comprehensive programme to aid re-thinking and to give additional training.

From the original number of roughly 32,000 officers, of whom about 10,500 are still serving, we shall succeed in taking on up to seven thousand as temporary servicemen for two years, and obtaining from them between 4,000 and 4,500 officers, including technical specialists, who will be able to serve in the Bundeswehr long-term. However, the establishment of an effective, stable corps of NCOs, as we know from the Bundeswehr, takes time. Here, at first, there will be both a quantitative and qualitative shortage. To compensate for this, considerable efforts are required to attract new recruits, as well as support from the Western Bundeswehr. In my view it will be an acid test as to whether we can find enough senior NCOs to serve in the new Länder for two to three years, accepting the strains on their personal and family situations and helping in the reconstruction.

While personnel strength in the units has fallen, in most cases, to less than fifty per cent, the formations have still almost the complete complement of weapons and ammunition, and are additionally burdened with those which had to be taken over from the armed organs which did not belong to the NVA. From approximately 400 units which are to be disbanded, about 130 will have been disbanded by 31 March 1991 and a further 250 by 30 June 1991. Parallel to this, major items of equipment which are to be destroyed or disposed of, are being collected together. Up to now, more than 2,300 major weapons systems have been brought together. Ammunition earmarked for disposal is being collected in certain depots and from there handed over to the Armaments Main Department and from then on to industry. By 30 June 1991 more than fifty-thousand tons of ammunition, from the units which are to be disbanded by then, must be collected together. The destruction or disposal of the materiel, and the hand-over for other uses, of bases which are no longer needed, is a task which is new in such a volume and, in order to be carried out, first requires suitable structures to be built up by the Bundeswehr, the public administration and industry.

The disentanglement and re-organisation of those public tasks which, in the long term, are not to be carried out by the Bundeswehr, are proving difficult, more so because the new Länder and the local authority structures are only now being created. It is clear that tasks such as heating civilian housing areas, running the public cultural and sports installations, or school and kindergarten canteens should not, in our view, be debited to the separate Budget Plan 14 but, until other bodies can take them over, transitional arrangements must be found. It is hard to imagine that, as a result of German unification, civilian housing areas should remain unheated, that in whole administrative districts cultural events and sport should no longer take place, or that children in kindergartens should no longer get anything to eat.

While the inheritance of the former NVA is being dealt with, the reconstruction of the all-German armed forces is taking place in the new Länder. The emphasis must be laid on this more and more – it will be the central task of 1991. Officers and NCOs have to be trained according to the principles of *Innere Führung,* either in courses, or by taking part in training in the Bundeswehr. Professional training must follow.

The Eastern Bundeswehr must achieve a normal training routine as soon as possible. The first step has been taken by starting basic training in the region of the Bundeswehr-Kommando Ost at the beginning of this year. Two-thirds of the basic training is still being carried out in units of the Western Bundeswehr. From the call-up of conscripts on 1 April we shall already be carrying out fifty per cent of the basic training. The aim is completely to take over the call-up and training procedures in the region of the Bundeswehr-Kommando Ost as soon as possible. The setting up of new units and offices has already begun. In forming further units as part of the intended structure, and introducing major equipment, it is intended that during this year operational companies, or perhaps battalions, will be created, and operational brigades next year. This is a demanding programme, but it can be fulfilled.

At the same time the pre-conditions for accommodating our servicemen – particularly living quarters, showers and kitchens – must be drastically improved to meet our minimum requirements; the first signs of this will be evident in 1991. This costs a great deal of money. The first improvements have already been made. Further measures will follow. During this year alone, four-hundred million Deutschmarks will be expended on this.

We have still not reached the position where we can transfer officers and NCOs from West to East without difficulties. Living conditions are still so different when one considers the infrastructure, the housing situation, schools, work for wives or leisure facilities. The housing situation, in particular, probably means that as a rule it will not be possible, for years to come, for servicemen transferred from West to East to move their homes. There is practically no empty housing accommodation available. Only if we succeed, in spite of all the difficulties, in exchanging personnel between East and West as soon as possible, shall we be able to become one Bundeswehr in our attitude of mind and in training. Here, the armed forces can make an important contribution to the growing together of Germany. An additional mission, until the end of 1994, is to help the Soviet forces in Germany in organising their planned withdrawal. The goal is: to ensure that action conforms to the treaty and that the agreed consideration towards the population is assured. In this respect the Soviet side is making strong efforts. After General Burlakov had taken over command of the Western Group of the Soviet Armed Forces (WGT), the overall withdrawal plan was quickly proposed. Between 1991 and 1994 more than half a million Soviet servicemen, civilian staff and family members are to be withdrawn from Germany, 150,000 of these in 1991. The Polish government's demand that transit be regulated by treaty has led to certain strains. However, the WGT shown flexibility in the use of transport facilities by withdrawing more personnel by sea. Even so, it is to be observed that every time there are difficulties concerning the withdrawal, efforts are made to persuade the German side to do more, particularly as regards finance. Relations with the Soviet forces are, on the whole, neighbourly. The psychological problems of last summer, and the tensions between the population and the Soviet forces, have been eased thanks, to a large extent, to the close contacts between the commanders of the Soviet forces and the German authorities.

The bases which have been vacated through the withdrawals, which began as early as 1988 [under earlier East-West treaties], are in general in a terrible condition. The damage and pollution in the training areas, too, are also great. The WGT is committed to observing German law on environmental protection and is, in principle, liable for damage. Responsibility for taking over the bases lies with the Federal Minister of Finance. On the whole, the impression is that the Soviet side is trying to fulfil its treaty commitments and itself has an interest in withdrawing its forces. Contact with the western way of life seems to be leading to concern regarding military discipline.

I sum up: until now we have been in the consolidation phase, now the reconstruction follows. On the whole, the transition has gone remarkably well, but a difficult road still lies before us. (...) Overall I am optimistic, in spite of all the difficulties. If the armed forces take the chance, in spite of the cutbacks, to achieve unity in the formations, they can fulfil a pilot function within the whole state. I am convinced that the efforts are worthwhile in view of the goal: to create united German forces in a unified Germany. We are well on the way towards that.

Tuesday, 12 March 1991

The British Defence Secretary, Tom King, visits the BKO region. We inform him of our task, our achievements so far, and then show him a few military installations, including a combat helicopter regiment equipped with the Soviet-made MI-24. Once again, the return flight over an undivided Berlin is impressive.

Thursday, 14 March 1991

An evening flight to Dresden to take part in the German-British 'Königswinter Conference'. Foreign observers seem to find it difficult to conceive of our political and psychological situation, our new conditions and needs. They overestimate the effectiveness of decades of Communist indoctrination and, on the other hand, underestimate the Germans' feeling of unity and the desire for freedom of the people in the East. We must clarify some of the incomprehension and explain a great deal – not least why we held back in the Gulf War. We need time to take in the new situation of the Federal Republic and adapt ourselves to the new role which a united Germany must play in the alliance, if it wants to do justice to the needs of its partners. It is argued at the conference that the First and Second World Wars distinguish Germany from other European countries such as Britain and France which, because of their colonial past, have a quite different attitude to the use of armed forces as a means of policy. Additional difficulties are being caused, it is said, by the differing interpretations of the Basic Law within Germany.

In the afternoon we visit the 'Green Vault' and the Dresden art gallery. It has been largely forgotten what cultural riches are present in these regions – particularly in Saxony and Thuringia. Afterwards I sat outside on a cafe terrace in sunshine and mild spring air. At 5 pm all the chairs are chained up and the terrace, as always according to the rules, is closed punctually. Neither the lovely weather, nor the wishes of the customers can change the attitude of the staff. Service according to the rules – but only inside the cafe! A not so rare leftover from the former era; here the interest of the proprietor is evidently still lacking. We visit Meissen and Moritzburg – almost forgotten architectural treasures. The cathedral church of Meissen is still in good condition. The smell of brown coal hangs over the small church square.

Monday, 18 March 1991

In the afternoon, at a small reception, I say farewell to 150 officers and NCOs from the BKO who are returning to their home units in the West on 1 April. Their six months in the East have been the greatest challenge, the greatest experience but also the greatest strain in their careers so far. Not one of them is leaving the same as when he came. All are changed, enriched, and have experienced and learned a lot. Like all the others who are taking part in the reconstruction, they are presented with a commemorative certificate with the coats-of-arms of the new Länder and Berlin, which is intended to recognise their personal commitment and to remind them of their shared experiences. It is a pleasure for me, on later visits to units in the West, to see some of these certificates hanging in the officers' workplaces and to hear them report proudly: 'General, that was a time we shall never forget.'

A civilian woman employee, who used to work in the GDR Ministry for Disarmament and Defence, breaks into tears because she still has no idea of what she is going to do after 1 July. She has helped us to reconstruct the BKO, but now the Armed Forces Regional Administration no longer seems to need her – the posts have been abolished. Her fate is not an isolated case, but affects many of the civilian staff who had applied to us for possible further work in the Armed Forces Regional Administration after the disbandment of the BKO. As their hopes have not been realised, we feel we ought to help them. It takes a long time for our joint efforts to achieve success.

Tuesday, 19 March 1991

Drive to Delitzsch, near Leipzig, to the NCO training school which is being established there and which will later take over the training of corporals to prepare them for the sergeants' course. The conscripts who started service in January make an optimistic impression. They are convinced they can deal with the difficulties facing them and that, after their service, they will find jobs. One of the older lieutenant-colonels from the West explains to me why he has come here: 'General, twenty kilometres from here there is a small industrial town with smoking chimneys. I was born in the shadow of those chimneys, and never thought it possible that I could return to my home area as a soldier. Now I am happy to be here again and to be training the young Bundeswehr NCOs.'

He is not the only serviceman from the West who has been brought back to the East by homesickness. Many feel challenged by the extraordinary task of creation of all-German forces on the territory of the former GDR, and they have devoted themselves to it. They are inspired, too, by the pioneering spirit which can be felt everywhere. It is the young officers, above all, who say to me: 'There's something happening here and we want to take part in it.' What is more, they do not always ask about extra payments for doing duty in the East and about personal favours. In the barrack blocks, building work is going on, hammering, painting: individual initiative and the readiness to make progress are becoming evident. A regular training routine can probably be started as early as May.

On the return journey I visit a Soviet barracks which has been empty since December 1990. It was built by the *Wehrmacht* and the fabric is solid, but the houses and installations erected by the Soviets do not meet our standards and are clearly ready for demolition. Everywhere the quarters are in an awful condition: the doors removed, the window openings covered with nailed boards, water taps and shower fittings gone, the roads full of holes. On the barrack square there is a scrapheap containing a hotchpotch of things – empty oil drums, rusty trucks, dummy missiles. Specialists who were brought in just for that purpose found a live hand grenade there a short time ago; fortunately it was not found by children at play. This seems to be only the beginning of the difficulties of clean-up and disposal which we shall be faced with. In addition, the Soviets even expect us to pay them for the buildings they have put up! I fear this will cause long drawn-out and difficult negotiations. As the Federal Defence Ministry is not responsible for this matter, it is one of the few bitter cups that will pass us by.

In the afternoon, talks with 'instructors' from the West: armed forces administrative officials who have been sent here to instruct members of the former Financial and Economic Service in the work of the Armed Forces Administration according to our budgetary laws. These very experienced officials are showing much initiative, but feel they are being left alone and not given enough help. They are not able to get down to their real training job because the officials of the forces administration – former NVA finance economists – are so overworked in their normal duties, because of the large numbers of servicemen who are leaving, that they have no time to study the federal budget law. However, this problem does not seem to have got through to Bonn. No one from the Defence Ministry has either spoken to or visited them yet, in order to learn the local conditions and difficulties. In view of this situation, I apply to Bonn for an extension of the officials' postings here, and I propose a change in the training of the members of the former financial and economic organs.

Wednesday, 20 March 1991

Conference of commanding officers in Strausberg, to which I have invited all commanders down to battalion level, in order to strike a balance and to bring to the fore what will be the most important task from 1 April onwards – the formation of new units. Some commanders are going back to their Western garrisons at the end of the month, after being in the East for six months. In spite of this great exchange of personnel, continuity ought to be assured and the credibility of the Bundeswehr maintained: the most important features of our work must remain the same.

After seven hours of discussion the mainly positive results are undisputed. The difficulties and confusion in the sphere of social welfare are gradually being cleared up, the incorporation of temporary servicemen is beginning and so is the planning for the training of officers and NCOs; in the first quarter of 1991 thousands of officers and

NCOs have already been sent to the West for training. The basic concept as regards materiel has been approved, the depots for collecting the materiel together have been chosen, and the infrastructure will be improved this year with an investment of 340 million Deutschmarks.

I point out the danger that, with increasing normality and conditions becoming similar to those in the West, Western regulations will be extended to our command region before the preconditions for that have been created. For this reason, too, I urge the commanders to work quickly. The feedback of information from below must be improved, as during my visits to units I frequently come across mistakes which should have been noticed earlier. This is still of importance for us: anyone who returns to the West should be an ambassador from the BKO region, and should make it clear that we are on our way to a united Bundeswehr, but that this can only be achieved if East and West work hand-in-hand, and each contributes what it can. At the end of the commanders' conference I have the impression that everyone is leaving in a confident mood.

After a meeting with the service chiefs, which follows, we take our leave from those of our colleagues who are returning to the West. Over time we have become a united team, have got to know each other better, and those who are leaving start to feel sad. A time of personal challenge and experience lies behind us. We go on talking with each other until early morning, latterly in my room. We are all moved by the same question: how can we bring about the creation of common armed forces of the Federal Republic of Germany? Are there alternatives to the course of togetherness on which we have set out?

Thursday, 21 March 1991

To the headquarters in Mauerstraße in East Berlin: the disbandment headquarters of the civil protection organisation, which is also subordinate to us. The disbandment is being carried out from Berlin by a small headquarters staff. The civil protection organisation evolved, early in 1990, from the civil defence organisation, which was of great importance in the GDR. It was organised 'under the authority of the Minister for National Defence as a system of state measures' and was financed with 260 million Ostmarks annually. At the civil defence headquarters there were about 300 full-time staff, with 330 in the regions and 700 in the local administrative areas. In addition, there were about 490,000 voluntary helpers from firms and industrial combines as well as from the local population. They were primarily intended to carry out life-saving and rescue measures and were equipped countrywide with the same uniforms, protective equipment and means of command; but they had no weapons. Training took place at the workplaces.

To protect the population, by the end of 1989, shelters which could be further enlarged had been provided for 85.5 per cent of the inhabitants! This is what the statistics say. When one sees the rundown houses it is difficult to imagine. It was intended that about one million children and their carers would be evacuated from thirty-one cities. For medical care about 240 hospital departments with 670,000 beds – including hospital trains and ships – were planned. Masks to protect against atomic, biological and chemical weapons were available to thirty per cent of the population. From early 1990 a start was made in transforming the civil defence organisation so that it could carry out the tasks of the new civil protection organisation, which took over all installations and equipment. Now the whole organisation is to be disbanded by us by 30 June. This can only be done only in co-operation with the new Länder, which are to be given the equipment needed to set up the future civilian protection organisation. Here, too, things are moving much too sluggishly. Some of the equipment needs to be serviced regularly, but we can no longer do this because of the costs involved and our shortage of personnel.

Wednesday, 27 March 1991

Along with Federal Foreign Minister Genscher I visit the 17th Motorised Infantry Regiment in Halle. Genscher is pleased to be visiting the Bundeswehr in his hometown. He has detailed discussions with soldiers of all ranks. This regiment is being disbanded on 30 June. However, the atmosphere among the soldiers is good. They all know what they are going to do after the disbandment of the regiment. In his final talk Genscher praises the commitment and initiative of the soldiers in particular. After our return to Strausberg, talks in the headquarters about our work, with members of the Bundestag Defence Committee, who all express strong approval.

In the evening a talk in Berlin with a leading official of the *Treuhand*. The conversation leads me to feel optimistic: there is progress, he tells me, but this is often not recognised; the complicated sphere in which the *Treuhand* is operating cannot be compared with Western German conditions either professionally or in human terms. What has been achieved, he adds, can be seen only through comparison with the previous terrible conditions. My informant tells me there is no one in the *Treuhand* or in the government who can sell these successes to the public. 'We need a man like Ludwig Erhard, who, with his cigar, even under the difficult conditions of the time was the symbol of economic success.' He agrees with my practice of speaking to people more, and always being ready to talk. He says that we need to give more explanations over here than we were used to in the West.

Thursday, 28 March 1991

Weekly situation meeting. The social unrest spreading in the population is causing me concern. We have no idea how far it could spread to the troops. It would be disastrous if, in this still unstable situation, soldiers were to start demonstrating publicly – it could have considerable consequences. If that happens, we want to prevent an escalation and intend to intervene immediately. We are prepared to be present at the first demonstration: I shall be there too, if necessary. The responsible commanders must be contactable around the clock, helicopters must always be available. The servicemen must know that we are ready to face the challenge. It is a good thing I have been to almost all of the garrisons and have spoken to all of the commanders.

In the afternoon, a speech to U.S. officers in Berlin, followed by discussion. They show great interest in everything we are doing. Mutual sympathy; one feels among friends. The questions show that they find it difficult to imagine how we can co-operate with the former Communists. 'Can you really trust the NVA officers?' is a question which, with variations, is continually repeated. By giving details of experiences that individual NVA officers had been through in their lives, I make it clear that we must not generalise. Each of them has his own fate – some have been misused or allowed themselves to be misused, and have probably also used or exploited others. However, the changeover and the ensuing completely new experiences have not been without effect on them. In any case, shouldn't they, too, have the right to make mistakes? Are we their judges? Anyway, prejudice and hate are bad counsellors here. The people need hope and a new feeling of self-esteem.

News reaches us of the murder of Detlev Rohwedder, Chairman of the *Treuhand*. This shocks me very much. He was helping to create unity in a comparable situation to mine, although in another sphere. I had often talked with him. During a joint talk with the Federal President at a reception in Berlin, the President had said that we two had taken on some of the most difficult tasks. How can one protect oneself against this senseless terror? The security analyses and the grading of dangers are obviously wrong time and again. The question has to be asked: what consequences were drawn after the assassination of the banker Alfred Herrhausen? Was everything that was humanly possible done?

Chapter 13

THE RECONSTRUCTION

Monday, 15 April 1991

At Strausberg again, and a headquarters meeting. The following confusing situation has emerged: because the weapons of some 'disbanded' formations could not be handed over by the planned date, these formations have unexpectedly been kept in service by drafting in detachments of three to four hundred soldiers. This makes these units the same size as the previous formations. However, the enforcement of discipline can no longer be carried out officially, because those in charge of the disbanded formations have, logically, no power to enforce discipline. Such a situation has not been accounted for in our regulations and none of us has thought about it. In this matter we have caused the difficulties ourselves! Now an order must be given to rescind the disbandment of the formations, until the weapons have been handed over and the remaining personnel have been released.

The situation report also tells me that on 9 April an observation team from a Military Regional Command was shot at by Soviet sentries while observing an ammunition depot of the Soviet forces. Thank God no one was wounded. All the same, I order that the sequence of events be clarified and that a repetition be avoided.

Finally, I say an official farewell to Major-General von Scheven, my deputy, who initially had taken over 140 sections of the central formations, which were then gradually disbanded or placed under another command. Tomorrow he will be installed as the Commanding Officer of the Corps and Territorial Command East; most of the soldiers stationed in the five new Länder will then be under his command.

Tuesday, 16 April 1991

The hand-over of the Corps and Territorial Command East to Major-General von Scheven. This is an important date in the establishment of the armed forces in the part of Germany which has acceded, because with it we are taking another step along the road towards normality in the Bundeswehr, and towards the acceptance of responsibility by the individual services – army, air force and navy – for their units.

The servicemen parade in their dress uniforms – for the first time in the BKO region. The uniforms had to be collected from many different regions, because we did not succeed in supplying the units with service dress by the end of March. The three services are on parade in order to make clear, too, their separate tasks. It is a sight we are familiar with from the Western Bundeswehr. The ceremony passes off as usual and it seems to me that our guests, especially the representatives of the Soviet armed forces, are impressed by the smooth way everything goes.

Thursday, 18 April 1991

At midday, we leave for Basepol to inspect Soviet HIND combat helicopters, a previously feared Warsaw Pact weapon on which no expense was spared. The question is whether this armoured, major weapons system should be kept in service or not. A check on the running costs has shown that in any case the system is too expensive.

I have arranged for one of the pilots to show me the capabilities of the system on a test flight and I fly with him in the engineer's seat. The pilot has completed done well over 2,500 flying hours, is a passionate professional and is burning to show me what aerobatics his machine can perform. I am almost made sick by the turns, ascents and dives that the armoured and fearsome-looking giant helicopter carries out with impressive ease. Man and system seem to be perfectly attuned. Nevertheless, I have to disappoint the pilot by telling him that we will probably not take over this weapon.

Later, a visit to the Military Regional Command VIII. I am welcomed with the report that the first fully operational unit is ready: the newly-formed army music corps. They play lively marches. A sign for the future? In a short speech, the unit's difficulties are outlined, but possible solutions are also proposed. Where there is no solution yet, they hope to be given decisions in good time – a positive picture.

From 6 pm until 10 pm, dinner with officers and NCOs from East and West; we talk about the growing unity of the Bundeswehr. A pleasant, relaxed atmosphere. The former members of the NVA speak appreciatively of the frankness and comradeship of the officers and NCOs from the West. The beginnings of a change in consciousness are becoming evident. There is also discussion of the present situation on the housing estates, where both dismissed and serving personnel are living next to each other. Naturally, tension is being caused by the changes inside individuals and in society, but evidently things are not so serious as they are in Strausberg.

One of the officers describes to me, once again, the permanent state of readiness in the former NVA and the effects of this, which extended right into the families:

> We had to be always reachable on six days and evenings in the week. From the central alarm system the alarm was sounded in the corridors of our block of flats. Twenty minutes later we had to be in the barracks and two hours later ready to move off. The permanent state of readiness, and the possibility of frequent alarms made us seek ways to avoid the strict supervision. Our wives and children did not understand why their husbands and fathers could not leave home even at weekends, and could not even go on an outing.

As a result, another officer explains to me, they tried to rent small garden chalets or allotments, in order to give these as their place of residence. There were no telephones in these, so, when there was a practice alarm, checks on their readiness could not be carried out as often. Sometimes, he tells me, they only used the allotments as a pretext, in order to be able to devote themselves to their private lives for an hour or two. In spite of this they had regarded the permanent state of readiness as part of their profession and had accepted it because they were conscious of belonging to an elite.

Does it now mean that it was all in vain? The family members feel they have been deceived. All of their past efforts seem senseless and unnecessary, the future material security of their families is no longer assured, and their earlier elitist view of themselves has turned into the opposite. They feel particularly humiliated and exposed in society.

An officer recalls the total control to which they were subjected. They were frightened of listening to western broadcasts because they did not know whether their children might let the cat out of the bag outside the family. Some of them hung an array of lights in their windows – something I had noticed several times in the dark. This was intended to prevent people seeing from the outside if the television was still on; as GDR television closed down early they were given away if they were seen staring at the television until late at night. In August 1987 there was even an order from the Defence Ministry, transmitted to the units, that television sets must be sealed up to block the transmissions 'of the enemy on Channel 25.' 'The enemy' – that was the western television stations. This, too, was part of daily life.

Social life – as we understand it in the West – did not exist in the officer corps of the NVA. They did not invite each other to their

homes, if only for fear that those not invited might suspect 'the formation of groups outside the party.' In addition the badly sound-
proofed flats were small – usually with only three rooms.

Another officer complains:

> And as regards our so-called privileges, General, basically we could not
> make use of them. Take cars, for example. The commanders could, it's
> true, occasionally give preference in allocating restricted numbers of cars,
> against payment, for special merit. But even when some of us received a
> Trabi or Wartburg in this way, we could hardly ever drive them, because
> we always had to be at home owing to the state of readiness. So it was our
> wives who drove them around, not us. Things were wrong from top to
> bottom. But if I'm honest it is only now that I realise this.

I find it depressing that all the possible doubts were suppressed so
successfully for decades.

Finally, we discuss the extent to which the question of a possible
'civil war' between Germans had concerned the members of the
NVA. Once again, I receive the unanimous reply that this question
was never discussed because, according to the way the GDR state
viewed itself, this problem did not exist. The GDR regarded itself as
an independent German state, it had disavowed a common German
citizenship, and so a war between the two sovereign German states
had never been seen as a civil war. They are surprised when I tell
them that, as young officers in the 1960s, we had often discussed
these questions, and that the theme was repeatedly a subject of discussion in the Bundeswehr training colleges. The question of
whether Germans would shoot at Germans, and of how the NVA
would act in case of a Soviet attack against NATO had really concerned us time and again. Now I receive confirmation that the NVA
would not have failed to follow the Soviet Union. A war would not
have been a civil war, but a defensive war against capitalist imperialists. All the more pleasing is the general change of consciousness,
the wind of change, which shows itself on this evening. All of us –
from East and West – have learned something from one another.

Friday, 19 April 1991

Staff work. It is still unclear on which airfields we can concentrate
our seventy to eighty thousand motor vehicles. There are different
views between the services regarding later use, the possibility of disposal, environmental protection precautions and guard duties. The
discussions move to and fro.

At midday it is reported to me that at the Altengrabow ammunition depot, about eighty kilometres west of Berlin, German officers
outside the depot have been shot at by Soviet soldiers. A major has
been wounded. It is the second time within a few weeks that Soviet

soldiers have shot at a German officer. It was only in early April that a German soldier was wounded at the same place. At the time I gave appropriate orders regarding the necessary action to be taken, intending to avoid a repetition. Evidently they did not get through to those 'down below'. This makes the new incident even more dangerous with regard to possible political repercussions.

Saturday, 20 April 1991

Countless press reports and commentaries about the incident in Altengrabow. The speculations go as far as the suggestion by a news agency that the shooting incident will affect my future employment in the Federal Defence Ministry. So quickly and recklessly are reports put out, speculations made and people allegedly suspended.

A meeting is held in Strausberg to assess the situation. In the meantime the actual sequence of events has largely been cleared up. Three soldiers of a Military Regional Command, driving in a Wartburg with NVA numberplates, wanted to reconstruct on the spot, what had happened in the first incident. In doing so, they photographed the fence installations and warning signs at the troop training area and the ammunition depot, without the Soviet headquarters having been informed beforehand. The soldiers, in uniform, were clearly recognisable as members of the Bundeswehr and were outside the fence as they took the photographs. However, after a short challenge in Russian, live shots were fired at them after they had got back into their car and were ready to drive away along the public road. In the view of the Soviets view they had trespassed on to the out-of-bounds territory on the edge of the troop training area without authority, so the Soviet sentries had to make use of their firearms in accordance with their regulations.

Here, too, it has been shown that we still have much to clear up with the Soviets, including the question of how far the Soviet guard regulations and use of firearms conform with German law. What is more, there have been suggestions made that nuclear arms are being stored at Altengrabow, which would explain the quick use of firearms. Haven't the Soviets publicly announced the withdrawal of the nuclear weapons?

Sunday, 21 April 1991

I drive to Altengrabow to see the place where the incident happened. A small village on the edge of a large garrison. On the main street only Soviet soldiers can be seen. An unreal sight. From the main street two small roads branch off, which are closed to civilian traffic – a strange situation in the middle of Germany. Using a hand signal, a traffic sentry of the Soviet army blocks my entry to the road leading to the barracks, even though there are no signs indicating that the road is closed.

We are all wearing civilian clothes and are in my civilian official car. So we follow the instructions. The atmosphere is oppressive.

Afterwards, I visit the wounded major, a former NVA officer, in hospital. He tells me calmly and in a matter-of-fact way what happened and rejects any accusation that he had acted recklessly. He had not wanted to play silly games, as he knew well enough how the Soviets behaved at their ammunition depots, and which of their security regulations must be respected by Germans. He had not left the public road where he was when the shot hit him ... Whatever the details of the incident may have been, we – and also General Burlakov, the Soviet commander – have had good fortune among the misfortune: namely, that the shots did not lead to a fatality. After all the shots were aimed.

Monday, 22 April 1991

Breakfast in Bonn with the minister and General Klaus Naumann, Commanding General of I Corps, to discuss some questions which we will soon have to solve together. The Altengrabow case also plays a part; the incident shows Soviet nervousness. In the evening, a drive to Mainz, and a speech to students. The audience is interested, many questions are raised. The most-often repeated key question is: 'Is it really necessary that you try to reconstruct the Bundeswehr with former Communists? Why can't they all be dismissed?' Here an explanation is needed: we cannot achieve unity without these people. I try to bring this home to the students by giving individual examples.

Tuesday, 23 April 1991

In Berlin, I attend an event held to honour Bundeswehr sportsmen and women. The minister makes awards to servicemen who have recently won medals in international competitions. The BKO is represented by a large group. One of them, a captain, and a representative of the athletes, describes the preconditions for competing successfully in the 1992 Olympic Games. They hope for long-term prospects and the retention of their good training facilities; their goal is to take part in international competitions. The self-confidence of the sportsmen is unbroken – nothing succeeds like success.

This evening I hold a meeting in headquarters together with General Foertsch about the consequences of Altengrabow. We decide to raise the incident with the Soviets and to condemn unequivocally the use of firearms. Although we have no wish to harm our newly established relations with the Soviets, we must make our position very clear.

Wednesday, 24 April 1991

I attend a reception for the President of Chile in Berlin. For the first time, a Bundeswehr guard of honour is drawn up in the park of

Bellevue Palace, the official Berlin residence of the Federal President. It is a special event for all who take part in it. Foreign Minister Genscher, in a conversation with me, stresses the special achievements of the Bundeswehr in support of the Allies in the Gulf War and in the reconstruction of the BKO.

The same day I appear before a meeting of the Bundestag Defence Committee concerning 'Altengrabow', which hopefully will now find a political solution. The clear condemnation by all political parties of the use of firearms, is causing the Soviets to soften their attitude. They evidently realise that there is no understanding in Germany of this incident. Further co-operation and clear agreements with the Western Group of the Soviet Armed Forces are intended to help to avoid a repetition. However, the incident still needs further clarification and must make us pay even more attention to the difficulties involved in the Soviet withdrawal.

Thursday, 25 April 1991

A meeting is held with the service chiefs. For the first time we have more discussion about practical routine military work than about the social welfare problems of the servicemen, pay, leave arrangements and exemption from service – some 'progress' at least! We concentrate on training, the collecting together of arms and ammunition, and personnel selection. We are progressing towards a state of normality and we note with relief that conditions are becoming more and more manageable.

In the evening, I attend a dinner in Bellevue Palace in honour of Queen Beatrix of the Netherlands. The Dutch queen and her consort, to whom we are presented, also show a lively interest in the process of unification and the changes in the military sphere.

Friday, 26 April 1991

A visit to the Western Group of the Soviet Forces, with Federal Minister Stoltenberg and Parliamentary Secretary Wimmer. The Chief of Staff of the Western Group, Lieutenant-General Kuznetsov, had signalled this afternoon, via Reuters news agency, a slight relaxation of tension in the 'Altengrabow' case. He expressed human understanding for those involved, even though they had earlier they had been brazenly declared guilty.

The welcome with military ceremonial is carried out according to protocol and in a disciplined fashion. The same young faces as those in Moscow in 1988. The army wants to show itself here intact and proud, in spite of all the political problems and doubts. The German national anthem is played solemnly by the Soviet military band – in front of the German Defence Minister. It is not only me who is moved.

Colonel-General Burlakov is approachable, polite but at first obviously tense. It is of importance to the Soviets that, in spite of the incident in Altengrabow, the federal minister has come. The delegation discussions take place in an open atmosphere and all important points are raised. A particular concern of Burlakov makes us Germans very pensive. He rightly complains that, more and more frequently, skinheads and other violent young people are attacking Soviet citizens, soldiers as well as their families, even including children and civilian personnel. Burlakov states that he will now improve security on the housing estates and will restrict freedom to go outside. He says that although it is only minorities that are becoming violent towards the Soviets, they are arousing considerable fear and are seen as threatening.

There have also been attacks on sentries which have already caused fatalities, he adds. Moreover, Soviet soldiers are being encouraged to sell weapons. The German police are, he says, not yet able to function, and rarely take action; but an over-reaction by Soviet soldiers to the actions of a few Germans must be prevented.

After the delegation talks the Soviets give an example of their famous hospitality with an opulent meal. The atmosphere is obviously relaxed. During the walkabout that follows, we are shown the large dormitories where everything is clean and tidy. One notices that things have been arranged, everything seems prepared. Next to a Russian television in the common room stands a Japanese video recorder which is worth a fortune in Soviet terms. The soldiers are wearing brand new uniforms; on some of the field uniforms one can in still see the folds caused by storing them in cartons. Combat firing practice, training, it all goes like clockwork. The officers say again and again that this is 'normal' training routine, this is a thoroughly 'normal' barracks with quite normal 'equipment' which includes a well-stocked shop. Only when answering detailed questions do they admit that, while in Germany things are fairly good, the supply situation at home is hopeless. A question about the tense personal situation of their troops is dismissed – everything is in order, they tell us.

At a press conference the intention of both sides to solve common tasks is strongly underlined. The Altengrabow case is to be cleared up by the joint German-Soviet commission and the necessary consequences drawn. In answer to a journalist's question, Burlakov states that in his area of responsibility there are no more nuclear weapons. From this statement, all those present take it that there are no longer any nuclear weapons at all in the five new Länder. How surprised we are when the Soviet Foreign Minister later announces that there are still nuclear weapons in Germany, although not under Burlakov's control – are they in Altengrabow after all?

After the press conference a concert is held in the great hall, with a choir and orchestra alternating. Russian songs are sung, Russian melodies played, but Glen Miller is also given his due. Russian soul, American heart, German feeling. Afterwards there is a lavish dinner, again in a relaxed atmosphere. The federal minister invites Burlakov to attend the disbandment of the BKO on 1 July. This visit has created the preconditions which will enable us to represent our interests with friendly firmness and to assist the Soviet withdrawal in word and deed.

Chapter 14

THE FEDERAL PRESIDENT
VISITS THE
EASTERN HEADQUARTERS

Monday, 29 April 1991

Arrival at Berlin's Schönefeld airport of the Federal President who, from the start, has shown great interest in our work and has twice invited me for detailed talks. So we are all the more pleased by his visit. Initially, the difficult weather conditions do not allow us to fly to the former NVA air force command centre in Fürstenwalde, southeast of Berlin, so at the airport I inform the Federal President and his party of the situation in the BKO region. Richard von Weizsäcker listens very attentively.

We land in Fürstenwalde about half an hour late, to a welcome from an air force guard-of-honour, and then visit the air force command centre. Here, we are able to show, on the spot, the close co-operation between former NVA officers and Bundeswehr officers in maintaining our air sovereignty over eastern Germany. The commanding officers of the army, air force and navy in our region report on the situation in their services. Reports by unit commanders show – at last – not only difficulties, but also signs of normalisation. Thanks to the commitment of personnel from the West, to sensitivity and close co-operation we have taken important steps on the way to our new armed forces. This co-operation is also becoming evident at work.

Afterwards, visit to the engineers at Storkow, near Fürstenwalde. We watch basic training in a relaxed atmosphere. At lunch in the open air, talks are held with officers from East and West. They seem confident that they will master their tasks. The recruits are happy to give information and are completely relaxed. I am impressed by the changes: in November I received very few answers from the then conscripts, and was met with great reserve and insecurity. Now, however, it is all different: the new intake of recruits has a positive and self-confident attitude towards the future. In that respect the proximity of Berlin has an important function. The staff sergeants and company sergeant majors explain to the Federal President the difficulties encountered in the transition from the former NVA to the varied and extended scope of duties and responsibilities in the Bundeswehr. They, too, seem to be tackling their tasks and to be learning from each other. Progress in the BKO is becoming evident.

Afterwards, flight to Potsdam, where the Federal President takes part in a conference of commanders from the Corps and Territorial Command. I had asked him to speak to the commanders and had proposed that two commanders should speak about their experiences: a divisional commander from the West, who took over his duties on 3 October, and a former divisional commander of the NVA, who was removed from his post on 2 October and now serves as a staff officer in the Bundeswehr. Because of the fundamental importance of these speeches extracts from them are reproduced below – first that of Lieutenant-Colonel Panian, now a staff officer and deputy commander of the Military Regional Command in Halle. Lieutenant-Colonel Panian was formerly, as a colonel, commander of the 11th Motorised Infantry Division in Halle:

The growing together of the German armed forces as seen by an officer of the former NVA

Mr Federal President! Gentlemen!
I have spoken once before in this room. It was 1982, I was a young regimental commander, and had to answer charges alleging 'breaches of Socialist relations' in my regiment. Today I speak as an officer of the Bundeswehr and to you, Mr Federal President, about the growing together of the armed forces as seen by the former NVA. Admittedly the comparison here is not appropriate, so very different are the subjects, but the uneasiness felt by the speaker is the same.

Since 3 October 1990 nothing is as it was. Anyone present who has ever seen the panoramic painting of the Peasants' War on the Schlachtberg in Bad Frankenhausen, which was a battlefield, can perhaps understand the following comparison. In one place, above a hill – at the foot of which the battle has ended – the message of peace is being brought by a symbolic figure, a mercenary *Landsknecht*. Behind the soldiers the world is shown still as flat but within a blue sphere. The sphere has been ripped open. The *Landsknecht* – the point of his sword has been broken off – is terrified and has clapped his hands over his ears.

That, or something similar, is how I would describe the situation of the officers of the former NVA around 3 October 1990. Their picture of the world had been torn apart, they were sick of the agitation and propaganda of a party army which they thought they had already escaped from by the spring of 1990.

Until 3 October the officers' feelings were subjected to many alternately hot and cold baths. We really experienced everything possible: from the theory – greeted with great applause and hope – of the continued functioning of the NVA within the framework of a temporary, but fairly long, parallel existence of both German armed forces, to the leadership vacuum and the loss of time in preparing for unification which was associated with it. As armed forces we had been defeated in peacetime, and that hit hard. The future was uncertain.

In any case one had difficulty in explaining things, within the family, to friends, and in public. Looking at the political events as we see them today, we have become – perhaps thanks to a historic chance – one state with united armed forces.

What expectations – for some, fears too – were there before the arrival of the generals, officers and NCOs of the Bundeswehr? Didn't we think that we knew everything about them? We had learned by heart the military structures and their formations down to the smallest detail. 'Keep the enemy clearly in view' was a motto which told us to study his operational principles exactly. About the actual people we knew little. Through meetings within the framework of the liaison groups between the Bundeswehr and the NVA, 'ordered from above', we had started to become pensive, perhaps just in time. Nothing more!

Never were so many questions posed at the commanders' meetings as in September 1990. These questions were, above all, a sign of the insecurity about what the *Wessis* intended. (...) Would the officers of the Bundeswehr accept us, ninety-five per cent of whom were members of the SED, imbued with the Soviet doctrine of being ready to rebuff imperialist aggression at any time and, until well into the 1980, to inflict an annihilating defeat on the aggressor on his own territory? Would they come as victors and feel themselves to be such, would they know everything better than we did and want to be constantly putting us right? The first impressions, and the whole of the past half year, have not confirmed the fears of the members of the former NVA. In spite of differing experiences, one can rightly say this. From the first minutes of our joint contacts objectivity, tolerance, frankness and polite manners were particularly noticeable. As for many of the former NVA officers, their absolute reserve in conversation, a wait-and-see attitude on the one hand and an exaggerated attention to duty on the other, had an effect which tended to be displeasing rather than helpful in creating the good working climate which was needed.

However, it was not only human values, but also the different views on how to lead people which stood out. In addition, there was professional competence and precision in daily work. And whether they were officers or NCOs they could, and did, listen. For me, as a former commanding officer, it was really surprising to see how quickly the servicemen from the West became attuned to the sensitivities of their new 'co-comrades' from the East and, above all, saw the weak points in their new environment and helped to change them.

Up until now, as far as I know, at such highly official events as today's, the servicemen from the West have been thanked for their work in the new Länder only by Western superiors. So, put simply, I am taking the liberty to do so, for once, as a member of the former NVA. If the servicemen had not been as we have experienced them, the Bundeswehr could not have set a good example in the all-German unification process.

There were two important concepts which we in the NVA did not know and which really – admittedly along with many other criteria – made the difference between the two armed forces. In this, the Western servicemen set us an example daily. I refer to *Innere Führung,* leadership through missions and mission tactics. It was precisely the concept of leadership, so important in *Innere Führung,* which was, after all, not a little strained under NVA conditions. It was a form of troop leadership in which the individual person had to serve Socialist construction in the Socialist collective. The function of protecting against outside attack was particularly important in that context. Here, we saw our place in society, acted in good faith and were honestly pleased with our results. Leadership then, as we experience it today, as a concept of humankind from Article 1 of the Basic Law, in which the dignity of humankind is the supreme precept, differs from our previous experience in that the state exists for the people and not the other way round.

Some of you will comment that I am talking as though I already understand everything. Quite wrong, there is still a long distance between realisation and action. I have observed excellent examples, which can be built on, particularly a caring attitude. Up to now the growing together of the armed forces has, in the main, been marked by success, for example through the high proportion of personnel who have been taken over, which went along with a reduction in their fear of contact; and also the increasingly common sight of empty barracks because the removal of materiel and equipment has now got under way. The situation which has been reached is the result of joint work, to which the former members of the NVA made a substantial contribution. This readiness can be further built upon. But there have also been times of insecurity and setbacks. Let me say something about these.

Here I do not want to put material and social-welfare matters in the foreground. Even in view of all the differences that still exist and which we officers of the former NVA – assuming the quality of our work is the same – feel to be an injustice, we have no reason to make undue demands at an inappropriate time. This is particularly evident when we draw comparisons with civilian life. To understand correctly, it is necessary to go into the problems of coming to terms with the past. In my view, the great extent of these problems, and the personal tragedies which are in some cases linked with them, are the root cause of the insecurity and setbacks as seen by the officers of the former NVA.

What sort of situation were we in or are we still in? The overwhelming majority of us believed that we were fighting for the good cause of Socialism. One need not be ashamed of that. It is now becoming clear to each of us individually, and not in some didactically pre-determined way: the ideal of humankind we learned is false, we had devoted ourselves to the goals of a leadership which was not serving humanity. And anyone who is trying to be honest with himself must consider whether he bears personal guilt. Only a person who believes himself not to be affected can deal with the burdens of the recent past more freely, cautiously and, with that, more reliably. One often has the impression that many of us are still suppressing this – just as it is evident all round that the attitude of people today is directed towards leaving the past behind. And with this it also becomes clear that this is the root of an often overdone sensitiveness.

I am of the firm conviction that one can identify with the free basic constitutional order – and particularly its concept of humankind – only if one can work through to the realisation that one has served a system that was, in part, criminal. That is personally very painful because it is often accompanied by the break-up of one's previous circle of friends. And this does not take place without conflict, as anonymous phone calls and letters prove.

Mr Federal President, you once said: 'One cannot overcome the past, one can only accept it.' And together we should do just that. Anyone has decided to serve in the Bundeswehr can do so only by looking to the future. The only measure for assessing the individual will be his overall democratic attitude at this time, which is not an easy period for us. Collective explanations of former actions should no longer be accepted as valid. The two parts which are growing together are called upon to cooperate in coping with the psychological situation of the people in the new Länder, including, above all, the former professional cadres of the NVA.

Inside of us there still lurks the readiness to conform and do as the others do, stemming from forty years' training (and some in this hall will think that in this speech I am conforming once again). People can only exist when they have self-confidence. More than ninety per cent of the 'reconstruction helpers', who have come from the West to the East of Germany, show us this daily in a convincing manner.

As an officer of the former NVA one is not used to adjusting to greater amounts of information and freedom in discussion. But this can be learned, because those we are talking with are different. And examples show that it must be possible to achieve self-confidence through training, and by having more contact with servicemen from the Western Bundeswehr. Thus, we can only hope that the dialogue will be continued on a broad front. And it is all one, whether this happens during a course, during training at one's workplace or during practical instruction of the troops. But the dialogue must not be too short! (...)

It has been said at length and often that a real integration of the armed forces can only come about if there are not only officers from the West serving in the East but if, vice versa, officers of the former NVA serve in the West. It remains to be hoped that this will soon happen and that the first instances of it are copied. The same applies to the language we use. Certainly, 'Western Bundeswehr' and 'Eastern Bundeswehr' do not sound good, but how else can one make clear the differences which still exist? So let us have some patience and then 'the Bundeswehr' will become accepted by all. The same applies also to the word *Kamerad*, which we Eastern servicemen still use very sparingly.

The Minister of Defence declared at the commanding officers' conference that in times when the situation is unclear it is comradeship, above all, which must prove itself. Many servicemen of the former NVA have already felt this comradeship, and vice versa. It is a guarantee that we shall fulfil our joint mission.

There follow extracts from the speech by Brigadier Kirchbach, who from 3 October 1990 was commanding officer of the 9th Armoured Division in Eggesin, and since 1 April 1991 has been commanding officer of the newly formed 41st Territorial Brigade in Eggesin:

The growing together of the German armed forces as seen by an officer from the old Länder

With this report I do not want to offer any scientific thesis and I am not relying on opinion polls or definite knowledge. My aim is to describe and assess personal experiences during the past seven months and from these to derive proposals for the process of the growing together of the armed forces of our Federal Republic of Germany. (...)

My knowledge of the members of the former Nationale Volksarmee was very limited. Certainly, we had heard a lot about the NVA: it was not an army of the people but a party army; ninety-nine per cent of the officers were members of the SED; the activity of political officers as a separate organisation within the armed forces; the activity of the Ministry for State Security within the armed forces; armed forces with a clear picture of the enemy; we ourselves a part of this picture of the enemy; military effectiveness on large manoeuvres to be seen now and again on television; the disciplined impression on parade.

All of this we knew, or thought we knew. We had heard of the poor structural condition of the military installations and of the high degree of combat readiness. Only in November 1989 did the picture begin to become a bit more concrete. The silence between the men serving in the two armed forces was replaced by the first, very cautious dialogue. During a leave trip to Dresden in May 1990, I myself got as far as the deputy commander of the 7th Armoured Division and made initial contact. During those talks I invited some young soldiers to Koblenz. That visit took place in September 1990. In the same month young officers from my brigade travelled to Dresden.

I was able to give a lecture to the staff officers of the 7th Armoured Division on the theme of *Innere Führung*, and I had discussions with the commander and his deputies until late at night. The predominant atmosphere was of scepticism. In answer to the question, posed after my lecture, of whether I would trust NVA officers to co-operate in restructuring common armed forces, I said I could not assess that. But I was convinced that we must make the attempt, and I found out, particularly among the young soldiers, how quickly the lack of dialogue could be overcome.

An experience concerning the second lieutenants from Dresden will end this short introduction. During an evening barbecue I was asked, as I was talking to the young Dresden officers, if someone could photograph me. I was surprised by the question and naturally agreed. 'I need this photo,' one of the young officers explained to me, 'to prove back home that in the West second lieutenants can speak and discuss things normally and intensively with the brigade commander, who holds the rank of colonel, on a comradely basis.' Insecurity, tension, scepticism and determination to conduct a dialogue, that is how I can sum up the atmosphere in which, on 3 October, the day of unification, I began my duties in Eggesin. (...)

My first impressions were contradictory. I notice soldiers who are obviously feeling uneasy about wearing the new uniform, I notice looks that avoid mine, I see scenes of surprising lack of discipline, I see quarters not fit for human beings.

Within a few days the impressions become clearer, but even more contradictory. Some soldiers are very open towards me, telling me about the confusing experiences of the past year, others hardly let themselves be spoken to. This is my first visit to the headquarters company and it takes a long time before the soldiers are ready to open up. I see NCOs who, lacking obvious initiative of their own, are awaiting what is coming to them in a state of extreme lethargy, and others who are immediately ready to plunge into a new task with great energy. In others I sense shame at the sight of the wretched armed forces, and muted pride at past military achievements.

I see excellently maintained materiel, but in many of the soldiers' quarters there are simple stools, broken fittings, wretched sanitary installations and kitchens which do not deserve the name. I come across locked and sealed offices and an almost absurd system for keeping trivial things secret. (...)

I discover an alarm system through which the NVA could be alerted – right down to the housing estates – from a central point or, ultimately, from Moscow. Like an engine left idling, it is still being tested until I order it to be switched off. I hear about the requirement for the eighty-five per cent state of readiness, which was kept in force for many years and which kept the soldiers away from their families for many weeks or even months.

I see soldiers who work into the night with great energy and drive to be able to meet requests for equipment for the Gulf War. And in contrast, I experience a training company which, on the day the recruits arrive, is left by the commander at 5 pm. I see soldiers who, in the evenings after duty, drink large quantities of alcohol sitting in their Trabis, because it is forbidden to serve alcohol in the barracks. First impressions, confusing impressions.

The first months are marked by insecurity. In times of insecurity rumours arise. They spring up more quickly than they can be countered through explanatory information. There is scepticism about the prospects of being taken on as temporary soldiers for two years – will it really happen? They would like to believe the promises of a fair chance, but really they do not. Clumsiness in personnel management contributes to the creation of rumours. How many servicemen will be taken on? When will decisions be made? Euphoria when the word goes round that far more soldiers will be taken on for two years than will finally be required; deep depression when a plan for the posts in the territorial brigade circulates, and they try to find themselves a place in this plan. The documents which come from the ministry departments dealing with different weapon types are not co-ordinated with each other and in the end are pointless; this only makes the insecurity worse. (...)

Discussions in my bungalow – Western officers, Eastern officers, regimental commanders, battalion commanders, company chiefs, with constantly changing participants. Free discussion about the past and the future. Openly expressed ideas about their own work, but also critical questions to me or to all of us who come from the West. Officers report back from courses and training in units in the West. Groups of soldiers experience the German Bundestag and democratic disputes. They see quarters and the military infrastructure in the West and experience the type of leadership practised there. As a rule I hear enthusiastic comments.

We receive the first dishwasher. I had never thought one could be so pleased about it. In the barracks building maintenance is beginning. Sanitary installations are being improved, barrack rooms wallpapered, stools being replaced with chairs. It is obvious that something is being done. This has an effect on the atmosphere. The first applications to be taken on have been approved. I proposed that the environmental protection group, which works untiringly and in an exemplary fashion, be taken over immediately. Only a few people were able, at least at first, to understand this but, as the approvals come in, the signal is understood. Around Christmas many more officers and NCOs are taken on. The word gets round that nearly all NCOs can expect to be taken on for two years. Slowly, hope is arising out of resignation. (...) I look self-critically at myself. My own attitude towards people is changing. I am more and more aware that I have an unlimited amount to learn. We must know how things used to be and we must talk about it. Only in that way can one understand, and only from understanding can trust grow. (...)

There are bitter setbacks. A young recruit is maltreated by older comrades when he does not want to carry out orders to clean a corridor. I hear of 'games' which are played by older soldiers with younger ones (...) Discussions are held with recruits who have been to the West for basic training. Many soldiers are enthusiastic, but some say they felt to be second-class soldiers and were, as *Ossis*, treated as such. Certainly, these were exceptions, but they really should not happen. Some soldiers are reduced in rank twice within six months. A major finds that he has become a lieutenant. I can understand his feeling of depression even though the reasons for what has been done are objectively understandable.

A weapon is missing. It has been stolen. With incredible recklessness some soldiers, led by an officer, left their weapons in the corridor and went to their barrack rooms, as the sergeant armourer was not immediately available. On the same day thirty soldiers from this block were dismissed. We experience short-stay visitors who, after looking round for two hours, believe that they then understand everything that must be done here, and how and why. We call them *Besser Wessis* and all of us are beginning to dislike this category of people. We find them in the civilian sphere, but sadly also in the military one.

I am fed up with slumming tourists. I no longer want to hear about how awful everything is, and I explain again and again that we are all pulling together to improve conditions, that there are successes and that things are moving. I have had enough of all those visitors who come only to confirm their own prejudices and show no strong interest. We are nowhere near our goal. The crippling lethargy has by no means been overcome in everyone. If this does not change we shall probably have to dismiss people as unsuitable after two years' service. A television programme creates a stir. Bundeswehr servicemen speak critically and in a whining way about their imminent service in Turkey. Some conscripts and also some of the short-service soldiers are refusing to do service. I am asked in a critical tone whether fear is a reason for conscientious objection. We are being seen in a more sceptical light. In the West, too, not everything that glitters is gold. (...)

We need dialogue. It must be continued intensively. We must not evade the past. We must come to terms with it, and do so together. We must place our hopes in a process of re-thinking and must leave time for that. Everyone has information which they did not have before, everyone has people to talk to whom they did not have before and everyone has freedoms they did not have before. Everyone will emerge changed from this process different from when he went into it – we too. The way to a new view of the world can be found, but it needs time. We have this time. We must maintain good comradeship; within the same ranks as well as right through the ranks. Every soldier from the West who is doing duty here should leave after two or three years with the feeling that he is leaving good comrades and friends behind. (…) We must not damn the proven professional ability of the former NVA. We must build upon it. Professional ability and the readiness to achieve achievement can be brought from the former NVA into the German armed forces as a positive inheritance. We must rely on open information and make opportunities available for people to experience the democratic process in Bonn, or elsewhere. We must help to sow the seeds of a new understanding of leadership not only in heads, but also in hearts. We must adjust ourselves to longer time-scales. In a ten-thousand metres race we have run the first hundred metres in a good time. Now persistence and staying power are needed. (…)

We have started on the road to common German armed forces. We have all realised that this goal can only be reached together. But confidence has grown that this task can, and will, be accomplished. Extra effort will be required from all of us for a long time, no matter where we come from. The goal does make the effort worthwhile. Not all salvation lies in the West. If we reconstruct the new armed forces together there is perhaps also a chance of correcting wrong developments, such as a whining attitude and bureaucratisation, and to prevent them from ever appearing in this part of our country. We shall overcome the gulf and we are in the process of creating a small piece of unity ourselves, not primarily in organisation, but a unity of people in action, in understanding and in trust. In this way we can help others to orientate themselves.

After these speeches the Federal President gives his assessment of the situation and expresses his appreciation of what we have achieved:

Gentlemen,
In recent months I have visited the five new Länder and have informed myself on the spot about the current situation. This is now my first visit to the Bundeswehr in the East of Germany. A day full of experiences and strong impressions lies behind me. To meet, here in Potsdam, servicemen of the German armed forces who are serving peace, moves me deeply. It was here in 1938, as an eighteen-year-old, that I joined the 9th Infantry Regiment to fulfil my duty as a conscript, and only a year later I was sent with my comrades into a war whose end was followed by the division of Germany and Europe. Hopes of peace and freedom were, in those days, distant and unfounded. We can be all the more thankful today for a free Europe, which is growing together in peace, with a united Germany in the centre of it. It is at one and the same time an expression and a result of the détente and disarmament which all of us have sought.

In this historic phase you have the responsibility, as military superiors, for a great and difficult task. Since the day of German unification we have had an all-German Bundeswehr based on our tested defence constitution. The time for preparation of this was extremely short; the formation in practice is nowhere near finished. But I have been convinced today that a good stretch of the road already lies behind you and that you are travelling in the right direction.

For me, it is a matter of course that servicemen of the former NVA have been given the chance to take part in this task. This accords with the idea of unity. But, it also means that previous potential adversaries are now taking responsibility for the joint cause. That is certainly not easy – for either side. After decades of separation and rigid confrontation, servicemen with completely different education and training backgrounds are finding their way from opposing each other to working together, are overcoming deep-seated reservations and are instead developing a firm feeling of togetherness.

The servicemen of the former NVA were trained in the spirit of class war and the 'concept of the enemy' of wretched memory. For them, the meaning of their profession is now revealing itself in a completely different context. The peaceful revolution in the GDR could not leave it untouched. For many it will have been very welcome, for among them were hearts and heads which in reality were concerned with freedom and its responsible defence. Now it is necessary to rethink further. Material worries are an additional problem. Because where, yesterday, there were secure livelihoods and good career prospects, today there are often anxious questions about the future course of one's own life. The overall opportunity for a new start in the East of Germany at first brought, for many individuals, a drastic change and an uncertain future. In the end each individual must personally come to terms with these difficulties. But all of those who bear responsibility are called upon to help with all their strength.

The psychological starting-point for the servicemen from the 'old Bundeswehr', who have taken over this responsibility here, is also not easy. They are the representatives of a social and value system which is now binding for all. They are moving within Germany but in many ways they are entering new territory. At the same time they are being required to change some of their attitudes towards the servicemen of the former GDR and to get rid of prejudices.

The difficult tasks – of that I have convinced myself today – are being fulfilled remarkably well. The servicemen of the Bundeswehr have been giving an example of German unity from the first day onwards. The former opponent is recognised as a fellow human being and accepted as a partner. Separation from each other for ideological reasons is increasingly a thing of the past. Instead of that, open-mindedness, willingness to learn and readiness to co-operate are in the forefront, but above all there is the rediscovery of the simple fact that we are all Germans. The challenges are being accepted and mastered together. This demands, from both sides, a high sense of duty and a strong commitment.

The Bundeswehr's contribution so far to the growing together of united Germany deserves the respect and recognition of all of us. You are taking part, with a particularly high degree of responsibility, in the dynamic process of social change, the course of which cannot yet be fully foreseen by anyone. For that I thank you. In scarcely any other sphere are the end of the Cold War and the opening to the East, more clearly visible than in the armed forces.

But I would like to strongly encourage you not to let up in your efforts. In the process of German unification we are only at the start of the common path. For the tasks lying before us we continue to need much patience and sensitivity. The division of Germany did not only leave its traces in the appearance of the cities and countryside, but it also marked the thinking and feeling of the people in both parts of Germany. Because of this no one should be asked too much. What are important in the togetherness of the citizens in East and West are personal experience, mutual understanding and the willingness to regard united Germany as the common homeland. Along with co-operation, trust is also growing.

Decades with no freedom to make political decisions, and with the suppression of personal initiative, are a poor initial precondition for gaining trust in the advantages of a balance of interests, based on pluralism in a free society. Competition is a dominant characteristic of a democratic order of society. The feeling of perhaps not being able to cope with that creates fears and doubts. If then, in the difficult transitional phase, the economic and social problems of daily life become dominant, the values of freedom and of a state based on law threaten to lose something of their attraction.

We have to meet this danger with energy and single-mindedness. For this two things are needed: firstly, social conditions in the Eastern Länder must be brought to the Western level as soon as possible. Secondly, we must practise the value system of our basic social order in word and deed. Not theoretical wisdom, but practical experience and good examples are decisive here.

Here the Bundeswehr also has an important role. The leadership and training of its servicemen are guided by the principles of *Innere Führung* and the model of the citizen in uniform. They mirror the essential political, ethical and legal foundations of our social order. Through that the serviceman experiences the value of this order, not as an abstract theory, but concretely during his daily duties. He knows what he is defending. This gives him the inner readiness to take on his duties as a serviceman and citizen. The tested principles of leadership in the Bundeswehr are certainly being understood and accepted by the servicemen in the five Länder, who until now had been used to another form of military training. The difficulties in adjusting should not cloud our view of the whole. Thanks to their internal structure the armed forces have an effect far beyond their own sphere. Indeed, they are helping to increase awareness of examples of freedom and democracy in the society around them. The unity of the forces is furthering the unity of the Germans.

The task of the leadership and the servicemen of the Bundeswehr is not, primarily, one of security policy or strategy, but is above all a human one. As in no other section of our society, human destinies are encountering each other in the armed forces drawn from East and West. I am highly impressed by the great sensitivity with which the commanding officer of the Bundeswehr-Kommando Ost and his staff have faced this challenge from the first day. They are doing all of us in Germany an irreplaceable service.

On this road the meaning and mission of the German armed forces are once more becoming clear: the Bundeswehr serviceman serves the law and the ethos of our constitutional system. He needs neither a concept of an enemy nor an ideology. And the impulse of class warfare to create hatred is foreign to him. His service is directed solely to the defence of the fundamentals and goals of our constitution and international law. In that he is a citizen among citizens.

Tuesday 30 April 1991

Press reactions to the visit of the Federal President are positive. It is becoming clear that part of our work is behind us and that the Eastern Bundeswehr is emerging. I am confident it will also be accepted by the population in the five new Länder.

At midday I learn that a young Soviet sentry has been murdered by unknown persons. Just what has happened is unclear and the Brandenburg police are investigating. After thinking it over briefly, I phone Colonel-General Burlakov on my direct line and express my sympathy to him that a Soviet citizen, as a soldier in Germany, has been killed in a time of complete peace. I just want to express my dismay from commander to commander. Burlakov is evidently surprised at my call, but he treats it with great seriousness. We both hope that the murderer will soon be found. An hour later I receive an indication that there is suspicion the soldier was killed by his own comrades. The crime must have been committed inside the barracks. All the same, I am pleased that I telephoned Burlakov and thus to have made a human gesture.

Together with the Chairman of the Bundestag Defence Committee, Fritz Wittmann, I visit a unit which is being disbanded. Here the difficulties of disbandment are clearly explained. A rear party of four-hundred soldiers is remains because they have not been able to hand over the tanks, and do not know where to move the ammunition. The officers are overcome by lethargy, they know that some of them will have to leave the service. Here vigorous leadership is needed, as well as more support from the West.

In the evening from 6.30 pm I receive the situation report. Positive results. The removal and collecting together of materiel are causing us the main difficulties.

Friday, 3 May 1991

In the evening in Potsdam, I inform the Chairman of the Social Democratic Party, Hans-Jochen Vogel, about our task. He and those with him are particularly interested in our activities and they express appreciation for what has been achieved so far.

Chapter 15

VISIBLE PROGRESS

Monday, 6 May 1991

Visit to an engineer battalion. On the way, we drive through the Havelland, the land of Theodor Fontane. Tree-lined avenues, willows, fields – a flat countryside. In the villages, everything looks weather-beaten. The houses are neglected and grey. Still, it is marvellous to be able to drive through this countryside again – on the track of Herr von Ribbeck, of Ribbeck in the Havelland, a character in one of Fontane's poems. In this battalion the atmosphere and results are poor. There seems to be something rotten in this unit, the selection of personnel must be improved.

On the other hand, in an armoured infantry battalion not far away there is a good atmosphere, in spite of the difficult situation. The commander has authority, has volunteered for the post and is staying in the East long-term. He identifies himself with the task and knows that he can master it through personal commitment and with the support of his officers. Personal commitment and strength of conviction on the part of the commanders, determine the results and atmosphere in the units more than the actual general conditions.

In Magdeburg, dinner with the Military Regional Commander, Colonel von Wagner, the Premier of Saxony-Anhalt, Professor Werner Münch, and the senior official of the Magdeburg administrative region. We sit in a small flat in a pre-fabricated block and hear the neighbours' voices which penetrate the thin walls. However, we quite forget where we are, because we are so concerned with the questions with which we have been faced so quickly. How do we complete unification among the people? Once again, I learn of the difficulties in finding suitable personnel in the administrative sphere, who are qualified but politically untainted. That cannot be done solely through 'western imports'. If we want to create trust, we must take on people from the East, even if they lack experience. However, problems are arising, so I am told, because yesterday's officials are still holding important offices after the political changeover.

I remember the case of a former SED legal adviser who in the meantime has become head of a town's employment office. In the mornings, I have heard, he goes through the waiting rooms of the job centre and taunts the unemployed: 'You all wanted this. Now you've got your tropical fruit and for that you've become unemployed.' That such cynicism increases anger and bitterness is easily imagined. In selecting personnel for the administrative authorities and offices, the lack of expertise is probably easier to accept, than the employment of the old cadres. An untainted political past is worth more here than a professional qualification, however high. An area administrative official told me that, after being elected, he had initially taken over all the existing personnel, but had quickly decided to replace all the senior staff with politically clean citizens. Although there had been a fall in efficiency, this had been offset by trust among the population, and in that fact he had seen proof that his decision had been right. Another area administrative official, on the other hand, has kept on the old 'cadres' and, together with eight newcomers, has taken over his office with a staff of 240. From the population's point of view, nothing has altered: there are still the same faces and the same behaviour – no noticeable change.

In Magdeburg I have to overnight in a hotel as there are no barracks quarters available. The hotel, which was formerly run by the SED, is outrageously expensive and the service is miserable. The employees give the impression that they are issuing food and beer on ration cards, and they treat the guests in an unfriendly and condescending way. A strange concept of hospitality and service! I hope that our pointed remarks have contributed to improving matters there.

Tuesday, 7 May 1991

Briefing at the Military Regional Headquarters in Magdeburg. Here, too, things are moving ahead and the strong commitment of the commanding officer once again confirms that personal commitment alone is the precondition for all further successes. The same can be seen at an engineer battalion that I visit afterwards. The commander is going to stay for three or four years, the recruits and training personnel make an excellent impression; the Western support groups are giving extraordinarily effective assistance.

I take the company commander, a former NVA officer, to one side and ask him whether he does not feel bossed around by the

Western support groups. This captain looks at me with surprise: 'General,' he admits to me, 'I sometimes feel that they are choking me. The officers from the West know everything better, are conversant with their regulations and are often impatient, while I have first of all to read through them. But after all, they are doing it because they want to help us. All the same, it is sometimes damned hard to accept that even a sergeant or sergeant-major knows more than I do.' Afterwards I speak to the chief of the support group and tell him about my conversation. He, too, is aware of the problem; but he says that as there is so much to do, he has little time for long explanations. I ask him nevertheless to be more considerate; after all, our goal that the former NVA officers should develop new self-confidence.

Next, a talk with battalion commanders of a territorial brigade, almost all of whom started their service on 1 April in order to reconstruct the new units. They exude self-confidence and optimism, are beginning their temporary transfers from the West as commanders, and are volunteers. They want to contribute their military knowledge and their personal experience to the unification process. Their families are in agreement with this. A few of them will be able to move house and they hope to soon find flats. They are aware of the many difficulties, but do not complain about them. Instead, they tell me how they intend to overcome them and where they need help.

Dinner with our Strausberg circle, formed from the heads of the regional office of the Federal Defence Ministry, the Military Regional Administration VII, the BKO, the Eastern Corps and Territorial Command and the German liaison staff to the Soviet armed forces. We have met regularly, because our departments are directly together, and over the months an extraordinarily close and trustful relationship has developed. In this context it is becoming clear that close co-operation between the military leadership and the military administration is a decisive precondition for mastering the special problems of the reconstruction – and also the cuts. Thanks to the very personal contacts many matters are being settled quickly and unbureaucratically – a relief for all.

Friday, 10 May 1991

Talks in the Federal Defence Ministry, primarily with the army Chief of Staff, about the rapid merger of the Western and Eastern formations into one German army. I strongly praise the support and co-operation between Western and Eastern units. This has proved successful, we must continue in this way.

Monday, 13 May 1991

I give a speech to the U.S. Chamber of Commerce in Berlin. An interested audience with many questions. Business people and economists from East and West Berlin participate – including some who held responsible positions in the GDR economy. In their contributions they express surprise about how smoothly the transition to the Bundeswehr has been carried out in the NVA. Some of our problems are similar to those encountered in the economy. However, as in the business world there is naturally no united organisation with a leadership corps trained on the same basis, it is extraordinarily difficult to bring about a united form of management. To solve economic problems, the differing situations of the firms require different principles and standards to be applied in each case, directed mainly towards efficiency. The main problem for business people is to find sufficient staff who are ready to take responsibility and who are capable of bearing this responsibility. Apart from the material difficulties, the market economy can only get going in the five new Länder if enough people can be found to tackle this task. Evidently, there are not enough volunteers in Western Germany who want to go to the East to help for a longish time. In that respect we are more fortunate in the armed forces. The readiness and extraordinary efforts of the many officers and NCOs is a good sign of their enthusiasm. Some business leaders recognise that the armed forces are really 'marching' in the forefront of developments.

Tuesday, 14 May 1991

A visit to the 39th Territorial Brigade in Erfurt. The commanders know their task, they know how to go about it and they are carrying it out with the necessary realism, but also with optimism. I encourage them to use their scope for action and to insist on the principle of 'leadership through mission fulfilment' rather than waiting for decisions from above.

On to visit an armoured infantry battalion which is also being built up. Here, too, there is a commander temporarily transferred from his Western unit, who is tackling his job with great passion. In the special basic training a few technical mistakes are still being made, but here too, the company commander, formerly NVA, makes a committed impression. However, he still has a lot to learn.

The training support teams have been sent over for three months, but the 'troops' would like them to stay longer. We must try to synchronise more effectively the disbandment of Western units with the reconstruction in the East. Our task will be to give the commanders on the spot the necessary help so that they can fulfil their task independently.

We drive to a little old Thuringian town and overnight in an old hotel. I took this opportunity to get to know one of the typical small towns, and had asked to be taken around the town and to discuss the town's future development. A choirmaster's wife acts as town guide. It is early evening. There is hardly anyone on the streets. We look round the oldest church, dating from 1280, which is well kept and restored, the town museum and a doll museum. The many beautiful squares and streets in the town are still partly paved with old cobblestones. In the evening in a restaurant I dine with the deputy mayor of the town, the head of the public order office, who moved to the GDR in May 1990, the choirmaster's wife who has guided us around, a veterinary surgeon and a former NVA officer – who was a senior 'reconnaissance' officer in the former division in Erfurt. The discussion goes on for four hours.

The head of the public order office explains that he moved from the West in May 1990 to help in building up the local administration. Naturally, he had rejected a demand that he should apply for GDR citizenship. In the registration document, in answer to the question about where he had served in the NVA, he had merely stated he had served in the Bundeswehr. Thereupon he had been ordered to report to the Volkspolizei and was interrogated by a police second lieutenant. However, in spite of these initial difficulties he was finally employed by the local authority and became head of the public order office after 3 October. The second lieutenant of the Volkspolizei who had interrogated him at the time is now one of his subordinates in the public order office.

This man has particular complaints about the behaviour of his West German countrymen:

> You know, General, many West Germans make a bad impression on me by behaving as though they were in darkest Africa. Only a short time ago one of my staff complained to me that cars from the West were parked on the marketplace where stopping is absolutely forbidden and that the drivers were not taking the slightest notice of the regulations. I then went to the spot and spoke to one of the car owners. He just tried to provoke me. 'Go away you Red, you can't order people around here any more.' But my Kassel dialect quite quickly showed him his mistake. I had a sixty Deutschmarks fine slapped on him and, with much shouting, he finally made himself scarce. But it didn't happen only once. Another driver from the West threatened to kick one of the Volkspolizisten in the behind. It is embarrassing to see that a few of our countrymen from the West behave so rudely here. It's just these few who particularly determine the image of westerners among the public here. That there are others who come here and work, and help to reconstruct and restructure the administration, is then easily forgotten.

Then the vet describes his experiences. He worked in a large animal production combine with 2,500 beef cattle and calves, but had difficulties because of his 'un-Socialist behaviour' and was dismissed. In October and November 1989 his son had taken part in demonstrations against the SED regime and was expelled from school – also

for 'un-Socialist behaviour'. The headmaster who had signed the
expulsion order and had explained the reasons for it to the father, is
still in his job – true, he is now only the acting head, but is nevertheless still there.

The vet explains:

> Now I am employed by the town administration and I am on the teach-
> ers' appointments committee which has been set up here. Unfortunately,
> too few volunteers are applying for the vacant head teachers' posts that
> we want to fill. At our grammar school the former headmaster is the only
> person to have applied. What should I do? A man who in the past served
> the system so loyally and expelled children from the school for un-Social-
> ist behaviour, really cannot be the headmaster today and teach our chil-
> dren about the essence of free democracy! That is absolutely implausible.
> So we won't fill the head teacher's post but will appoint someone in an
> acting capacity until we have found a man or woman who is less tainted.

Are there really not enough teachers in the West who are ready to
make a personal contribution to the unity of Germany?

At this point the former NVA officer interrupts the vet: 'I must say
one thing: my wife is a teacher too and she is also being investigated
at present. I think that this political snooping by the Westerners is
unbearable. We cannot go along with that, we must reject it.' I strongly
disagree. The term 'political snooping' is completely incorrect in this
context, I say, rather it is a question of finding out whether teachers
are credible supporters of the Basic Law, and can teach the fundamentals of our democratic state based on the rule of law.

The vet then touches on a problem that used to concern many
people: the possibility of travelling to West Germany – to a 'non-
Socialist foreign country'. An aunt of the vet's who lives in the West
had invited him to her seventy-fifth birthday celebration. He then
applied for permission to visit her, and had provided all the necessary documents to the department responsible. A short time later it
was discovered that the aunt no longer had the surname which the
vet had given to the Volkspolizei. The vet's explanation, that she had
married for a second time, was rejected. In addition, he was told, it
could not be certain that this was the same aunt, it could all be a
trick. Several visits at official departments, as well as explanations,
had no result. Neither had a reference to the fact that he had received a written invitation to the birthday celebration. It all led to
nothing. That in the end the vet was able to visit his aunt was due to
an irony of fate – in the meantime the Wall had come down.

Our town guide tells us about her husband who, as choirmaster,
was able to visit the West frequently with the choir, but of course
without his family. In the summer of 1989, when her husband was
with the choir in West Germany, the Hungarian frontier had been
opened and her son had made a spontaneous decision to flee by way

of Hungary. She was able to inform her husband in the West and to tell him that their son would arrive in Ulm on a train. 'My husband was able to arrange to travel to Ulm,' the woman says, 'and he waited there for trains coming from Austria in order to meet our son. It was real luck, fateful, that father and son met. My husband welcomed my son in the free West and then said goodbye as he himself had to return to the East. The weeks that followed put a particular strain on us. But I could understand our son's action. Now I'm all the more happy that he has come back again and wants to set up his own business here in our town.'

After these detailed personal accounts the former NVA officer feels compelled to explain his viewpoint. We are very keen to hear how he will justify himself – the atmosphere is really tense. He refers to the heavy workload in the service and the restrictions on personal freedom. 'Looked at from that point of view what we received was not a privilege, but payment for the large amounts of overtime we worked. We got more money, that's true, but to get it we worked much, much more than anyone else in the GDR. We could hardly take advantage of those so-called privileges. And, anyway, we servicemen contributed to peace and stability. Only on that basis was it possible for things to develop as they have done.'

Naturally there are further questions, and a lively debate begins. We all know that we shall have to do a lot more talking about our separate and so different pasts. But we do all agree with the summing-up given by the vet at the close of the evening: 'That we are sitting together like this tonight and having this kind of discussion shows that the Bundeswehr is something quite different from the NVA. Such a conversation would have been unthinkable a year ago.'

Wednesday, 15 May 1991

In my hotel I have heard doors slamming since 5 am, as my room is opposite a toilet and shower. I have to wait about half an hour to get in, and am successful only at the fourth attempt. As a special favour I had been given a key for the shower and toilet the previous evening, but as there were only two shower rooms for all the bedrooms on the corridor I did not lock up a shower room just for myself – so in the morning I just had to wait. On the news I hear by chance that water consumption per head in the five new Länder is three times as high as in the West. How can that be explained in view of these sanitary conditions? It's certainly not due to the individuals, but is possibly caused by industry, old machines or leaky pipes.

A surprise visit to a military sub-regional command in a small town. As is often the case with surprise visits it falls at an awkward time. In this case: the commanding officer is on leave, his deputy not reachable, and a former NVA officer is trying to set up the head-quarters which, according to my documents, has already been set up. Everything is confused, furniture is being carried to and fro, it certainly couldn't be called an organised reconstruction. What is written in black and white is sometimes like one of those little flags on a military situation map – it cannot always be relied on.

Afterwards, a visit to a troop training area of the former frontier troops, which now belongs to the Bundeswehr and where ammunition is to be stored temporarily outside. We are having to arrange extra places for storing ammunition so as to speed up the disbandment of the units. The first idea – to store this ammunition in ventilated underground installations – has been turned down as we do not have enough experience of this. Now we only have the option of storing the ammunition outside – if we cannot hand it over to other users. I commission a report on how we can store the ammunition safely. Earth walls and anti-lightning equipment must be provided, and all the guard arrangements organised. This place is quite suitable for the purpose. The main difficulty is in transporting the ammunition for the final kilometre over narrow tracks, as the rail link ends outside of the training area.

While we are pushing on with these plans, citizens' groups are calling for the handing back of the training area so that leisure facilities can be created on the site. A symptomatic development which we are encountering often and which is causing us difficulties. The Bundeswehr, it is true, does not want to keep all of the former training areas of the NVA, the Western Group of the Soviet Armed Forces and the frontier troops, but it still needs areas for training and exercises. In addition, extra space is, as I've mentioned, needed for the temporary storage of ammunition and the parking of between seventy and eighty-thousand vehicles.

Thursday, 16 May 1991

Meeting with the three BKO service chiefs. We are still concerned with many problems, but the atmosphere is more relaxed than five or six months ago; this, too, is progress. The tasks have become more manageable. Solutions are in sight. An interim appraisal shows that in the reconstruction and disbandment of units it is largely a matter for the local commanders to determine the atmosphere and the speed of work.

In the sphere of forces' administration there have been, and still are, difficulties. The first complaints are coming in about the change-over in the system of paying wages, from that of the to that of the Bundeswehr, as wages have often been paid late or not at all. This is leading to criticism and unrest, which is made worse because the staff have practically no savings. The units are being informed about these difficulties and instructed to make generous use of the possibility of giving advances. All the same we are throwing away trust.

Tuesday, 21 May 1991

Stayed in Berlin over Whitsuntide and took a boat trip on the Berlin lakes. The Berliners' passion for water sports is no longer obstructed by frontiers. Berlin and Potsdam, as seen from the lakes, made me feel at home.

Breakfast meeting with a journalist from *Time* magazine, who shows extraordinarily great interest in how we are educating former Communist servicemen to become citizens in uniform. I tell him that not all of the officers were convinced Communists. Membership of the party does not mean that someone was a fanatical supporter of the regime. As I am explaining our concept and how we intend to proceed, I meet with some scepticism. As he has enough time, I recommend that he looks around among the units and I provide him with an accompanying officer. In this way it is possible for him to visit very differing units in the BKO region, and to hold discussions with servicemen of all ranks. At the end of his tour we talk again and he tells me that he has found confirmation of what I told him at the start. His visit, he says, has taught him some surprising things and has been very convincing. Above all, he is impressed by the natural way that officers from East and West are behaving towards each other and working together. He later publishes a very positive report in a special issue about Germany.

Next I hold talks with an area administrative official about the situation in his area. A pastor by profession, he has been elected as area administrator because he was an early member of the opposition. One of his friends, who had been intensively involved with economic issues, told him early on that, if only because of the economic facts, the GDR could not go on existing for much longer. This, he says, strengthened him in his oppositional role. After he was elected as administrator for the area he started to build up the administration. He too has had difficulties in finding enough suitable and efficient staff members, and has therefore decided to retain the overwhelming majority of the former administrative staff, and to appoint only a few new people. He says that although he sees the problem of a possible loss of trust among the public, it makes it all the more important that he change the behaviour of the staff so that the public, too, understands that things have changed. He has found enough investors for his administrative area and must now start a planning procedure – of which he has no experience at all. He has therefore appointed a Western German company to oversee the planning. He says it is primarily individual men and women who are getting things moving.

I am surprised again and again at the vigour with which 'lay people' seek to solve problems without knowing their full complexity – will they perhaps learn step-by-step how to master the difficulties? It can sometimes be a good things not to know the full extent of problems at the start.

In the evening I have an extensive view over lit-up Berlin from the *Funkturm*. It is reunified, the streams of traffic are no longer cut off by the Wall. Only in lighting do the Eastern and Western parts of the city look different – otherwise, from above, one no longer sees any difference.

Wednesday, 22 May 1991

In the morning, talks in Potsdam with the rapporteur group of the Bundestag Defence Committee, who want to gain a first impression of the situation in the BKO. We find all-party understanding for our situation, and a readiness to help in solving our problems. Our success to date leads us to expect further support from Parliament. Afterwards I visit a consolidation depot where tanks are being collected together. I want to find out why things are moving so slowly. As so often, it is due, in part, to innumerable individual problems which are together causing great difficulties: there are no longer enough drivers to fetch the tanks from the railway, there are not enough technicians to remove and store the batteries; in addition, the required parking space has been wrongly calculated. Then on to the 37th Territorial Brigade in Dresden. The recruits undergoing general basic training make a spirited and enthusiastic impression. In broadest Saxon dialect, which I have long since got used to, they talk about their hopes and fears – here, too, the atmosphere is basically positive. Through a discussion with sergeant-majors from the West I try to find out what has prompted them to come to the East. They say that, to start with they came over to take on a new task – for a limited time. However, the longer they work here, and the more they get to know the region and the people, the more they consider coming to the East permanently. This readiness, they tell me, is increasing because units in the West are being disbanded; however, the difficult housing situation, the rotten conditions in the schools and the lack of job opportunities for working wives have practically ruled out moving to the East in the next few years. It is therefore important for them not to be stationed too far from their home areas. They feel that more than four or five hours travel time is unacceptable. 'Who gets married to live from a coat hanger, General? At the weekends we want to go home, we work hard for it during the week!'

In the evening a visit to the Semper opera to see *Don Giovanni*. The festive, brightly coloured auditorium is impressive. It is amazing that the SED was ready to rebuild this magnificent opera house.

Thursday, 23 May 1991

Visit to the Military Regional Headquarters in Dresden and then on to the 571st Motorised Infantry Battalion. The commanders have a view of the future, they know what they want and how to get it. Even so, they are rightly annoyed that they still have to drive the old Wartburgs and Ladas with NVA numberplates, whereas their colleagues in the administration and the business world have already got Western German cars with new plates. Thanks to the active help of the 'Western' army we are, it is true, able to arrange the delivery of a fairly large number of cars to the East, but this is to the detriment of Western units. We also try to fit all vehicles of the former NVA with the 'Y' numberplate of the Bundeswehr but it takes a total of ten months before the last NVA plate has been removed. A really long time – too long for something reminiscent of a regime which was swept away by the people. The psychological pressure which forces us to act is difficult to explain to technocrats and bureaucrats – in their world such problems do not exist; such a mass exchange of numberplates was not provided for in the regulations.

At the Military Regional Headquarters VII in Leipzig the situation reports show that the challenges have been recognised and that the staff know how to deal with them. The headquarters staff is amazingly united. Afterwards, dinner and discussion with officers. A captain, at present doing service as a company commander but who has not been taken on as a temporary serviceman, describes to me the events in Leipzig at the time of the political changeover:

> There was a great deal of unrest in the units, and the conflicts extended to the families. My wife told me that she too wanted to go to the demonstrations, and so she did. How in the world were we supposed to behave? Finally, I called a meeting of my company in which we talked to each other fairly openly. The majority of the conscripts and NCOs then spoke out against any use of arms. I too, of course! How could I have given an order to shoot if my wife was on the side of the demonstrators? Moreover, nearly all of my NCOs were in the NVA so they could go to college when they had finished their service, they did not want to be soldiers. I doubt whether they would have fired a single shot. In October and November even the commanding officer of our military region spoke out clearly against calling out the Nationale Volksarmee. In spite of this I had trouble on account of the company meeting and received a disciplinary punishment.

Another captain, formerly the commander of a motorised infantry regiment and later the deputy commander of a division, was serving, in 1989, as a lieutenant-colonel in a colonel's post. He has been demoted by two ranks: firstly, to major, after the unification of Germany, and secondly, to captain, when he was taken on as a temporary soldier. He tells me:

When I became an officer of the NVA I was firmly convinced that I was serving the most just cause in the world. I grew up here. I felt that our country was threatened by capitalism and wanted to do something to defend it. I had a good career in the NVA; I was given responsibility while young and I had the classic career of an NVA commander. In principle I had in no doubts about the system; I believed that in time the few weaknesses it had would be removed. When I saw our fraternal Socialist states I was even proud at what we had achieved in the GDR.

When the first demonstrations started I really believed at first that it was a counter-revolution. Everything went exactly the way the start of a counter-revolution had been explained to us. However, as the demonstrations grew larger and larger, it became clear to me that this was more than a counter-revolution, namely a form of people's movement. In discussions at home I noticed that my family was contradicting my views and my daughter told me that she, anyway, would take part in the demonstrations. All the same I did not really understand what was happening then. Only now do I realise that we lived apart from society, isolated – evidently myself even more so than my family. That was not surprising. As the commanding officer of a motorised infantry regiment I was in such a high position that no one dared to speak frankly to me and no one expressed their opinion. I did not grasp what was actually happening. It was like living beneath a cheese cover.

In answer to my question about what he had felt as he was demoted for the second time, and what his wife had said when he had come home as a captain, he admits:

When I was suddenly only a captain, I wept for the first time as a soldier. Nonetheless, I am determined to stay in the Bundeswehr because I think I have the best chances there. If I am once again given disciplinary powers as a company commander, I could really learn about the Bundeswehr from the inside. Perhaps then I would have the prospect of career advancement in the Bundeswehr. Anyway, I want to stay a soldier because that's what I have learned. My wife has encouraged me on this path. But she would also have understood if I had left. My daughter sees it somewhat differently but she accepts my decision – after all, we must all make a new start, me included.

Then came the anxious question: 'General, do we really have a fair chance?' Once again, I explain the structural problems, the directives and the criteria for personnel selection, and add that an officer like him, who shows commitment, is seriously trying to find his way in the Bundeswehr, and has independent judgment, certainly has a good chance.

Finally another captain comes to me and says:

General, I have been impressed, above all, by the fact that you as our commanding general have been wearing, since 3 October, the same uniform as us and not the walking-out uniform. We have only seen you in this olive-green NATO uniform. That would have been impossible in the NVA. We are all impressed that the Bundeswehr officers have shown solidarity with us in this way. By this, you have that you are serious in saying that you want to reconstruct the Bundeswehr together with us.

Our staff and our countrymen take in more than one generally assumes.

Friday, 24 May 1991

Our weekly situation report. Things are moving forward everywhere – only the dispersal of material is moving too slowly. The size of the total task, the problems with the enormous quantities of materiel that we have to find space for, have in many cases still not been grasped. The pressure for a rapid winding-up process will grow. In spite of the various tasks they have, the commanders must give more attention to the reconstruction.

Sunday, 26 May 1991

At the weekend we drive in the footsteps of Fontane by way of Fehrbellin through the Rhinluch, to Wustrow, the birthplace of Ziethen, and on to Lindow, Neuruppin, Rheinsberg, Stechlin and Gransee. Each name revives an almost forgotten memory: the rambles of Fontane and Tucholsky, things my parents told me. Even the Communists could not destroy this Prussian countryside. We see many storks in the Rhinluch.

In the evening in East Berlin, we visit acquaintances of friends. The husband works for the state-owned telecommunications company and was recently sent to work in West Berlin. On the first day he was greeted by the departmental chief with the request to dress differently, as he looked like an *Ossi*. 'We don't need you and haven't asked for you,' it was made clear to him on his arrival, 'but we have been ordered to employ you. So do us a favour and don't irritate us!' The man recounts this very calmly and in a matter-of-fact way, but with bitterness. He used to work for the GDR post office as a technician, but his GDR college education is not fully recognised by us. Does he have to be treated like this? This is not helping Germans to grow together. Anyway, in this case it is a question of 'clothes don't make the man'.

A lawyer and notary, who grew up in the East and is now opening his practice there, tells about his personal history and his experiences during the political changeover. He says that the decisive precondition for the upheaval was the feeling that one no longer needed to fear the state authorities. A state built on fear collapsed like a house of cards when there was no longer any fear. He then explains the sublime methods of surveillance and the means of repression. He

was in the Ministry for Foreign Trade, responsible for contract negotiations with the Comecon states, lived in East Berlin and had a telephone. One evening, a woman neighbour came to him, and asked if
she could telephone an extremely sick relative in West Berlin. The
very next morning he was ordered to go to his departmental chief
and was asked by him if he had anything to report. When he said no,
he was asked why he had not reported the phone call to West Berlin.
All of his explanations about the neighbour and her sick relative
were not accepted. He was threatened that his telephone would be
removed if he ever made another call to the West that was not immediately reported to the security service of the department.

Monday, 27 May 1991

All day spent in Eggesin with the 41st Territorial Brigade. What
progress from October until now! In all the formations there is an
enthusiastic atmosphere. Everywhere things are being renovated or
repaired. German perfectionism has also arrived. In a completely
renovated block to my surprise I find a 'boot-washing installation' for
cleaning dirty boots – as if we had no other worries. Discussions with
the soldiers are more open, the recruits are more relaxed than
before, as are those in charge too.

Wednesday, 29 May 1991

Visit to the 40th Territorial Brigade in Schwerin and Sternbuchholz
in Mecklenburg. Here, too, compared with the way things were, it is
like the difference between day and night. The former NVA officers
can scarcely be distinguished from their Western comrades.

In the evening, more discussions with officers and NCOs during
dinner in the open air. The relationship between officers from East and
West has become freer and more natural. A former regimental commander, then a lieutenant-colonel and now a captain, tells me how he
experienced German unification. He, too, must still get used to the
new conditions. He could not believe, he says, that in the Bundeswehr
the weapons, artillery and tanks were not fully loaded with ammunition
and in a state of readiness. So he could not understand why, on the
order of the BKO after the political changeover, he had to remove the
ammunition from his unit and collect it together in the local depot.

Like all his comrades he complains of the pressure caused by the
permanent state of readiness in the NVA.

> I could not even stay at home at Christmas or the New Year. If I, as a reg-
> imental commander, was away from home for more than twenty minutes
> I had to report to the duty officer and say where I was and when I would
> return. My wife did not understand why we had to maintain this high
> state of readiness, as the overall political situation was really quite relaxed.
> When we heard, after the political changeover, that the Bundeswehr had

only had a very low state of readiness we felt that we had been cheated and misused. Now it is completely clear to me that it was all unnecessary, but one still has to come to terms with it. Our personal commitment, the sacrifices of our wives and children – all in vain and for nothing.

Monday, 3 June 1991

Visit to the navy in Warnemünde, a suburb of Rostock. I go to sea in a modern minesweeper of the former *Volksmarine* and am given the necessary information. The officers and petty officers in the ships' crews – including the captains – have a special labour contract and will be dismissed this year. The minesweepers will not be taken over, so the crews are only staying in service as long as they are needed to keep the ships functioning technically. As soon as the ships have been sold or scrapped, the crews will be dismissed. How long that will take no one knows at present. I feel that is unacceptable for the men and intend to press Bonn for quick decisions.

The captain is the same one whom I met in October. His application to be taken over as a temporary serviceman has been turned down as he is not needed, but has caused his father, a former colonel in the Ministry for State Security, to ban him from his house. He is refusing to talk to his son because he regards him as a traitor – 'you take an oath only once'. However, the captain is an enthusiastic seaman and has had an excellent naval career without drawing any privileges from his father's connections. Even so, he cannot be taken on as we have no need of him. He must leave the navy with a master's certificate which is not valid for the merchant navy.

Once more I come across a rumour: the crew members with special labour contracts tell me that after 1 July, when the new pay regulations come into force, they will be paid less than now. They say that if this is really true they will quit the service immediately, because their unemployment benefit will otherwise be reduced as it will be based on lower pay. I tell the crew members that they can be sure that a regulation to maintain their pay levels will be applied. I add that we have a great need for them for as long as we have to keep the ships operational.

Conversation in the evening with officers in the Volksmarine guesthouse – beautifully situated but furnished in a petty bourgeois style – is revealing. The former NVA officers knew that the West German navy was, unlike their own, scarcely in readiness at weekends. During exercises they noted, with envy, how the ships of the West German navy returned to port at weekends, while they dropped anchor at sea and waited until the 'enemy' came out again on Sunday or on Monday morning. 'But, General, we were powerless against the system.'

An officer describes his five years of training in Baku and later in Leningrad. In Baku he was also able to get together with officers from the Developing World. He met one of them again a few years later in Leningrad. In the meantime, a new regulation had banned contact with officers from those countries. He kept to this ban because he did not know which of his 'comrades' was the snooper from the Stasi. 'Friendship between the peoples'? Experiences in the Soviet Union showed many officers that the Communist system there was not functioning but that the Socialist system in the GDR was fairly successful. To a certain extent they had been proud of that.

Wednesday, 5 June 1991

A visit to the so-called Document Depository where all the documents of the former NVA Defence Ministry are kept in archives, including protocols of the National Defence Council. In a number of cellars there are documents and card indexes ordered by years and subjects. We know that from November 1989 until September 1990 large numbers of documents were destroyed – particularly those from the 'Operations Administration'. Nevertheless, pointers for further research can be drawn from the ministry's diary and which, in the end, enable the reconstruction of documents which have been destroyed. Thus our experts have gained reliable knowledge about the intentions and capabilities of the NVA in case of war. The documents show that operations directed at Schleswig-Holstein were a central mission. During a headquarters staff exercise, the following was predicted for the final phase: 'Transition to the use of nuclear arms, planning of combat action for the occupation of more of the Jutland peninsula and for fulfilment of tasks on the North Sea coast.'

In 1985 and 1986, exercises simulated major attacks against conurbations and cities, and in a war game the conquest of Berlin was worked through. Analysis of all the documents will take years, but results so far are depressing enough. They meant it seriously and it would probably have really been carried out if situation had arisen – but if we had said that no one would have believed us.

Tuesday, 11 June 1991

A visit to the 42nd Territorial Brigade in Potsdam confirms the picture I have seen during my visits to units in the past few days; things are moving ahead.

Next, a visit to a former NVA depot for transport services which reveals the perversity of the previous system. Stored here are rails for the construction of eighty to a hundred kilometres of railway lines, parts for railway bridges, hundreds of road signs, five-hundred aluminium containers in which tools and equipment can be transported, thousands of brooms, hammers and shovels. In addition, there are earth rammers, bulldozers and giant tractors for bridge building. They had planned, in case of an advance, to repair railway lines or build new ones so they could immediately take over traffic control. Evidently they wanted to introduce GDR road signs in case of an advance into West European countries. It is amazing what was thought out and on which this worn-out state went on spending money.

Wednesday, 12 June 1991

Visit to the 4th Army NCOs School which, on the troop training area at Annaburg, about eighty kilometres south of Berlin, runs a final exercise at the end of the NCO training course. The first course is coming to an end. It shows how much still needs to be done to train the instructors to such a level that they are really good instructors for our new NCOs. But, thanks to the strong commitment of the officers serving there we shall succeed, step-by-step, in achieving good NCO training.

Then a visit to Bad Frankenhausen to two battalions which are being formed there. The general basic training is satisfactory. The recruits make a pleasing impression. A talk with the company sergeant major shows that everyone, whether from the West or the East, feels they need more help from the West. The former NVA sergeants feel overtaxed as company sergeant-majors, they complain primarily about the large amount of form-filling and the whole 'admin and office business'. They are surprised when I tell them that the education and training of the NCO corps, as well as their personal approach to the soldiers, is more important than 'paper stuff'. Paper, I say, is patient, but people are not and many need help but are afraid to say so.

There are complaints that there are not enough lockers for the soldiers arriving on 1 July even though there is a surplus in the West as units there are being disbanded. I am told they have been trying to get lockers for months. At my request the teleprinter messages concerned are shown to me, and in fact nothing has been done on the Western side. Finally we succeed, through the Military Regional Administration VII, in ensuring that the lockers are brought from West to East. Concerning oneself with such details is important, because only in that way does it become clear that we are all pulling together. We must not have shortages in the East while there are surpluses in the West. In many minds the former inner-German frontier has not yet been overcome.

During an evening discussion with officers and NCOs, again the same themes arise – but with the firm conviction that we can move forward only when there is readiness on all sides. Each person must come to terms with his past by himself, but we ought to know more about each other. I learn that rejection by the general population of former NVA members who have been taken on by the Bundeswehr is diminishing and that approval of the Bundeswehr is increasing. NVA members who have left the service are becoming more inquisitive; they would like to know how the Bundeswehr differs from the NVA. Then, the usual problems: the reconstruction of the NCO corps requires a lot of time, the forces administration is understaffed, accounting is taking far too long and building works are getting under way too late. Still, things have started moving.

We visit the Peasants' War panorama by Werner Tübke, the Leipzig painter. A strongly expressive and symbolic depiction of the era of upheaval in the sixteenth century, which had special importance for the GDR state leadership in expressing the revolutionary spirit of Thomas Münzer. Our guide explains to us – we are in uniform – the historical context and the symbolism without making any reference to Socialism. One of the former NVA officers accompanying me tries to curry favour by saying: 'A year ago he explained that quite differently. He really has learned quickly!' Certainly – but have not the former NVA officer and his comrades not also 'learned' quickly?' Who has the right to throw the first stone?

I overnight in a hotel which has recently been renovated recently and have a long talk with the couple who are leasing it. They believe that their efforts are worthwhile and will in time be repaid. The hotel is tastefully appointed and makes a well-run impression. The leaseholder has turned down an offer from the Black Forest because he wants to help the reconstruction in his home region. He hopes to profit from the flow of tourists to the Peasants' War panorama on the Schlachtberg.

Thursday, 13 June 1991

A visit to a missile artillery battalion. There is a shortage of specialist personnel here even though this battalion is to get the army's most modern artillery system. Once again I realise that official channels often take too long and that the right information does not get through. Unofficial channels do not yet exist. In the afternoon at Strausberg, a briefing for the Finnish Commander-in-Chief who, in conversation afterwards, expresses great sympathy about developments in Germany. He is surprised at how well East and West are getting on together. Our common ground in language and culture evidently could not be fully wiped out by forty years of Communism – it is amazing how many forget that.

Tuesday, 18 June 1991

Press trip to the area of the 40th Territorial Brigade in Schwerin. The number taking part is very large. Does that only indicate curiosity or is it a readiness to give us serious consideration? The unit makes a good impression and from one of the journalists from the new Länder there escapes the remark: 'They look like federal German soldiers.' I reply: 'They don't just look like it, they *are*.'

Thursday, 27 June 1991

My farewell visit to the Eastern Corps and Territorial Command, which for two-and-a-half months has been responsible for all army units in the BKO region. Here, the transition has been successful, a good team has been built and is working successfully.

Afterwards, a visit to a Military Sub-Regional Command and to an industrial plant where number of employees has been cut reduced from two thousand to six hundred, of whom it will be possible to employ only four hundred permanently. The plant was regarded as the most modern in the GDR, but compared to Western plants it looks hopelessly out of date. The machines are too old, almost all the spare parts are made on the spot. Working conditions, so far as undue noise, dirt and security standards are concerned, are almost unbearable.

The technical manager explains earlier difficulties in obtaining precision instruments and computer-controlled machine tools from the West. As a 'show plant' they were supplied in part by the firms of Schalck-Golodkowski. However, they often received the requested equipment too late and incomplete. One could not rely on anything, he says.

The members of the works council are extraordinarily objective and, for their part, are accepting the personnel cuts. In spite – or because – of this, they have been re-elected. There is a realisation that only in this way does the plant have a chance of survival. However, everyone is hoping for vocational training measures. In common with the forces, they are faced with the problem that some of their efficient skilled workers are already moving West. The mayor describes the difficulties in building up his administration, the concerns of the population and what has been achieved in construction so far. He fears that they will be hampered by Western administrative regulations before they are even in a situation to implement the necessary pump-priming measures for the economy. Moreover, they lack experienced local authority officials from the West and the money to pay them if they find any.

I am accompanied on my visit by the commanding officer of the Military Sub-Regional Command who, like the mayor, confirms the good relationship between the Bundeswehr and the citizens. He also reports that relations with the Soviet soldiers are quite good, even though the Soviets have lots of problems. For instance, some time ago the sewage pipes in the 'Russian housing estate' became blocked but the Soviets could not have repairs done, either by a cleaning firm or the town's cleansing department, as they had no money. The situation became unbearable. Finally, he began negotiations with the Soviet *Kommandatura* and the town to reach a satisfactory solution. Now, he says, he is so often and so willingly called in that his advisory work has become almost a full-time job.

I learn that, some time ago, a Soviet helicopter regiment was to be transferred from a nearby airfield back to the Soviet Union. It is reported that the wives demonstrated on the airfield in front of the helicopters to try to stop them taking off. They would only agree to the transfer back to the Soviet Union once they knew that they would not have to spend the winter in tents.

Friday, 28 June 1991

We carry out final work in the headquarters, clearing up. At 4.30 pm we are given a farewell by the U.S. Berlin brigade with the ceremony of 'beating the retreat', which has a personal note. A military event which is also a friendly one.

Saturday, 29 June 1991

Dinner with Colonel-General Burlakov and his wife in Schloss Wilkendorf, the guesthouse of the former ministry. I had asked Burlakov some weeks ago if he and his wife would accept a private invitation from the Schönbohms. He was surprised, but accepted with thanks. So we have the chance, aided by our interpreters, to have a detailed talk in which we discuss official, but also private, problems, going as far as the vocational training of our children and their prospects for a life in peace and growing prosperity.

Burlakov again mentions the attacks by German citizens on Soviet servicemen and civilians and gives some examples: on 23 June an officer cadet was shot at in the dark and the next day a sentry was wounded; a week previously young people attacked and beat up three officers, two of whom will have lasting damage to their health. In May a captain was attacked by skinheads in front of a restaurant, and was later found dead in a canal.

Burlakov refers to the difficult psychological state of his soldiers and also their families. He knows the difficulties which our police face and regards it as his duty to take precautions to give extra protection to his people. He also mentions the difficult housing situation in the Soviet Union and underlines that he can leave only when there are enough flats. He knows about the difficulties in his own country and continues to hope that we will help.

By the end of the evening we come to see some of the Soviet requests in a different light. We have more understanding of the needs and concerns of the other side. We are all agreed that we want to make a contribution to better understanding between our people, and we hope that our grandchildren will be able to travel between Russia and Germany as we in Western Europe can do. We talk about Dostoyevsky and Tolstoy and also about Gorbachev and effects of his policies. We feel like neighbours who, for the first time, are discussing their neighbourly relations and the future. What a change from my first frosty meeting with the military leadership in Moscow!

Monday, 1 July 1991

The disbandment of the BKO and the hand-over of responsibility to the Chiefs of Staff of the three services takes place in the usual Bundeswehr way. For the first time the whole headquarters are drawn up in dress uniform. We want to make it clear to the public that it is a normal occurrence when a military ceremony is conducted according to Bundeswehr standards, as in the West. At the hand-over I sum up my thoughts again and express my thanks to all:

Federal Minister, servicemen, civilian staff, honoured guests:
Today the Federal Minister of Defence concludes the duties of the headquarters staff of the Bundeswehr-Kommando Ost and hands over the responsibility for the units to the Chiefs of Staff of the individual services. An important period in the history of the German armed forces lies behind us – the end of the NVA, its disbandment and the start of the reconstruction of a Bundeswehr in which citizens from the five new Länder also have their legitimate place; this also includes members of the former NVA, if they commit themselves to the free and democratic basic constitutional order.

I am happy that on this day, which is so significant for the Bundeswehr, so many of you, our most honoured guests, have come, as by doing so you are visibly underlining your interest as well as your support and sympathy. Servicemen and civilian staff, behind us lie months of the greatest effort, great strain and challenges. We came from two different armed forces, which faced each other in two alliance systems, and we now want to be servicemen together in one Bundeswehr so that we can faithfully serve our fatherland – the Federal Republic of Germany.

There has been much discussion as to whether former servicemen of a lawless Communist state can be servicemen in the Bundeswehr, armed forces which are committed to our democratic state based on law. Today I say clearly: servicemen of the former NVA also understand the differences in principle and in fundamentals, and are ready to serve our united Germany – they have made a start with this since 3 October and they will prove it in the future. Decisive in this is that they honestly come to terms with their own past and commit themselves, out of inner conviction, to our democratic state based on law – this individual process needs time, help and encouragement. We must realise that this is a task for all servicemen and only through this can we find the way towards togetherness in one Bundeswehr.

The last nine months have given us reason for self-confidence. Together we have created something which was earlier regarded by many as unlikely:

- We have taken over the units of the former NVA in a largely ordered condition.
- We have disbanded the NVA and completed the transition to common German armed forces without public controversy and without endangering the security of our citizens and our country.
- We have taken enormous quantities of arms and ammunition into safe keeping, reduced the forces from ninety thousand to fifty-six thousand servicemen, disbanded 350 units and built up 250 new ones. Discipline, and readiness to achieve results are growing.
- We are contributing to making the armed forces, as a visible sign of the sovereignty of our state, a symbol of the unity of Germany as well.

Our joint achievement gives reason for confidence in the future of our united Germany. We have trodden the particularly challenging path of transition successfully and without eruptions. The creation of new units and formations, and the training of our conscripts and young volunteers according to the principles of *Innere Führung* is now the challenge for us all; here we must prove ourselves. We want to achieve in the armed forces that which corresponds to the desire of our people: unity in thinking and feeling too.

We must, therefore, consistently continue on the way towards common armed forces. Since 3 October about two-thousand officers and NCOs, together with about three-hundred officials, all from the West, have been voluntarily doing long-term service here in order to take an active part in the reconstruction. I have noted a pleasing amount of commitment and readiness to achieve results. Tact, but also clarity in gaining acceptance for our basic democratic viewpoint, have complemented each other – the concept of *Innere Führung* has proved itself.

We have likewise determined that our tactic of leadership through mission fulfilment offers the only possibility for solving complex problems in difficult conditions. Our mission was not foreseen in any service regulations. We had to find solutions for difficult tasks which often could only be carried out locally and independently. Those in charge, in particular the commanders of units, have acted to fulfil missions and have used the scope for action which was granted to them. For that I thank them specially. In dealing with the challenges which will face the armed forces – and particularly the army – in the future, it is necessary really to apply fully the tactic of mission fulfilment, to open up the scope for action and to trust our commanders. If we continue on this road I will not worry about the common future of our armed forces.

Our conscripts have already realised that we are doing all that we can to improve their living and training conditions. Our young conscripted citizens, through their service in the old or new Länder, can make just as great a contribution to the growing together of Germany as their older comrades. The experience which they gather in the other part of Germany, or which they take there, will improve our knowledge of each other and our understanding for each other. This getting to know each other is an enrichment for the whole Bundeswehr and also for our country.

If, in this situation of radical change, we are striking a successful provisional balance in spite of all the difficult problems, including the personal ones, that is the result of our joint efforts, our joint struggle to find the right way. We have talked to each other a lot and explained a lot – may it stay that way.

Everyone who is today completing their individual task with me will go to their next task as a changed person. For us, Germany has changed not only politically and geographically, but above all in a human and cultural sense. We have got to know people who are weighed down by their past, with which they must first come to terms in order to become free inside themselves – but who are seriously wrestling to do this. We have experienced a great readiness to work and a sense of duty from those who stayed with us for only a short time. We know that time is needed before the deep scars of arbitrary Communist rule disappear from the people and the environment. I am, however, confident that together we shall succeed in healing these scars and the remnants of oppression.

We have reason for self-confidence and hope if we keep our goal of a Bundeswehr embedded in the democratic state based on law firmly in view. I thank you all for your personal commitment and readiness to work under difficult conditions. I thank your families for accepting the separation from husbands and fathers so that they can make their contribution to the reconstruction of the Bundeswehr in the five new Länder. Our fellow citizens here in the East of Germany have struggled for the unity of our people. Servicemen from East and West are engaged in shaping this unity in the Bundeswehr. In so doing they are visibly underlining the sovereignty of our people. We are proud of what we have achieved so far. We are thankful that it was made possible. Our goal is now to realise the high expectations demanded of us by our national anthem: Unity and Law and Freedom, for the German Fatherland.

From 5 pm we invited all staff members of the BKO, along with their families, to say farewell; we – that is those officers who are returning to the West. I am pleased that a number of former staff members have also come: that is officers and staff, along with their families, who left on 30 December. We invited them because they too played a part in our task. In bright sunshine we sit outside on the meadow behind the conference centre, servicemen from East and West united in friendship. We eat sausages, drink beer and chat. We start feeling almost a kind of melancholy about our imminent departure. I again thank all those who have taken part and shown personal commitment – particularly those whose future career was so uncertain. Together we have carried out the mission of the BKO, have trodden the path towards unity and have proved that forty-five years of Communism and division could not completely separate Germans from Germans. There remains the task of completing inner unity.

EPILOGUE

We have now been united for five years and we still do not know enough about one another to understand each other. Unity came overnight and we West Germans have been pushed out of the spectator's box into the arena where events are taking place. Before unification we knew little about the daily life and living conditions of our countrymen, who also include our relatives; the GDR was a neighbouring country, cut off by the Wall and the barbed wire. We accepted that fact as normal, and repressed our knowledge of how inhumane the system was. Our media reported on Chile, Nicaragua and South Africa, about the difficult living conditions and the situation of youth in those countries, but rarely said anything critical or even descriptive about the reality of life and daily routine in the GDR, about the needs and worries of our countrymen, or about the destruction of nature and of minds and hearts.

Our countrymen in the East had only seen the West through their own eyes if they were over sixty-five or were officials who were allowed to travel. Most of them were able to picture the 'FRG' only from what others told them or from West German television. Naturally, this picture naturally did not show the reality of West German daily life with its emphasis on performance. These pictures could not reveal the need for efficiency, work directed towards success, decisions which were based on rationality and which were understandable, as well as the readiness and ability to make independent decisions and thus to take on responsibility. Indeed, scarcely anyone could have had any idea of these things.

The majority of the population of the GDR – like their countrymen in the West – had accepted the division of Germany and had accommodated themselves in the GDR. They were better off than the populations of all the other states in the Socialist camp, they had work, a roof over their heads and a livelihood; they conformed. A large section of the elite fled before the Wall was built, a smaller section subsequently. Those who remained became, on 3 October 1990, as it were overnight, citizens of a state which in its constitution was realising all the values they had only dreamt of until then. However, that state and its citizens were alien to them. Unity came upon us when we were so unprepared and had little knowledge of one another and no common experiences. Only a few had a real integral part in preparing for unification, and felt they were concerned with it, but it concerns us all.

In the East living conditions have changed drastically within a few months, the old bureaucracy has been replaced by new regulations and form-filling, unemployment is becoming apparent and is bringing new, depressing experiences, re-training measures are being offered and people are facing new qualification procedures. Some are overstretched and others are no longer needed – they have been rationalised out of jobs. Only for a few in the East is life continuing on its usual path – for almost everyone in the West nothing has changed.

Amid these general conditions the Bundeswehr, after a short preparatory period, faced the take-over of the NVA. The whole Bundeswehr very quickly came to regard this task as a shared task, and from the first servicemen and civilian staff volunteered in large numbers for deployment in the East – many saw unification as a national task. It does after all still exist, that much-disparaged patriotism. At the time of the take-over the NVA was on its way from being a party army to being an army in a democratic state based on law, but without having come to terms with the past or having changed its leading personnel. Owing to the rapid turn of events the career and short-service men of the NVA were deeply insecure. They saw themselves being faced with the same social and personal problems as all employees who must learn a new profession; the standard bearers of Socialism had turned into doubting job seekers in an alien world.

However, the decisive question will be how our countrymen come to terms with their past, and whether they can gain new self-confidence from their efforts in the era of upheaval and transition. People in Eastern Germany, whether they are inside or outside of the Bundeswehr, need a genuine chance to realise that all was not in vain, and need to be able to hope that their previous life was not pointless. The previous system gave them no freedom to develop. To flee, to take part, to conform: those were the alternatives for the majority; only a few had the inner strength to enter into open opposition.

It is to be admired all the more when today they take their lives into their own hands, throw off the restrictions and oppression of the past and find courage and strength for the common future. From the experiences of the past we can gain important signposts for the future. The length of time it will take to overcome the scars of past ravages will depend to a large extent on the readiness for togetherness, and the will to learn from each other and to speak with one another.

The unification process is much more than just bringing into line the economies of Eastern and Western Germany, although that too is very important. Germany is more than the common currency area of the Deutschmark. We can combine our differing experiences, and apply them for the benefit of Europe. Our people in eastern Germany have experience and knowledge of our Eastern neighbours, just as we have about our Western neighbours. For long periods the Germans in the GDR shared many hardships with the peoples of the Soviet-bloc countries, while in the West prosperity was growing.

To our neighbours, the process of German unification is a test case. If the rich Federal Republic is not able to rebuild the new Länder states and to win the people for democracy, then our Eastern neighbours will have little chance of mastering their own, even more difficult, task. They have to rely much more on their own efforts, and they must burn away the terrible inheritance of Communism through kill-or-cure economic and social measures – with all the pain that entails.

Let us Germans therefore be thankful that unity has come now and not later – under still more alarming conditions – and that we have sufficient people among us who are willing to make their very own personal contribution to inner unity; let us not be impatient. The two parts of a nation which were separated by force for forty-five years, and which stood in hostile camps, cannot be unified in a few years without any fractures. We Germans situated in the centre of Europe have -through division and unification – gained experience unlike that of any other people. Can we not manage, with this experience and our common capacity for work, to lay the basis for a happy future?

In the Bundeswehr togetherness has emerged, and the armed forces have, to a large extent, achieved unity. In the meantime, the Bundeswehr's daily routine has taken over in the garrisons of the new Länder. Units in the East and West can be distinguished only by their dialects, not by their commitment – they are soldiers of *one* Bundeswehr.

To sum up: six-thousand officers and eleven-thousand NCOs of the NVA were taken into the Bundeswehr on a trial basis for two years. On the basis of suitability and requirements, about three-thousand officers and 7,600 NCOs were then taken on for longer periods of service. Anyone who wanted to become a career officer had to be screened by the 'Independent Committee for Suitability Screening'. Today, former members of the NVA are serving in both East and West. The Vocational Assistance Service has given further vocational training to more than twelve-thousand former NVA servicemen and thus enabled them to make the transition into civil life.

Many conscripts are, of course, being called up from the old Länder to serve in the new Länder, and vice versa. Thus, conscription is helping us to get to know an understand each other better and, as a result, to complete the achievement of inner unity.

Ten thousand of the weapons and major weapons systems, which we took over, have been destroyed in accordance with our commitments in the treaty on conventional forces in Europe. In order to decommission the 300 thousand tons of ammunition, industry created a considerable capacity for making it safe, so that by now about ninety per cent of the stocks have been processed.

The refurbishing of the four hundred bases, which are to be used militarily in the long term, is going ahead rapidly; living quarters and conditions for the servicemen have been noticeably improved, as has the situation regarding hygiene and sanitation. By the end of 1994 about 3,500 million Deutschmarks had been expended on this, and invested predominantly in the new Länder. In future, too, about one-thousand million Deutschmarks will have to be invested annually in order to equalise Bundeswehr living conditions in East and West.

In spite of the difficult infrastructure situation in the East, installations and formations of the Bundeswehr are being transferred from a good infrastructure in the West into the new Länder. The best-known example is the army officers' training academy, which is being moved from Hanover to Dresden. As a result, each army officer will undergo an important part of their training in Dresden – a city rich in tradition – and the army will become the army of unity. In this way, we are overcoming the division by sharing.

In Strausberg the Regional Military Administration VII has been set up, with responsibility for the whole region of the new Länder. The staff – about twenty-two thousand – used to serve mainly in the NVA, and have been prepared for their new duties by means of numerous training and re-training measures. Thanks to their commitment they are guaranteeing a functioning and effectively operating military administration.

The successful take-over and disbandment of the NVA, as well as the reconstruction of new units including former members of the NVA, is a credit not only to the Bundeswehr as a whole, but also to those NVA servicemen who, after the political changeover, felt committed to the common goal of all-German armed forces. For everyone in the new Länder it was a special challenge to take part in this task and to help make it possible for us to say together: 'One people, one state, one armed force.'

SELECT LIST OF NAMES

Blücher, Gebhard von: Field-Marshall, Prussian army commander during the Napoleonic Wars, one of the historic figures exploited by the GDR regime in its efforts to instil a 'Socialist patriotism'.

De Maizière, Lothar: 1940- . Lawyer and chairman of the GDR Christian Democratic Union (CDU) 1989-1990. The first democratically elected GDR Prime Minister, from March to October 1990. After German unification De Maizière was appointed Federal Vice-Chancellor and elected a deputy chairman of the all-German CDU. In December 1990 he resigned from these two posts after being accused of having co-operated with the Stasi during the GDR era, which he denied.

Fontane, Theodor: 1819-1898. Berlin novelist and poet.

Herrhausen, Alfred: A director of the Deutsche Bank, murdered in November 1989 by a left-wing terrorist.

Honecker, Erich: 1912-1994. First Secretary and from 1976, General Secretary, Socialist Unity Party (SED), until 1989. Chairman of the State Council (Head of State), 1976-1989.

Honecker, Margot: 1927- . Wife of Erich Honecker. GDR Minister of Education 1963-1989.

Janka, Walter: A leading East German communist publisher, who was imprisoned by the regime for alleged dissidence.

Mielke, Erich: 1907- . GDR Minister for State Security, 1957-1989. From 1980, with rank of General.

Milosz, Czeslaw: Polish author and poet, holder of Nobel Prize for Literature (1980).

Münzer, Thomas: c. 1490-1525. Protestant preacher, leader of the Peasants' Revolt. After the defeat of the revolt in 1525 he was beheaded.

Rohwedder, Detlev: 1932-1991. Industrialist in 1990 was appointed Chairman of the *Treuhand*. Murdered in March 1991, extreme left-wing terrorists claimed responsibility.

Schalk-Golodowski, Alexander: 1932- . From 1975-1989, Permanent Secretary, GDR Ministry of Foreign Trade. He master-minded often secret deals with West Germany and other countries to obtain much-needed foreign currency for the GDR.

Tucholsky, Kurt: 1890-1935. Left-wing, pacifist writer. Emigrated to Sweden 1929. The Nazi regime deprived him of German citizenship in 1933. Committed suicide 1935.

Ziethen, Hans-Joachim: 1699-1786. Prussian cavalry general in the army of Frederick the Great.